Privacy in the Age of Social Media: Beyond the Like

I0875879

Privacy in the Age of Social Media: Beyond the Like explores the hidden dynamics of social media and the ways our online behavior is tracked, analyzed, and monetized, offering an accessible overview of the interaction between social media engagement and personal data privacy.

This book dives into the heart of social media's greatest paradox: the pursuit of connection versus the protection of personal privacy. It reveals how everyday online interactions drive engagement, targeted advertising, and predictive analytics; build detailed user profiles; shape the content we encounter; and influence how platforms operate.

This book explores ethical considerations, regulations, and practical strategies for protecting personal and organizational data, while identifying emerging trends in social norms and technology that may shape the future of privacy and social media. Through case studies, expert insights, real-world examples, and accessible explanations, readers are equipped to understand the hidden mechanics of social media, engage online with awareness, and safeguard their digital footprint. The authors also illustrate how the simple "Like" button transformed the digital landscape—what began as a quick tap of approval has become one of the most powerful tools in the online ecosystem.

This compelling book is essential reading for marketers, business professionals, and those working in the fields of social media, cybersecurity, and data privacy, as well as organizations seeking to understand how platforms operate behind the scenes. It will also be of interest to students and researchers in the fields of social media, marketing, cyberpsychology, data privacy, digital media, and business management.

Dr. Manimuthu Arunmozhi is a cybersecurity academic and technology entrepreneur. He is Assistant Professor at Aston Business School, Aston University (UK), where he teaches cybersecurity management and business analytics. A patent holder and finalist for the 2025 Innovation Award (Young Innovator category), he is also the Founder and CEO of Q Safe, focusing on Quantum Security, digital trust, privacy, and responsible technology adoption.

Luan Wise is a seasoned marketing professional with agency, client side, and consultancy experience. She is a chartered marketer and fellow of the Chartered Institute of Marketing (FCIM), and is currently pursuing a PhD by Portfolio at the University of Lancashire (UK). She delivers training and offers insights on the latest industry developments to organizations and at events worldwide.

"An essential read for a time when every interaction on social media and in AI feeds an invisible system designed to predict and subtly influence our behaviour. Luan and Manimuthu ask some probing questions which we should all be mindful of as our relationship with technology becomes ever more complex."

Drew Benvie, *CEO of Social Media Consultancy Battenhall, and Founder of youth social media safety nonprofit, Raise*

"Dr Manimuthu Arunmozhi and Ms. Luan Wise offer a thoughtful, well researched, and deeply relevant examination of these challenges. Their combined expertise spanning cybersecurity, digital risk, marketing, and behavioural insight provides readers with a rare, holistic perspective on what it truly means to live in a data driven world. This book not only demystifies how platforms collect and use our data but also empowers readers with practical strategies to navigate social media more safely and responsibly. It is a valuable resource for students, professionals, and everyday users seeking clarity in an increasingly complex digital environment."

Dr Vincent Charles, *Programme Director, Queen's University Belfast*

"This book resonates because it speaks to a reality many of us sense but rarely articulate; that our everyday online interactions carry deeper consequences than we fully understand. With clarity and care, the authors unpack these complexities while keeping the reader grounded in real-world implications. It is an engaging and meaningful work that invites reflection as much as it informs."

Dr Tatiana Gherman, *Associate Professor of AI for Business & Strategy, University of Northampton*

"At a pivotal moment for online privacy, this book is an essential wake-up call. Luan Wise and Dr Manimuthu Arunmozhi lift the lid on the uncomfortable truth: data collection isn't a side effect of social media; it's the business model. They unpack the hidden mechanics of tracking, profiling and monetisation, exposing how the 'control' users think they have is often an illusion, and why every internet user has the right to understand, challenge, and protect how their digital lives are being turned into profit."

Alison Battisby, *Social Media Strategist and Founder of Avocado Social*

"An eye-opening and enlightening look into the privacy issues concerning the social networks we all use daily. Arunmozhi and Wise provide a deep look into how our every click, scroll, and post is tracked, used, and all too often, abused. A must-read for anyone who has clicked 'accept' on terms and services they haven't read...which is all of us."

Jon-Stephen Stansel, *Social Media Consultant, Founder of Saturn 9 Media and author of* The 10 Principles of Effective Social Media Marketing

Current Issues in Cyberpsychology

Current Issues in Cyberpsychology brings together books that explore the psychology behind human interaction with digital technology, and the impact of the internet on individuals and society as a whole.

It showcases books that will be relevant to both an academic and professional market, bringing together the work of established and emerging authors. The series spans a range of topics relating to cyberpsychology; including the influence of technology on behavior and attitudes, the effects of social media, human factors in cybersecurity, and digital identities. Ideas for new books are welcome.

The Psychology of Cybersecurity
Hacking and the Human Mind
Tarnveer Singh and Sarah Y. Zheng

Human Factors and Cybersecurity
The Psychology Behind Online Safety and Security
Lee Hadlington and Chloe Ryding

Privacy in the Age of Social Media: Beyond the Like
Dr. Manimuthu Arunmozhi and Luan Wise

For more information about the series, please visit: https://www.routledge.com/our-products/book-series/CIIC

Privacy in the Age of Social Media: Beyond the Like

Dr. Manimuthu Arunmozhi and Luan Wise

Routledge
Taylor & Francis Group
LONDON AND NEW YORK

Designed cover image: KTSDESIGN/SCIENCE PHOTO LIBRARY / Getty Images

First published 2027
by Routledge
4 Park Square, Milton Park, Abingdon, Oxon OX14 4RN

and by Routledge
605 Third Avenue, New York, NY 10158

Routledge is an imprint of the Taylor & Francis Group, an informa business

British Library Cataloguing-in-Publication Data
A catalogue record for this book is available from the British Library

Library of Congress Cataloging-in-Publication Data
Names: Arunmozhi, Manimuthu author | Wise, Luan, 1977– author
Title: Privacy in the age of social media : beyond the like / Dr. Manimuthu Arunmozhi and Luan Wise.
Description: Abingdon, Oxon ; New York, NY : Routledge, 2027. | Series: Current issues in cyberpsychology | Includes bibliographical references and index.
Identifiers: LCCN 2026018961 (print) | LCCN 2026018962 (ebook) | ISBN 9781041102823 hardback | ISBN 9781041102816 paperback | ISBN 9781003654322 ebook
Subjects: LCSH: Online social networks | Privacy, Right of | Social media
Classification: LCC HM742 .A78 2027 (print) | LCC HM742 (ebook)
LC record available at https://lccn.loc.gov/2026018961
LC ebook record available at https://lccn.loc.gov/2026018962

ISBN: 9781041102823 (hbk)
ISBN: 9781041102816 (pbk)
ISBN: 9781003654322 (ebk)

DOI: 10.4324/9781003654322

Typeset in Times New Roman
by codeMantra

Contents

Figures

Tables

About the Authors

Dr. Manimuthu Arunmozhi is a cybersecurity academic, researcher, and technology entrepreneur whose work focuses on digital privacy, trust, and responsible technology use. He is Assistant Professor at Aston Business School, Aston University (UK), where he teaches cybersecurity management, digital risk, and business analytics.

Before moving into academia, Manimuthu worked in infrastructure engineering, cloud platforms, and cybersecurity operations within large, structured organizations. This practitioner's background continues to inform his research and teaching, helping bridge technical systems with human behavior and governance.

He is a patent holder and was named a finalist for the 2025 Innovation Award (Young Innovator category), recognizing his contribution to cybersecurity innovation and societal impact. He is also the Founder and CEO of Q Safe, a Quantum security company focused on improving digital trust, privacy, and responsible technology adoption.

His research spans digital privacy, data exploitation, trustworthy AI, digital twins, smart data governance, and cyber governance, supported by interdisciplinary projects and international collaborations.

Luan Wise is a seasoned marketing practitioner with 25 years of agency, client-side, and consultancy experience. She is a chartered marketer and fellow of the Chartered Institute of Marketing (FCIM) and is currently pursuing a PhD by Portfolio at the University of Lancashire (UK), focusing on B2B marketing and technology adoption. Luan is a LinkedIn Learning Course Instructor and Meta Lead Trainer, and delivers training for professional bodies, university business schools, and organizations across the world. Her 2024 TEDx talk focused on the role of social media as a force for good.

Privacy in the Age of Social Media: Beyond the Like is Luan's seventh book—she has previously published *Relax! It's Only Social Media, Planning for Success: A Practical Guide to Setting and Achieving Your Social Media Marketing Goals, Using Social Media for Work: How to Maintain Professional Etiquette Online, Smart Social Media: How to Grow your Business with Social Media Marketing,* and *Marketing and Psychology: Understanding Customer Behaviour with the ABC Approach* and she also contributed a chapter to *The Future of Charity Marketing.*

Foreword

I have spent a great deal of my career studying why people behave the way they do online: what draws them in, what they share without thinking, and what they later wish they hadn't. What strikes me most, still, is not the complexity of the technology. It is the gap between what users believe is happening to their data and what is actually happening. That gap is not accidental. It is, in many cases, designed.

Drawing from my earlier research on social media privacy (or the lack of it), one theme surfaced repeatedly across contributions from researchers in cybersecurity, psychology, law, and public health: we have built extraordinarily sophisticated systems for capturing human behavior, and extraordinarily poor ones for helping people understand what that means for their lives. Social media platforms know more about our habits, preferences, and vulnerabilities than most of our closest friends, and they know it in real time, at scale, and with commercial intent. Privacy, in this context, is not simply a matter of adjusting settings. It is a matter of literacy, power, and rights.

This is precisely why this book matters. It takes a subject that has too often been the preserve of specialists: data scientists, regulators, and legal scholars, and opens it to the rest of us. It asks what really happens when we tap a like button, accept a cookie notice, or share a location. It traces the journey from that small, instinctive gesture to the vast data economy it feeds. And it does so without either sensationalizing the risks or retreating into technicality.

What I find particularly valuable here is the pairing of two perspectives that rarely appear together in a single volume: the technical and the human. Cybersecurity research tends toward systems and threats; marketing practice tends toward behavior and influence. Together, they shed some light onto something neither fully captures alone: the experience of being a user inside a machine that was not designed with your interests as its primary concern. Understanding that experience, clearly and honestly, is the first condition for changing it.

We are at a moment when the questions this book raises are moving from academic concern to urgent public debate. Regulators are catching up, slowly, imperfectly, but genuinely, with the realities of surveillance capitalism. Artificial intelligence is reshaping what platforms can infer from the data they hold. Users, in growing numbers, are asking harder questions about the bargains they have implicitly accepted. This book equips its readers to participate in that conversation with knowledge, confidence, and, crucially, agency.

Privacy is not a niche concern for the technically minded. It is a condition of autonomy, dignity, and trust in a digital age. I am delighted this book exists, and I hope it finds the wide readership it deserves.

Professor Vladlena Benson MBE
PhD MSc BSc CISMP SFHEA
Editor, Handbook of Social Media Use: Online Relationships, Security, Privacy, and Society

Acknowledgements

We would like to extend our thanks to our colleagues and peers who supported us throughout our research and writing journey. Your encouragement, conversations, and shared perspectives have played an important role in shaping this work, and we are truly grateful.

We are especially grateful to our early reviewers: Alison, Drew, Vladlena, Jon-Stephen, Tatiana, Vincent. Your thoughtful feedback has been invaluable in shaping the final version of this book.

We also want to express our gratitude to the team at Routledge for their guidance and support throughout the publication process.

From Mani: I would like to extend my heartfelt gratitude to Luan for being an incredible collaborator on this journey. Your perspectives, clarity of thought, and dedication have enriched this work in ways that go far beyond what I had envisioned. This book is as much yours as it is mine. I am deeply grateful to my family, especially my wife, Dharshini, and Son, Magilshreesai, for their unwavering support, patience, and encouragement throughout this process. This work would not have been possible without you.

From Luan: Thank you to Mani for inviting me to collaborate on this project—it's been a joy to work on it with you. You've opened my eyes to the technologies and challenges in the world of social media, and I hope our guidance will support our readers in navigating this ever-evolving digital world with confidence. As always, thank you to my husband, Steven, for everything you do to support me.

Introduction

Since the early 2000s, the rapid rise of social media has reshaped how people interact, communicate, and consume information—and the shift has added enormous value globally. As of 2025, over 5 billion people use social media worldwide and billions more benefit from the economic impact: social media advertising alone has grown into a multibillion-dollar industry, with global ad spend surpassing US$275 billion and still climbing.

However, despite the benefits, it is also evident that this digital transformation has come with some serious costs. Its use can impact mental health, well-being, and social connection, increase exposure to misleading or polarizing content on social media, influence politics and policies, and threaten our privacy and human rights.

Social media platforms operate within a data-driven economy, a system in which personal information is treated as a valuable resource that fuels business models and drives revenue. Every interaction—from likes and shares to clicks and comments—generates data that is collected, analyzed, and monetized, often in ways users cannot see or control. Even simple online actions contribute to detailed profiles that companies and organizations use to predict interests, influence decisions, and shape the content users encounter.

This was not part of the vision for the web, as inventor of the World Wide Web, Tim Berners-Lee intended. In his book, *This is for Everyone,* he said:

> I had known for a while that something was wrong with the web. What was intended to be a tool for creativity and collaboration had become divisive, polarizing and toxic. I had often talked publicly of the two Cs of the web: creativity and collaboration. After 2016, I began to talk of a third C: compassion. I was greatly concerned that the human element of the web was beginning to disappear. In its place we had large, faceless systems which spied on and manipulated the user.

Today, the reality is dominated by massive social media networks with billions of users worldwide, where personal data has become the cornerstone of a multibillion-dollar industry. The scale and concentration of power in the hands of a few platform leaders, combined with the global reach of these networks, means that the ways data is collected and used affect people on an unprecedented scale.

DOI: 10.4324/9781003654322-1

For individuals, this makes privacy critically important. It's not just about deciding what to share, but about understanding the consequences of your online actions—how seemingly small interactions reveal patterns, habits, and preferences that can affect your personal, financial, and professional life. For organizations, privacy matters because mishandling user data can damage trust, harm reputations, and lead to legal and financial consequences.

Social media and digital technologies have transformed privacy. Data is collected constantly and at an unprecedented scale, stored indefinitely, and used in ways that are often invisible to users.

In this connected world, being aware of how your online behavior generates information—and why that information matters—is essential for protecting yourself and for holding organizations accountable for the ways they use it.

Yet, most users remain unaware of the full extent of how their data is collected, analyzed, and used; and this raises important ethical dilemmas: platforms profit from users' personal information through mechanisms that are often invisible or poorly understood, raising questions about consent, transparency, and fairness. The scale and complexity of these networks also make it difficult for governments and regulators to manage how data is collected and used. When users do not fully understand how social media platforms operate within a data-driven economy, they cannot make informed choices about their online actions or the information they share.

Research shows that this lack of understanding is widespread. Only a minority of social media users are aware of how their data is collected, processed, and monetized, and many underestimate the degree to which even passive interactions contribute to profiling and targeted content. At the same time, surveys indicate that concern about data privacy is high: a 2023 Pew Research Center study found that 81% of adults are worried about how companies use their data, while 67% report having little to no understanding of what happens to their personal information once it is collected. Academic studies also show that lower awareness of privacy risks is associated with greater self-disclosure on social media, meaning people often share more than they might realize.

This gap between concern and understanding highlights why education about data practices, ethical considerations, and privacy is increasingly essential—not just for individuals, but for society as a whole.

By exploring these issues, this book takes readers beyond the like—uncovering what happens behind the scenes when you interact online, how your data is collected and used, and the ethical and privacy implications and the challenges of managing these complex systems at scale—so that you can navigate social media with greater awareness, control, and confidence.

Who Is This Book For?

This book is written for anyone curious about the complex and often confusing world of social media and data privacy. If you're an everyday user scrolling through

Facebook, Instagram, X, LinkedIn, or TikTok and wondering what really happens to the information you share, you'll find clear explanations here. It's also a helpful guide for business professionals and marketers who rely on social platforms to build brands, connect with customers, and run campaigns, but want to make sure they're using data ethically while still meeting their goals.

Students and academics in fields such as digital media, cybersecurity, business ethics, and law will discover a foundation for understanding the unique privacy challenges that come with today's social platforms. And if you're a privacy advocate or policymaker working to shape digital rights and regulations, this book offers insights that can support informed decision-making.

And beyond all of that, we believe this book is essential reading for every citizen. In a world where our personal data is constantly collected, analyzed, and used—often in ways we don't see—understanding how social media works behind the scenes isn't just helpful; it's a vital life skill in a digital age.

What Readers Will Learn

This book brings together aligned expertise from two areas: a cybersecurity academic who studies the mechanics and risks of our digital lives, and a marketing practitioner with recognized knowledge of how social media works in the real world.

The idea for this collaboration began when we met as speakers at TEDx Aston University, on the theme of the ripple effect—the ways small actions online can create far-reaching consequences.

By combining our viewpoints, we've created a guide that explains the complexities of digital privacy in a way that's both informed and approachable.

Understanding the Realities of Social Media Privacy

We start by lifting the lid on what actually happens to your data—how platforms collect it, how long it stays around, and what it's used for. Along the way, you'll explore:

- The hidden risks that come with everyday scrolling
- Why privacy breaches can have long-lasting consequences
- What metadata and behavioral tracking reveal about your habits

The Ethics Behind the Platforms

We then look at the business models powering social media and the ethical questions they raise. You'll gain insight into:

- How companies balance growth with user rights
- The influence of AI, algorithms, and targeted advertising
- Why transparency and accountability matter more than ever

How Laws and Regulations Fit In

Next, we take you through the global rules shaping today's digital landscape—without the legal jargon. You'll learn about:

- Key privacy laws such as General Data Protection Regulation and the California Consumer Privacy Act
- Why enforcing regulations across borders is so challenging
- The evolving roles of governments and tech companies in protecting digital rights

What the Future Might Hold

We also explore where things are heading, from technology to culture, including:

- New privacy-enhancing innovations
- The rise of decentralized platforms and user-owned data
- The growing push for ethical, human-centered technology

Practical Steps You Can Take

And throughout, you'll find clear, simple actions you can take to protect yourself online. This includes:

- Strengthening your personal privacy
- Navigating platform settings with confidence
- Building digital literacy that lasts

A Call to Action

Privacy in the digital age requires active participation. By understanding the risks, implementing best practices, and advocating for responsible digital policies, individuals and organizations can build a more secure and ethical digital environment.

You'll see the word "manipulation" used periodically within this book. That term can sound heavy or threatening, and that's understandable—in everyday language it often carries negative connotations. But in the context of digital privacy and social media, we use it in a specific, descriptive, and practical way.

In *Manipulation: What It Is, Why It's Bad, What to Do About It*, Cass Sunstein—drawing on decades of work in behavioral science—offers a definition tailored to our digital age. He explains that manipulation refers to ways in which information, algorithms, and design can steer choices or behaviors behind the scenes, potentially undermining individual autonomy or well-being. Importantly, this isn't about suggesting everyday use of social media is inherently harmful—it's about recognizing how certain unseen influences can shape decisions and why awareness matters.

Throughout this book, our aim isn't to alarm you. It's to equip you with greater understanding. We hope that after reading, you'll be better positioned to make informed decisions, protect your privacy, and engage with digital platforms with confidence.

References

Berners-Lee, T. (2025). *This Is for Everyone.* Macmillan

Lee, J., & Attablayo, S. (2023). Examining the impacts of privacy awareness on users' self-disclosure on social media. arXiv. https://arxiv.org/abs/2303.07927

Pew Research Center. (2023, October 18). How Americans view data privacy: Risks, personal data, and digital privacy laws. Pew Research Center. https://www.pewresearch.org/internet/2023/10/18/views-of-data-privacy-risks-personal-data-and-digital-privacy-laws/

Statista. (2025). Social media – statistics & facts. Retrieved December 4, 2025, from https://www.statista.com/topics/1164/advertising-spending/

Statista. (2025). Social media advertising – worldwide market forecast 2025. Retrieved December 4, 2025, from https://www.statista.com/outlook/dmo/digital-advertising/social-media-advertising/worldwide

Sunstein, C. R. (2025). *Manipulation: What it is, why it's bad, what to do about it.* Cambridge University Press.

1 From Connection to Commodification—The Evolution of Social Media

How many times have you tapped the "thumbs up" or "heart" button on a social media post today? Did you pause to consider what that really means, or what happens next?

Yes, you've sent a clear signal to the person who shared the post, but that's just the beginning. Every "like" you add feeds into an invisible algorithm, shaping what you see next, nudging what your friends see, and subtly influencing how content spreads. That simple tap is both a personal expression and a tiny drop in a massive digital ripple, with effects that reach far beyond the post itself.

Social media has become such an integral part of modern life, shaping the way people connect, communicate, and consume information. From personal interactions to business engagements, platforms such as Facebook, Instagram, X (formerly Twitter), LinkedIn, and TikTok have revolutionized digital interactions.

But, every time we engage online, we leave behind traces of our behavior: the posts we like, the videos we watch, the comments we leave. These digital footprints are collected and analyzed, forming detailed profiles of who we are, what we care about, and how we behave.

Social media platforms use this information to tailor content, suggest new connections, and, in many cases, drive advertising that feels eerily precise. Over time, these traces—so casually left behind—become part of a vast, data-driven economy, where our information is treated as a currency. And while the benefits of social media are real—connection, convenience, entertainment—the trade-offs are often invisible, subtle, and far-reaching.

The very fact that our every move online is observed, analyzed, and monetized raises a concern about the boundaries of privacy in this digital world. And so we ask: Can privacy exist in an era where digital interactions are constantly monitored and monetized?

It is an important question because the answer touches the core of how we live, work, and communicate online. Data fuels the platforms we rely on, shaping not only the content we see but also the choices we make. It influences marketing strategies, political discourse, and much more.

DOI: 10.4324/9781003654322-2

Connection, Creativity, and Community

Social media began as a space for connection, creativity, and community. It offered users the thrill of real-time communication, the novelty of self-expression, and the joy of shared experience across borders. In its early days, logging onto a platform felt like entering a global gathering—messy, earnest, and brimming with potential. Facebook, for example, launched with the mission "to give people the power to share and make the world more open and connected." We were not just users; we were participants in a new social fabric.

But as these platforms matured, their core purpose quietly shifted. Behind the familiar interfaces and curated feeds, a new engine began to hum—one that ran not on connection but on data. Likes, comments, and shares morphed from social gestures into data points. The more we engaged, the more we revealed—and the more valuable we, as users, became the product.

What began as a digital commons for human expression transformed into a vast marketplace of behavioral prediction.

This chapter retraces the arc of that transformation. From the optimistic birth of online communities to the emergence of platforms designed to surveil, predict, and monetize human behavior, we explore how social media's business model has pivoted.

We examine not just the evolution of technology, but also the changing behaviors, expectations, and vulnerabilities of users navigating these systems. As we peel back the layers, a clear narrative emerges: the tools built to connect us are now finely tuned instruments of observation and influence.

In tracing this trajectory, we may begin to see social media not as a neutral platform but as a powerful force—shaping what we see, how we feel, and even who we become. Understanding this evolution is important for taking more control in a digital environment where attention is often treated as a commodity and privacy remains a key consideration.

The Birth of Digital Social Spaces

The early 2000s marked the dawn of a new era in online interaction. Platforms such as MySpace and Orkut invited users to explore a virtual landscape centered on profiles, friendships, and personal expression. These early platforms offered basic features—adding friends, posting testimonials, or sharing music—but they were revolutionary for the time. Social media was not yet a business strategy; it was a cultural experiment in connection.

Self-Expression and Digital Identity

A defining feature of early social media was the creative freedom users had in curating their digital presence. MySpace, for instance, allowed users to customize backgrounds with HTML, embed music players, and adopt unique screen names. These personal touches turned user profiles into digital canvases—representations of personality, taste, and mood. The emphasis was not on performance for an audience, but on identity-building and belonging.

Users became amateur web designers, musicians, bloggers, and community builders. Unlike today's more polished feeds, early social media was often messy, unfiltered, and raw. But therein lay its charm—it was authentic, imperfect, and grounded in play rather than performance.

Community before Algorithms

These platforms fostered a sense of community that was often intimate and supportive. Friend groups formed naturally, based on real-life connections or shared interests in music, fandoms, or hobbies. Groups and forums flourished, enabling niche discussions and peer-to-peer interaction. The absence of engagement metrics such as likes or follower counts at this time meant interactions were driven by genuine connection.

In this early phase, users controlled their own visibility. There were no algorithmic feeds shaping what you should see or engage with. Content appeared in the order it was posted, allowing users to interact on their own terms. This chronological design encouraged intentional engagement and reduced the performance anxiety we often see on today's modern platforms.

> To note: It is possible to change timelines to a chronological order, however this is no longer the default option on most platforms.

A Business Model Yet to Be Born

In its early days, the social web lacked a clear revenue model. While some platforms experimented with banner ads, sponsorships, or premium features, most were funded by venture capital and focused on building and retaining users.

Users were explorers, testers, and creators in an unfamiliar digital terrain. Digital footprints existed, but they weren't systematically analyzed for behavioral targeting. Privacy, though not always explicitly discussed, often felt like a default assumption rather than something that required constant attention.

Do you remember what it was like to log on to a social platform for the first time—the novelty and excitement of sharing a post, seeing friends' updates, or reconnecting with old school friends and distant relatives?

A Lost Digital Innocence

Looking back, this era can feel almost idyllic. Users weren't subject to personalized ads, nudging algorithms, or feeds curated by predictive models. Social media was participatory, not predictive—a patchwork of communities woven together by curiosity and creativity.

As technology has evolved and connectivity grown more sophisticated, some of that openness has shifted. That early period holds a sense of digital innocence:

a time when platforms were primarily about connection, experimentation, and shared experience rather than data monetization.

This origin story isn't meant to evoke nostalgia alone; it's instructive. By understanding where social media began, we can better trace how and why it transformed—and consider the ethical, social, and regulatory questions that come with its current form.

The Rise of Engagement Metrics and Platform Capitalism

We now turn to how social media evolved from a space for connection and creativity into a data-driven ecosystem, where engagement metrics became central to both user experience and business strategy.

From Communication to Optimization

As social media platforms became more firmly established, the original ethos of connection and creativity gradually evolved into a focus on optimization and measurement.

A pivotal moment came in February 2009 with the introduction of Facebook's "Like" button—a simple, intuitive feature that changed the way people interacted online. According to *Like: The Button That Changed the World* (Reeves & Goodson, 2025), the feature was initially met with skepticism, with concerns that it might cheapen interactions by reducing meaningful engagement to a single click rather than thoughtful comments. Nevertheless, the Like button provided a scalable way to measure user preferences and engagement, giving advertisers far richer data and laying the groundwork for the highly targeted advertising model that followed.

Since then, the like-button concept has spread widely. LinkedIn added "Likes" in 2012, while newer platforms such as TikTok and Instagram incorporated similar features from their launch, cementing single-click engagement as a standard across social media.

What started as a simple way to show appreciation quickly became central to the data economy. Each like, comment, share, reaction, or view offered a glimpse into user preferences, helping platforms understand what captured attention. Over time, these signals became the core currency of social media, shaping not only the content people saw but also how platforms designed experiences and connected with advertisers—all while influencing the ways we interact, share, and engage online.

The Attention Economy and Metrics Mentality

With engagement metrics now in focus, platforms began to structure their interfaces to maximize attention. This shift contributed to what Herbert A. Simon describes as the "attention economy"—an idea that human attention is a scarce and valuable resource, and that our focus has become something platforms actively compete for.

As user engagement became central to platform design, the more time users spent online, the more data they generated, creating opportunities for targeted

Table 1.1 Engagement Metrics vs. User Experience

Engagement Metric	*Platform Goal*	*User Perception*	*User Impact*
Likes	Measure popularity	Validation	Self-worth tied to numbers
Shares	Amplify content reach	Influence or trendiness	Pressure to go viral
Follower Count	Signal social status	Community size	Fear of missing out (FOMO)
Time-on-Platform	Ad revenue optimization	Convenience	Loss of time, digital fatigue
Comments	Engagement feedback	Conversation	Exposure to harassment or echo chambers

advertising. Features such as infinite scroll, autoplay, push notifications, and algorithmic content suggestions were introduced to maintain engagement, often without users' conscious awareness. Table 1.1 illustrates this dynamic, showing common engagement metrics alongside the goals platforms pursue, how users perceive these features, and the potential impacts on user behavior. For example, likes and shares can foster validation or a sense of influence, but they can also lead to self-worth being tied to numbers or pressure to go viral. Similarly, features designed for convenience or conversation may enhance community feeling but can contribute to digital fatigue or exposure to harassment. These patterns—how engagement metrics shape behavior, perception, and experience—are themes we will continue to explore throughout this book.

This engagement-centric design also reshaped how users interacted with content. Posts increasingly drew attention through visual appeal, emotional resonance, or timely relevance, encouraging likes, shares, and conversation. These changes give a picture of how platforms learned what kept people engaged and how users, in turn, responded. The metrics began to guide the kinds of posts people created and the ways they participated, shaping the rhythm of everyday social media experiences.

Algorithmic Feeds and Behavioral Engineering

Around the mid-2010s, one of the most significant technological shifts was the move from chronological feeds to algorithmically curated timelines. Instead of showing posts in the order they were created, platforms like Facebook, Instagram, and Twitter (now X) began displaying content based on predicted engagement. TikTok later amplified this approach with its *For You* feed, delivering a highly personalized stream of videos from both friends and strangers, making algorithmic curation central to the user experience.

It was during this period that behavioral engineering emerged as a key feature of platform design. These algorithms—powered by artificial intelligence (AI) and machine learning—analyze user behavior to determine what content is most likely to hold attention. Feeds started to become personalized spaces, designed not only to inform or entertain but also to encourage longer and more frequent engagement.

This shift created a feedback loop. If a user pauses on emotionally charged videos, controversial posts, or highly polished content, for example, the feed responds by showing more of the same. Over time, this pattern can be used to steer attention and behavior—shaping what people see, how long they stay, and even how they feel—as we'll soon start to explore in more detail.

Monetization: The Pivot to Platform Capitalism

As engagement metrics grew more sophisticated, so did the business strategies behind them. Social media platforms increasingly embraced platform capitalism, a model where infrastructure is owned by a few centralized corporations, and value is extracted from user activity at scale.

This approach built on existing advertising revenue but intensified with data monetization, turning interactions into increasingly valuable insights for advertisers. Detailed behavioral data allowed platforms to reach micro-targeted audiences with remarkable precision, with every click, pause, and scroll contributing to a user profile that could be leveraged for profit.

In essence, users were no longer the audience—they were the product. Their attention was the commodity, their data, the asset. What had started as a place to connect had become a machine to measure, predict, and capitalize on human behavior.

The Metrics Mentality: Shaping User Behavior

As users and organizations became aware of how visibility depended on metrics, their behavior changed. Posts were optimized for reach and engagement. Content creators and brands alike began studying algorithms, trying to decode the best times to post, the most effective hashtags, and the types of content that would attract attention.

Even everyday users began curating their digital lives. Photos were filtered, captions crafted for maximum appeal, and self-worth increasingly tied to online validation. The metrics mentality seeped into social behavior, subtly redefining how people presented themselves, what they chose to share, and how they gauged their standing or approval within their networks.

Figure 1.1 illustrates the evolution of social media over time from early community-focused platforms to data-driven, commodified ecosystems, where

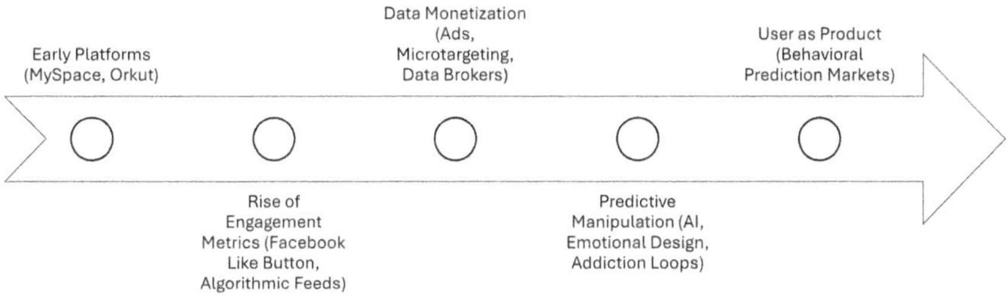

Figure 1.1 The Evolution of Social Media—From Connection to Commodification.

user interaction was largely chronological and driven by the choices users made about who/what to follow and engage with.

Engagement metrics, such as Facebook's Like button and algorithmic feeds, shifted the focus toward measuring and optimizing interaction. This shift marked a move from neutral content display to engagement optimization, where visibility and interaction became measurable and strategically incentivized. We see the transition to data monetization, where user activity is systematically harvested for targeted advertising, micro-targeting, and data brokerage.

Here, personal data becomes an economic asset, embedding surveillance and profiling into platform business models. The next stage shows the rise of predictive design, where platforms use AI, emotional design, and engagement-driven loops to anticipate user behavior. Content is optimized to capture attention, encourage interaction, and sustain retention, shaping how users experience the platform. This evolution culminates in the "user as product" phase, where behavioral data becomes the core value of the platform.

A Silent Shift with Lasting Implications

This rise of engagement metrics and monetization did not happen overnight. It was gradual, subtle, and largely unchallenged—normalizing a digital environment where users' emotional and behavioral data became fuel for corporate growth.

What was lost in this transition was nuance and authenticity. Interactions were no longer just about meaning or connection; they became performance-driven, shaped by unseen algorithms and monetized in real time. The tools of expression had been repurposed into instruments of influence, steering not just what users saw, but also how they acted.

Understanding this evolution is vital to understanding the modern digital landscape. The next sections will explore how this monetization model paved the way for large-scale surveillance, behavioral profiling, and the ethical dilemmas that now define our social media experience.

The Monetization Shift

As platforms attracted millions of active users, many adopted a model of "free access," offering their services at no direct cost while generating revenue from advertising.

Platforms monetized the behavioral data users produced, turning interactions into highly targeted marketing opportunities. The value of these platforms came not only from their technology, but from the rich data trails users created.

Behavioral Data as Currency

Every click, like, share, pause, or scroll creates a data point. Aggregated across millions of users, these micro-behaviors reveal preferences, routines, and even emotional cues. Platforms turned these patterns into predictive insights, enabling precise audience segmentation and real-time programmatic advertising.

Users had little visibility or control over this process. However, as we are learning, their activity frequently generated value for the platform without their full awareness or explicit consent.

The rise of microtargeting—delivering ads or content tailored to very specific user attributes—was a key development of this model. Advertisers could target users based on niche criteria: not just age or location, but recent purchases, emotional tone of posts, or inferred political views.

This level of targeting created a significant opportunity for marketers and political strategists. For instance, consumer brands could deliver personalized promotions based on browsing habits, past purchases, or even the emotional tone of posts, increasing the likelihood of engagement and conversion. During election cycles, platforms were used not just to share messages but to subtly influence voter behavior, shaping perceptions, emotions, and engagement.

Social media platforms also became central players in a larger data economy involving third-party developers, data brokers, and advertising networks. Applications integrated via Application Programming Interfaces (APIs)—tools that allow different software programs to communicate—often collect user data for purposes far beyond their stated function.

In some cases, data was sold or shared without explicit user knowledge. This ecosystem became difficult to trace, as user data moved between companies, often bundled, anonymized, and repurposed for marketing, research, or political campaigns. The now-infamous Cambridge Analytica scandal involved the unauthorized collection of millions of Facebook users' data, which was then used to create targeted political advertising during elections, highlighting serious privacy and consent concerns.

These examples highlight the thin line between persuasion and manipulation. Once exposed, these practices led to changes in governance and regulation around targeted online messaging.

As public awareness grew about how personal data was being collected, shared, and monetized, trust in social media platforms began to erode. High-profile cases, combined with increased media scrutiny and regulatory attention, prompted users to question how much control they really had over their digital identities and the value being generated from their activity.

This shift in understanding raised critical ethical questions: Who owns the data? Should users be compensated for the value their data generates? For the most part, platforms sidestepped these debates by relying on Terms of Service (ToS) agreements—long, dense documents that research consistently shows are rarely read in full, yet are routinely accepted in order to access the service.

When was the last time you read a platform's ToS from start to finish?

This widespread acceptance without engagement is an example of what is often referred to as passive consent. But is it ethical for platforms to rely on users agreeing to terms they rarely read?

Despite growing concerns, most users stayed. The convenience of connection, the design of the platforms, and the lack of viable alternatives made opting out difficult. This revealed the depth of dependency—and how the use of social media has become deeply ingrained, shaped not just by data, but by habit, routine, and perhaps our need to maintain connection.

Looking Ahead: Monetization with Accountability?

As users become more privacy-conscious and regulators intervene, platforms are under increasing pressure to review their monetization models. Most now offer subscription tiers in addition to traditional advertising, while others explore decentralized networks—social systems built on distributed, peer-to-peer protocols rather than a single corporate owner. In such networks, users retain greater control over their own data and governance decisions, as seen in federated platforms like Mastodon and Bluesky, where independent communities connect without centralized data harvesting.

In September 2025, Meta introduced a subscription option in the UK and EU that lets users pay a monthly fee to use Facebook and Instagram without ads. Subscribers' personal data is not used for targeted advertising, while those who continue with free access see ads based on data-driven targeting.

This change followed legal challenges and regulatory pressure. Earlier in 2025, the tech giant agreed to stop targeting adverts at a British woman, Tanya O'Carroll, after she filed a lawsuit claiming Facebook's targeted advertising system fell under the UK's definition of direct marketing, giving individuals the right to object. Data watchdogs in the UK and EU contested Meta's previous model, where personalized ads were the only option, arguing it didn't provide a real choice.

Still, the legacy of the current system persists. To make sense of where social media is heading, it helps to first understand where we are now: a digital economy built on the large-scale collection and use of personal data, alongside emerging options—like subscription tiers and decentralized networks—that aim to give users clearer insight and more control over how their information is used.

The Architecture of Surveillance

Modern social media platforms are not neutral communication tools—they are sophisticated systems engineered to capture, retain, and monetize user behavior, as we are beginning to realize in this book. At the heart of these systems is surveillance capitalism, a term coined by Shoshana Zuboff to describe an economic model centered on the commodification of personal data with the goal of predicting and influencing behavior. Unlike traditional capitalism, which commodified labor and goods, surveillance capitalism commodifies human experience itself. Social media platforms are not merely participants in this model—they are its most powerful architects.

Every element of the interface—whether visual, interactive, or functional—serves a dual purpose: enhancing user experience while generating data that can be analyzed, monetized, and used to guide behavior. Features like infinite scroll, autoplay videos, and reaction emojis are not just conveniences—they encourage longer engagement. These design choices increase the time users spend on platforms, which in turn produces richer, more detailed behavioral data. The longer someone remains on a platform, the more granular their digital footprint becomes, and the more it can be used to inform algorithms and guide advertising.

AI is also central to this dynamic. As Mark Zuckerberg explained on Meta's Q2 2025 earnings call, AI-driven recommendation systems have helped increase the time users spend on Facebook by 5% and on Instagram by 6% in a single quarter. These systems learn what content users find "interesting and useful" and steer them toward more of it, keeping people engaged longer—especially through video and other interactive content.

Meta reported that in June 2025 more than 3.4 billion people used at least one of its family of apps daily—up 6% year-over-year. Video consumption rose by 20% year-over-year, thanks to AI-powered ranking optimizations and the promotion of original content. Even Threads, Meta's newest platform, saw similar increases in time spent due to the integration of large language models (LLMs) into its content recommendations.

Together, these developments show how platform design, video prioritization, and AI-powered personalization work together to extend engagement and deepen the data captured.

Every second of attention carries both experiential and economic value, shaping individual experiences and underpinning the broader surveillance and monetization of social media.

Persistent Tracking and Data Retention Policies

Even when users are not actively posting or engaging with content, social media platforms continue to monitor background activity through tools like cookies, pixels, and device fingerprinting.

As a reminder: cookies are small files stored on a user's device that track browsing behavior across websites. Pixels are tiny, invisible images embedded in web pages or emails that report when content is viewed or interacted with. Device fingerprinting collects information about a user's device—such as operating system, browser, and screen resolution—to uniquely identify and track them even without cookies. Software Development Kits (SDKs) embedded in third-party apps extend tracking further, allowing platforms to monitor activity across multiple apps. SDKs enable platforms to track off-platform behavior, such as browsing other websites, using unrelated mobile apps, or interacting with connected services.

This collected data doesn't simply disappear once the activity ends—it can be stored, analyzed, and reused, creating long-term records of user behavior.

Data retention policies often extend indefinitely. As already noted, these practices are typically outlined in platform ToS and Privacy Policies—documents rarely read in full by users. Posts that appear deleted may persist in backups; interactions that seem fleeting—likes, comments, or ephemeral stories—can be archived for later analysis. Metadata, including time stamps, location, and device information, is similarly stored long after its immediate relevance has passed. While data protection laws require that personal data be kept only as long as necessary for the purpose for which it was collected, in practice platforms may retain data for technical, security, or analytical reasons before deletion is completed. For example, major social networks may hold user data for weeks or months after account deletion as part of normal retention processes.

Together, these practices raise important questions about consent, necessity, and privacy. Users may assume that deleting content removes it entirely, but in reality, their data can remain accessible within platform systems.

Surveillance Layering: Beyond the Platform

Social media surveillance is not confined to a single app or platform. Through cross-platform integration, companies can build unified behavioral profiles using a combination of browsing data, location history, purchasing habits, and social connections.

For example, a user may log into multiple services using a single sign-on (SSO) system like Facebook Login or Google Sign-In. While convenient, this consolidates user data across platforms, giving the parent company broader visibility into the user's digital life. Combined with third-party data brokers, this surveillance layering becomes more invasive and less transparent.

Have you ever used your social media account to sign into other apps or services—perhaps while connected to public Wi-Fi in a coffee shop? Figure 1.2 illustrates how a single login can link multiple platforms and share data with third parties, revealing the hidden paths your information can take.

Invisible and Inescapable

The true danger of this surveillance architecture lies in its invisibility. Unlike physical surveillance, which you can usually see and is limited to a specific place—like a security camera in a store—digital surveillance is silent, persistent, and embedded in everyday behavior.

Tracking not just what you post, but how long you hover, where you pause, what you delete, and even how quickly you scroll.

For many, avoiding social media is not a realistic option. People rely on platforms to stay connected with friends and family, while organizations run aspects of their business, professional networking, and customer engagement through them. This integration into daily life makes it difficult to step away from social media without withdrawing from the digital world entirely.

The deeply embedded nature of these surveillance systems has shifted the balance of power in digital life. What once began as tools for connection has gradually evolved into infrastructures that guide behavior (see Chapter 5 for a deeper discussion of psychological influences).

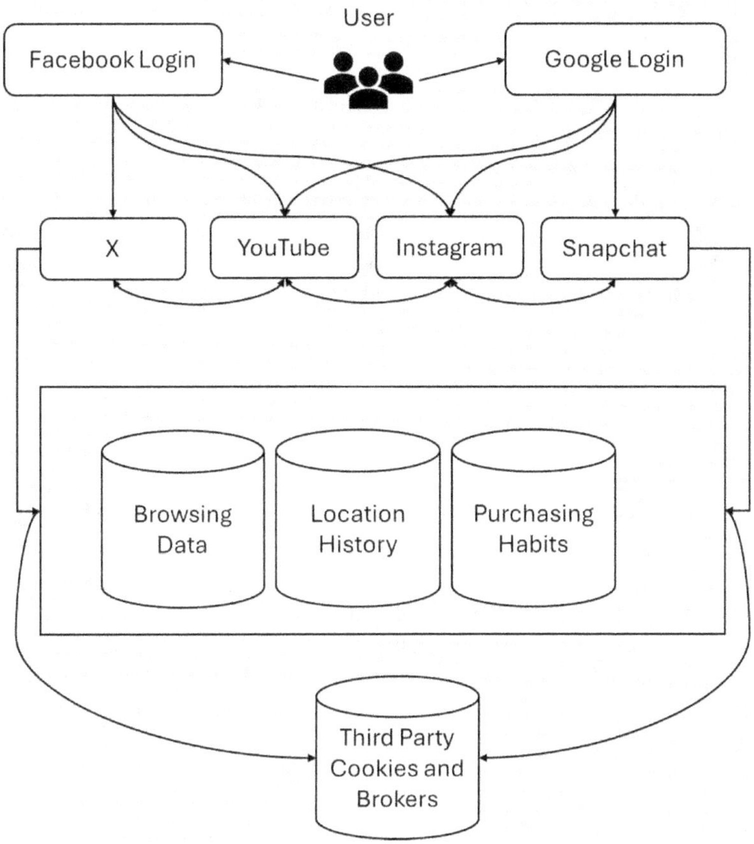

Figure 1.2 The Single Sign-On System.

The Social Contract of the Digital Age

In traditional societies, the social contract was an explicit or implicit agreement between citizens and institutions: citizens followed rules, and institutions provided protections and services in return. On social media, a new kind of social contract exists—though it's far less visible.

By using social media platforms, we agree to share our personal information, post content, and engage with others. In return, platforms provide connection, entertainment, information, and community. But unlike traditional contracts, the terms here are often opaque. The social contract in the digital age has shifted the balance of power. Platforms collect and monetize vast amounts of behavioral data, while users gain access to valuable services—but often without full awareness of what is being traded.

This situation raises the ethical dilemma: how can platforms innovate and remain profitable without exploiting user data? Supporters argue that personalized services, free access, and data-driven optimization improve user experience. Critics counter that these benefits come at the cost of autonomy, equity, and psychological well-being.

The real challenge lies in rethinking digital value: is success measured by engagement and monetization, or by empowerment and trust? Can business models evolve to reward transparency and user agency rather than exploitation?

Understanding the mechanics of surveillance capitalism and this digital social contract is a necessary step toward reclaiming control over our digital lives. It invites us to ask not just what platforms do, but what kind of society they are helping to build.

From Interaction to Instrumentalization

At first glance, social media seems harmless—even helpful. But over time, what began as tools for connection and expression have gradually been instrumentalized: interactions and content are increasingly treated as means to an end, whether that's engagement metrics, advertising revenue, or behavioral prediction. These changes didn't happen abruptly—they were incremental, layered, and subtle. By the time users noticed, many of the platforms they trusted had already transformed into highly efficient systems of behavioral engineering.

What's concerning is that this exploitation is rarely framed as such. Instead, as in Figure 1.3, it hides behind the language of "personalization," "user engagement," and "enhanced experience"—phrases that soften the reality that platforms extract time, data, and emotional energy for corporate profit.

One of the most subtle shifts is how engagement metrics—likes, views, followers, and shares—have redefined users' sense of identity and social worth. These metrics were originally introduced as feedback mechanisms, intended to signal interest or appreciation. But they quickly became social currencies—a way to measure popularity, influence, and value.

As users began optimizing content for more likes and comments, the line between authentic self-expression and performative posting began to blur. Many users, both individuals and on behalf of organizations, tailor their content to fit algorithmic preferences or peer approval, crafting a curated online identity that may differ significantly from reality.

In this way, users are not just participating in digital culture—they are being subtly guided and conditioned by it, often without realizing the extent to which their behavior is shaped by the platforms themselves. This shaping of behavior doesn't stop at content creation—it extends to what users see and engage with.

Figure 1.3 The Engagement–Extraction Loop in Social Media Platforms.

One of the most effective ways platforms capture attention is by provoking emotion—especially anger, fear, and outrage. Algorithms have learned that emotionally charged content generates more engagement and, as a result, prioritize it in users' feeds. Users are therefore repeatedly exposed to provocative posts, controversial opinions, or shocking headlines—not necessarily because they are the most accurate or balanced, but because they drive interaction.

Emotionally charged content is just one way platforms shape user behavior. Many of the most "engaging" features—notifications, likes, streaks, and infinite scroll—are designed using insights from behavioral psychology, particularly techniques borrowed from gambling.

Intermittent variable rewards—rewards that arrive unpredictably—are especially effective at creating habit loops. Every time users check their phone, they might encounter a new like, message, or follower. This unpredictability encourages repeated engagement, often without conscious awareness.

The objective is less about improving user experience than maximizing time-on-platform, a key metric for advertising revenue. By keeping users returning frequently and staying longer, platforms increase opportunities to monetize attention and behavior.

Digital Labor without Consent

Every moment spent on a platform contributes to a system of value extraction. Whether users are creating content, reacting to others, or simply consuming, their behavior is being converted into data. That data, in turn—justified by pointing to user consent through ToS agreements—powers advertising algorithms, content recommendation engines, and insights that can be sold to third parties.

Yet for most users, contributions are neither compensated nor fully transparent in how they are used, even though some professional creators can earn some revenue from their content.

This arrangement benefits the platform disproportionately. Social media companies profit immensely from user activity, while most users often receive little more than short dopamine hits, curated content, and social comparison in return.

To reclaim the original promise of social media—as a tool for communication, creativity, and community—users, developers, and policymakers must critically examine how platforms define and reward engagement.

Only by recognizing the subtle shifts that have taken place, and the challenges they create, can we begin to address them and reclaim a more balanced digital experience.

Building a New Digital Ethic

The evolution of social media tells a story that is both remarkable and sobering. It began with a sense of wonder—a digital frontier full of possibility, where people could express themselves, reconnect, and form communities across borders. Early on, platforms thrived on creativity, authenticity, and experimentation. But as these platforms scaled and matured, their orientation has shifted. What was once a social tool gradually became a commercial enterprise, then an engine of surveillance.

This transformation wasn't, we believe, driven by intentional malice. It has been incremental—nudged along by market demands, technological innovation, and the increasing appetite for personalization and immediacy. But somewhere along the way, the promise of connection gave way to a commodification of attention, emotion, and user behavior.

From Playful Participation to Predictive Control

In the early years, participation was playful. Users experimented with content, expressed opinions freely, and curated digital identities without fear of being watched, judged, or profiled. But with the rise of engagement metrics, algorithmic feeds, and monetization models, participation took on a different meaning. Every post became a data point, every click a signal, every pause a micro-expression to be analyzed and monetized.

Today, users are no longer just expressing—they're performing. They are performing for an algorithm they do not understand, optimizing for attention and reach. Their digital presence is curated for visibility, their behavior subtly steered by psychology-driven nudges. They are playing the game to get results. This is not the freedom social media once promised—it can be considered predictive control disguised as choice.

The Emotional Cost of Engagement

This shift has not come without consequences. As platforms push for more engagement, some users report more anxiety, more comparison, more fatigue. The constant pressure to be seen, validated, and relevant takes a toll.

We now live in a world where social validation is quantified, privacy is transactional, and time spent online often benefits others more than ourselves. The emotional cost of engagement is real, and yet rarely acknowledged in the business models that drive it.

Responsibility without Blame

It is important to recognize that users are not to blame for this shift—nor are developers, marketers, or even platforms alone. The rise of surveillance capitalism and platform commodification reflects a larger systemic issue: a digital economy that rewards scale, speed, and attention above ethics, well-being, and trust.

The architecture of today's social media is the result of deliberate design choices—but also of cultural and economic forces that incentivize short-term gain over long-term responsibility. Acknowledging this helps move the conversation from individual blame to collective responsibility.

Taking time to reflect on the journey from connection to commodification is more than an academic exercise—it's a necessary step toward regaining agency. If users don't understand how platforms have changed, they cannot push for change. If designers and developers don't reflect on the consequences of their tools, they cannot build better ones. Reflection invites awareness. And awareness invites action.

This moment demands more than criticism—it calls for ethical imagination. Can we build platforms that value attention without exploiting it? Can we design systems that recommend without manipulating? Can we prioritize privacy without sacrificing connection?

The future of social media is not fixed. Just as it has evolved over the past two decades, it can evolve again—toward systems that are more transparent, and more accountable. We are now starting to see this with countries moving to restrict the use of social media for under 16s. But this future requires deliberate effort from everyone involved: users who demand better, regulators who enforce standards, companies that choose responsibility over reach.

We have traced the path from connection to commodification, from dialogue to data mining, from freedom to feedback loops. This journey sets the stage for what lies ahead.

Looking Ahead

As we reach the close of Chapter 1, we reflect on our fundamental question: How can privacy thrive in an era where digital interactions are widely monitored and monetized?

What would it look like for our digital lives to feel intentional and human—where we connect, share, and explore online with awareness and confidence, rather than perhaps simply following the flow of the platforms?

Drawing the line is the first step. The next is building something better—a new digital ethic, where platforms earn trust, users understand and exercise their rights, and privacy, respect, and well-being are integrated into the system by design.

References

Ahmadon, M. A. (2025). Digital privacy: Trends, challenges, and the future. *Computer*, *58*(3), 45–54. https://doi.org/10.1109/MITP.2025.3546433

Aisha Malik. (2026, June 15). These are the countries moving to ban social media for children. TechCrunch. https://techcrunch.com/2026/06/15/social-media-ban-children-countries-list/

Albulayhi, M. S., & El Khediri, S. (2022). A comprehensive study on privacy and security on social media. *International Journal of Interactive Mobile Technologies*, *16*(1), 277–291. https://doi.org/10.3991/ijim.v16i01.27761

BBC News. (2025, September 2026). Facebook and Instagram to get £2.99 UK subscription fee to stop ads. *BBC News*. https://www.bbc.co.uk/news/articles/c5y4xl5x8q7o

Meta Platforms, Inc. (2025, July 30) *Q2 2025 Earnings Call* https://investor.atmeta.com/investor-events/event-details/2025/Q2-2025-Earnings-Call/default.aspx

Metzler, H., et al. (2024). Social drivers and algorithmic mechanisms on digital media. *Perspectives on Psychological Science*. https://doi.org/10.1177/17456916231185057

Neves, J. (2024). Privacy concerns in social media use: A fear appeal perspective on SNS behaviour. *Computers in Human Behavior Reports*. https://doi.org/10.1016/j.chbr.2024.101956

Obar, J. A., & Oeldorf-Hirsch, A. (2020). The biggest lie on the internet: Ignoring the privacy policies and terms of service policies of social networking services. *Information, Communication & Society*, *23*(1), 128–147. https://doi.org/10.1080/1369118X.2018.1486870

Ojokoh, B. A., et al. (2025). *Privacy and security in recommender systems: An analytical review*. Artificial Intelligence Review. https://doi.org/10.1007/s10462-025-11333-4

Pereira, C., et al. (2025). Security and privacy in physical–digital environments: Challenges in mixed reality and the metaverse. *Future Internet*, *17*(2), 83. https://www.mdpi.com/1999-5903/17/2/83

Reeves, M., & Goodson, B. (2025). *Like: The button that changed the world*. Harvard Business Review Press.

Shrestha, A. K., Barthwal, A., Campbell, M., et al. (2024). Navigating AI to unpack youth privacy concerns: An in-depth exploration and systematic review. arXiv Preprint. https://arxiv.org/abs/2412.16369

Shrestha, A. K., Bobkova, Y., & Shouli, A. (2025). Covert surveillance in smart devices: A SCOUR framework analysis of youth privacy implications. arXiv Preprint. https://arxiv.org/abs/2510.24072

Simon, H. A. (1971). Designing organizations for an information-rich world. In M. Greenberger (Ed.), *Computers, communications, and the public interest* (pp. 37–72). Johns Hopkins Press.

Zuboff, S. (2020). *The age of surveillance capitalism: The fight for a human future at the new frontier of power*. Profile Books.

2 The Age of "Like" and the Price of Privacy

Social media has rapidly evolved from a simple means of communication into an essential part of modern life, shaping how individuals and organizations connect, share information, and present themselves to the world.

Among the many platforms that have reshaped digital interaction are Facebook, Instagram, X, LinkedIn, and TikTok. Each serves different social, informational, and professional functions—yet they all contribute to a digital environment where engagement is instant, content is continuously generated, and personal data becomes a fundamental part of the online ecosystem.

For many, social media started as a way to bring people together; today, those same platforms operate as vast networks of digital surveillance, where every interaction, click, share, and engagement is tracked, stored, and analyzed.

Do you know what happens to your personal information every time you like, share, or comment online?

Social media platforms gather vast amounts of information not only through interactions but also through location tracking, device identifiers, and metadata such as browsing history—often in ways that are not immediately apparent.

While many users assume they can manage their digital exposure privacy settings, the reality is far more complex, and much of their online behavior can still be tracked, shared, or inferred. Privacy settings may give the impression that you are managing your data, but understanding what is actually collected and shared requires navigating the often dense and complex privacy policies.

And although privacy settings can limit visibility to other users, they do little to prevent data collection by the platform itself.

As a result, the control users believe they have is largely illusory: adjusting settings may create the impression of some forms of protection, but in practice, platforms continue to collect, analyze, and share personal information.

Privacy on social media is heavily influenced by the platforms' business models. Since these services rely on collecting and analyzing user information to generate revenue—for example, via advertising—the control we think we have over our data is often more limited and conditional than it seems. The lack of transparency in these practices has sparked ongoing privacy concerns, regulatory scrutiny, and ethical debates surrounding data ownership and user rights.

DOI: 10.4324/9781003654322-3

Pervasive data collection transforms user activity into a commodity, feeding a broader surveillance economy. In this system, individuals can become products rather than users, with their attention and behaviors commodified for profit. This shift challenges the traditional notions of autonomy and consent, compelling both individuals and organizations to consider the ethical dimensions of digital participation.

Meanwhile, regulatory bodies struggle to keep pace with the rapid evolution of digital platforms, resulting in a fragmented landscape of privacy laws that vary across jurisdictions. From the European Union's General Data Protection Regulation (GDPR) to the California Consumer Privacy Act (CCPA), legal frameworks attempt to enforce user protections, yet enforcement remains inconsistent, and many companies have found ways to navigate around these restrictions.

This chapter sets the foundation for an in-depth exploration of privacy in social media. It examines how the evolution of digital engagement has created an intricate web of data exchange, where users trade personal information for connectivity.

Later chapters will dissect the mechanics of data collection, analyze the ethical dilemmas surrounding user surveillance, and provide insights into how individuals and organizations can navigate this digital landscape responsibly. Ultimately, this book aims to empower readers with the knowledge to make informed choices in a world where social media engagement and privacy might be seen to stand in opposition.

The Trade-Off between Connectivity and Privacy

One of the greatest paradoxes of social media is the trade-off between connectivity and privacy. *The Social Dilemma* (2020), a Netflix documentary, examined this tension by unpacking how social media platforms are intentionally engineered to maximize user engagement through persuasive design, behavioral prediction, and large-scale data collection. The film highlights the asymmetry between users and platforms: while individuals believe they are simply connecting and consuming content, the underlying systems continuously monitor, analyze, and monetize their interactions.

Users willingly share personal information to engage with friends, family, and online communities, yet they often underestimate the consequences of their digital footprint. Every post, photo, and comment contributes to an individual's online identity, which can be tracked, aggregated, and used in ways beyond their control, including:

- Targeted Advertising: Social media companies use collected data to serve highly personalized advertisements based on user interests, search history, and behavioral patterns.
- Algorithmic Content Curation: Platforms prioritize content that maximizes engagement, often creating echo chambers where users are exposed only to information that aligns with their previous behaviors.
- Third-Party Data Sharing: Many platforms share user data with external partners, advertisers, and data brokers, raising concerns about consent and security.

- Surveillance and Profiling: Governments and corporations utilize social media data for monitoring, predictive analytics, and behavioral profiling, often without full user knowledge.

This interconnected web of data collection raises serious concerns about user autonomy, as individuals often have little insight into how their digital personas are being used. The long-term implications of this trade-off are profound, impacting everything from consumer behavior to political polarization and digital security.

The Broader Implications of Data Collection

The consequences of unchecked data collection extend beyond individual privacy concerns. As social media platforms become increasingly integrated into daily life, the ethical, legal, and societal ramifications of their data practices come into sharper focus. The rise of misinformation, the shaping of public opinion, and the potential for biased outcomes from AI-driven content recommendations—such as promoting extreme, sensational, or one-sided perspectives—underscore the broader implications of the surveillance economy. The more data that is collected and stored, the greater the potential for breaches, identity theft, and other malicious exploitation, highlighting the ways these risks directly affect users and society.

These issues are particularly evident in three areas:

- Political Influence: Data-driven strategies have been used to influence public opinion, as seen in cases such as the Cambridge Analytica scandal and the impact of US and UK elections.
- Cybersecurity Risks: The aggregation of vast amounts of personal data makes social media platforms attractive targets for hackers and cybercriminals.
- Regulatory Gaps: Existing privacy laws struggle to keep pace with technological advancements, leading to inconsistent global protections and enforcement challenges.

Understanding the Data Economy

The data economy is the backbone of modern social media platforms, where user-generated data fuels business models that rely on targeted advertising, predictive analytics, and personalized experiences. Every interaction on a platform—whether liking a post, watching a video, or sharing content—creates valuable data that is collected, analyzed, and monetized by social media companies.

The Data Flow in Social Media

The journey of user data, as shown in Figure 2.1, follows a structured flow, from its initial generation to monetization. The process involves multiple stakeholders, including social media platforms, advertisers, data brokers, and regulatory bodies.

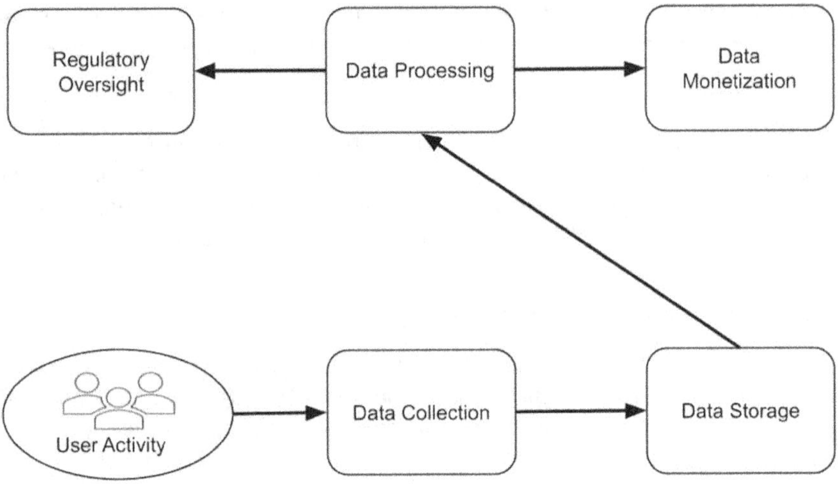

Figure 2.1 Social Media Data Flow: Illustrating How User Activity Leads to Data Collection, Storage, Processing, Monetization, and Regulatory Oversight.

Below is a step-by-step breakdown of the data flow:

1 User Interaction: Users engage with social media by viewing, liking, commenting, and sharing content. Each action generates data that reveals user interests, behaviors, and engagement patterns.
2 Data Collection: Platforms track user activities using various tools such as cookies, tracking pixels, and APIs. This collection extends beyond visible interactions to include metadata like device usage, location tracking, and time spent on content.
3 Data Storage: Collected data is stored in extensive databases, where it is categorized based on user behaviors, demographics, preferences, and predictive trends.
4 Data Processing and Analysis: Machine learning models and AI algorithms process stored data to extract meaningful insights. This enables platforms to refine content recommendations, predict user engagement, and personalize user experiences.
5 Data Monetization: Platforms generate revenue by offering advertisers access to highly targeted audiences. Advertisers can use microtargeting techniques to reach users based on certain behaviors, interests, and demographics.
6 Regulatory Compliance: In some cases, social media platforms sell or shareuser data with third-party companies, data brokers, and business partners. Theseentities further refine and repurpose data for marketing campaigns, political influence, and consumer research. Governments and regulatory bodies enforce data privacy laws such as GDPR and CCPA to ensure ethical data handling. However, compliance varies across jurisdictions, and enforcement mechanisms often lag behind technological advancements.

The implications of the data economy extend far beyond simple advertising. The widespread collection and analysis of personal information have led to significant concerns regarding privacy, security, and ethics, including:

- User Awareness and Consent: Many users remain unaware of the full extent to which their data is harvested and monetized. Privacy policies are often lengthy and complex, leading to uninformed consent where users agree to terms without fully understanding their implications.
- Privacy Risks and Data Security: The storage of vast amounts of personal data increases the risks of data breaches and cyberattacks. High-profile incidents have demonstrated how improperly handled user data can be exploited for political and commercial gains.
- Ethical Concerns and Surveillance Capitalism: The transition of social media from a communication tool to a commercial enterprise has raised ethical questions about digital surveillance. The commodification of personal data means that individuals effectively become products, with their behaviors continuously analyzed and monetized.
- Regulatory Challenges and Legal Compliance: The rapid evolution of data collection technologies presents challenges for regulators. While laws like GDPR and CCPA aim to protect users, enforcement remains inconsistent, and companies often find ways to bypass stringent regulations.

The Role of Artificial Intelligence

AI can be defined as "Software that is developed with one or more of the techniques and approaches and that, for a given set of human-defined objectives, generates outputs such as content, predictions, recommendations, or decisions influencing the environments they interact with."— European Union Artificial Intelligence Act, Article 3(1), 2023.

AI has been part of social media's evolution since the early 2010s, when platforms began using algorithms to personalize feeds and recommend content. Early AI systems primarily relied on rule-based approaches and basic machine learning models, analyzing likes, shares, and connections to determine what users saw. Facebook, for example, initially used a system called EdgeRank to rank posts in users' newsfeeds, considering factors such as user affinity, content weight, and recency. Over time, these algorithms evolved into far more sophisticated machine learning models, enabling real-time personalization at scale. Instagram and X followed a similar trajectory, gradually replacing chronological feeds with algorithm-driven timelines as the default.

A particularly notable milestone came with TikTok's "For You" Page, which exemplifies a fully algorithm-first feed. Unlike earlier platforms, TikTok delivers content based almost entirely on its recommendation algorithm, using user interactions, device data, location, and behavioral signals to predict what will maximize engagement. This model demonstrated the power of AI-driven curation, influencing other platforms to further prioritize personalized feeds.

Today, social media platforms operate as sophisticated data collection networks, leveraging AI and machine learning to tailor user experiences. By analyzing behavior patterns, platforms curate content, predict preferences, and optimize engagement to maximize time spent online. While this level of personalization enhances user experience, it also creates an environment where individuals unknowingly contribute to their own digital profiling, feeding into an ecosystem that thrives on constant data extraction.

AI plays a crucial role in processing the massive volumes of data generated on social media. AI-powered recommendation engines curate content feeds, detect emerging trends, and optimize advertisements in real time, ensuring that platforms can deliver ever-more relevant—and profitable—experiences to users. The rise of generative AI further expands these capabilities, deepening the ways platforms analyze, predict, and shape user behavior, cementing AI's central role in the social media data economy.

The Future of the Data Economy

The data economy is constantly evolving, with new technologies and policies shaping its trajectory. Emerging trends include:

- Decentralized Data Ownership: Technologies such as blockchain offer the potential for users to regain control over their personal data, enabling more transparent and secure data transactions.
- Privacy-Enhancing Technologies: Innovations such as differential privacy and homomorphic encryption aim to balance data utility with user anonymity (i.e., the ability to operate or engage online without revealing one's real identity, thereby reducing risks of profiling or exposure).
- Stronger Regulatory Frameworks: Governments worldwide are exploring stricter data protection laws, with a focus on user consent, transparency, and corporate accountability.
- Ethical AI and Algorithmic Accountability: There is growing demand for ethical AI practices that prioritize fairness, explainability, and user empowerment in data-driven decision-making.

Understanding the data economy is essential for navigating the modern digital landscape. Social media has redefined personal privacy, making it imperative for users, organizations, and policymakers to engage in responsible data practices. The next section will explore privacy concerns in a hyper-connected world and the measures users can take to safeguard their data.

The data economy is the backbone of modern social media platforms, where user-generated data fuels business models that rely on targeted advertising, predictive analytics, and personalized experiences. Every interaction on a platform—whether liking a post, watching a video, or sharing content—creates valuable data that is collected, analyzed, and monetized by social media companies.

Privacy in a Hyper-Connected World

The digital landscape has redefined the concept of privacy, challenging traditional boundaries between personal and public spaces. As social media platforms continue to expand their influence, users are increasingly embedded in a hyper-connected world where privacy is no longer a default condition but a personal responsibility. In this environment, every online interaction—whether posting a status update, sharing a location, or engaging with content—contributes to an extensive digital footprint that is constantly being analyzed, stored, and repurposed.

While connectivity offers numerous benefits, including instant communication, access to information, and global engagement, it also presents significant privacy concerns. The erosion of personal boundaries, the rise of real-time data tracking, and the commodification of user information have placed individuals in a position where privacy can be compromised in exchange for convenience (Figure 2.2).

The Expansion of Digital Footprints

With every interaction on social media, users generate a vast amount of data that is meticulously tracked and cataloged. Unlike traditional forms of communication, where conversations remain private and localized, digital interactions leave a persistent trail that can be analyzed, archived, and monetized. This shift has led to the phenomenon of context collapse, where private and public personas merge, exposing individuals to unintended audiences and potential privacy breaches.

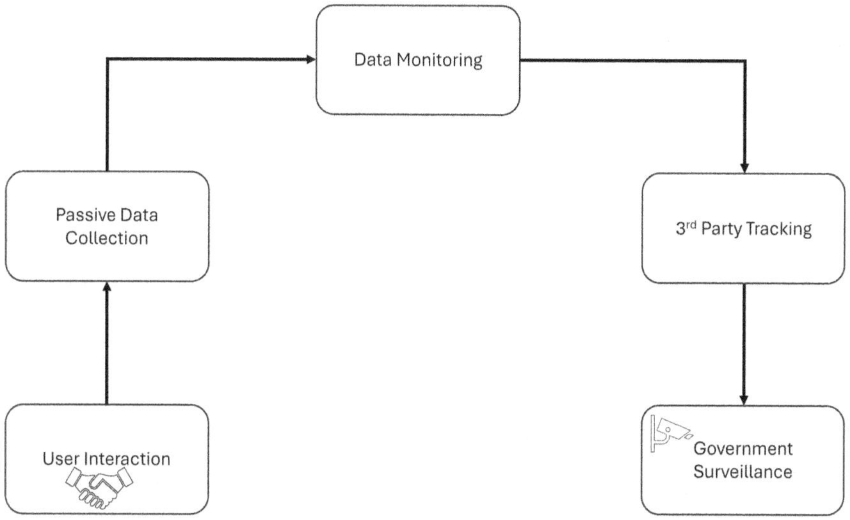

Figure 2.2 Real-Time Surveillance Mechanisms—Showing How User Interactions Contribute to Passive Data Collection, Algorithmic Monitoring, Third-Party Tracking, and Government Surveillance.

Key contributors to expanding digital footprints include:

- Social Media Sharing: Users voluntarily share personal details, images, and opinions, often without considering long-term implications.
- Location-Based Services: Many apps and platforms collect and store geolocation data, providing insights into user movements and behaviors.
- Cross-Platform Data Collection: Companies track user activity across multiple platforms, aggregating information to create detailed behavioral profiles.
- Biometric Data and Facial Recognition: Advanced AI-driven technologies analyze photos and videos to identify individuals and their associations, further eroding anonymity.

Emerging Threats to Privacy

The convergence of new technologies with social media is creating additional threats to personal privacy, many of which users may not yet recognize. One growing concern is the rise of deepfake technology—AI-generated images, videos, or audio recordings that convincingly imitate real people. Because deepfakes can be difficult to distinguish from genuine content, they pose risks to reputation, identity security, and the spread of misinformation.

Another development is the expanding use of big data and predictive analytics. Social media companies gather vast amounts of behavioral information and use advanced algorithms to predict what users might do next. These predictions can shape what people see online and subtly influence decision-making processes, often without the user's explicit awareness.

Cybersecurity threats further amplify privacy risks. As social media platforms store more personal data, they become attractive targets for hackers and cybercriminals seeking to access or exploit this information, with consequences for both individuals and organizations (see Chapter 6 for further details).

Finally, the integration of social media with the Internet of Things (IoT)—from smart speakers to fitness trackers—extends data collection beyond the screen. Many IoT devices connect to users' social media accounts or can be linked through shared logins, allowing offline behaviors to be associated with online profiles. This connection allows platforms to integrate data from multiple sources, building richer behavioral profiles that can shape what users see in their feeds, the ads they encounter, and the content that is suggested to them. IoT thus adds another layer of exposure and complexity to social media privacy.

The Ethics of Social Media Privacy

As social media platforms continue to shape digital interactions, ethical concerns surrounding user privacy have become increasingly pressing. The ethical dimensions of social media privacy involve questions of user consent, transparency, legal compliance, corporate responsibility, and ultimately data ownership—as highlighted in Figure 2.3.

While social media has provided individuals and organizations with unparalleled opportunities for connection and engagement, it has also introduced serious dilemmas regarding how personal data is collected, stored, shared, and monetized.

The tension between corporate profit and user rights is at the heart of this ethical debate. Social media companies justify data collection as a means of improving user experience, personalizing content, and optimizing platform functionality.

Consent is a cornerstone of ethical data collection, yet it remains one of the most problematic aspects of social media privacy. Many users unknowingly grant extensive access to their personal information through long, complex terms of service agreements that are difficult to understand. Informed consent is often more theoretical than practical, as users rarely have a full grasp of what they are agreeing to. Platforms further complicate this by collecting data passively—tracking behavior even when users are not actively engaging—and using design elements such as pre-checked boxes, misleading prompts, or hidden settings to nudge users into sharing more than they might intend. These practices raise serious ethical concerns about whether consent can ever truly be considered informed.

Transparency and corporate accountability are equally important. Ethical social media practice requires that users understand how their data is being collected, used, and shared. Yet, many platforms provide minimal disclosure, eroding trust. Ideally, privacy policies should be clear and accessible, data usage should be regularly reported to users, and companies must take responsibility for breaches, promptly notifying users when security is compromised.

As we discovered in Chapter 1, a central ethical issue is the commodification of personal data. Social media business models rely heavily on user data as

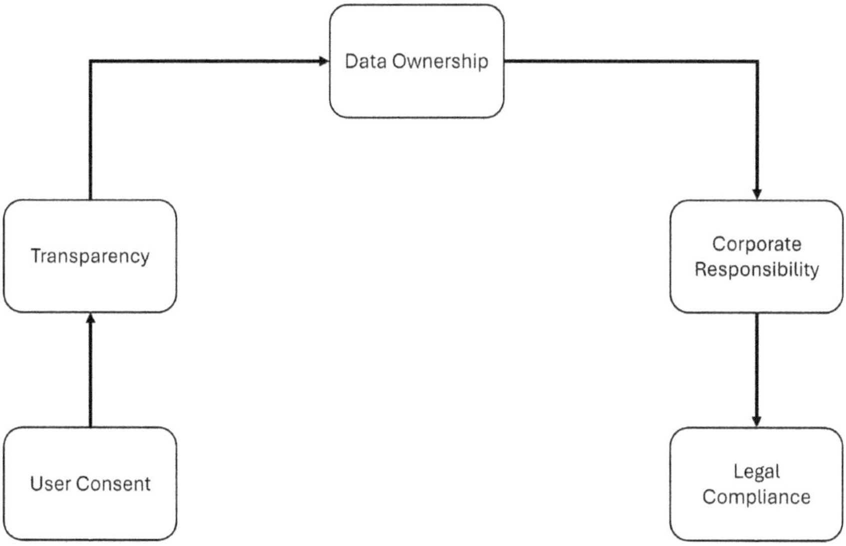

Figure 2.3 Ethical Dimensions of Social Media Privacy.

a revenue-generating asset, often selling insights to advertisers, data brokers, and third-party organizations. Users are frequently treated as the product rather than customers with rights, and behavioral data fuels highly targeted advertising campaigns. Many users are unaware of the extent to which their information is collected and used to shape content, ads, and recommendations. Data sharing with third parties without explicit consent further complicates the ethical landscape, highlighting concerns about misuse and inequitable power dynamics.

AI and algorithmic decision-making add another layer of complexity. AI-driven systems power personalized content, recommendations, and moderation, but they can also reinforce biases, exacerbate misinformation, and create filter bubbles. Algorithms may inadvertently privilege certain groups or viewpoints, while automated moderation struggles to balance free expression with the need to curb harmful content. These challenges underscore the ethical responsibility of platforms to ensure that AI supports fairness, accuracy, and transparency.

Government surveillance and law enforcement use of social media data further raises ethical dilemmas. State-sponsored monitoring of citizens, collaboration between platforms and authorities, and gaps in legal protections leave users vulnerable to overreach. While data sharing may support criminal investigations, it also risks undermining civil liberties and privacy rights in jurisdictions where regulatory frameworks have not kept pace with technological capabilities.

Addressing these ethical challenges requires action from both platforms and users. Social media companies should, we believe, prioritize user empowerment through privacy tools, adopt comprehensive ethics policies, and submit to independent audits to ensure compliance. Legislative protections must evolve to provide clear standards and enforce accountability. For individuals, strengthening personal privacy measures, advocating for ethical technology use, and challenging norms around data collection are key steps toward reclaiming control.

The ethical concerns surrounding social media privacy are complex and multifaceted, requiring cooperation among corporations, regulators, and users. Responsibility cannot rest solely on individuals adjusting settings; it must be embedded in corporate policies, AI systems, and business models. As social media continues to evolve, ethical considerations will remain central to debates about technology, governance, and human rights. Transparency, accountability, and respect for user autonomy are essential to balancing digital innovation with ethical responsibility.

We hope this book serves as a guide for navigating these complexities. By understanding the mechanisms of data collection, the role of AI in user profiling, and the impact of emerging technologies, you will be able to make informed decisions about protecting your personal information. Having explored the foundations of social media ethics and privacy, the next chapters will dive deeper into these mechanisms, examining how digital behavior is tracked, monetized, and influenced in an increasingly connected world.

The Future of Privacy in the Digital Age

As awareness of digital privacy issues grows, governments, advocacy groups, developers, and users are all exploring ways to strengthen protections and regain control over personal data. This shift is driven by a recognition that transparency, consent, and data security must be central to how digital platforms operate. Regulations such as GDPR and CCPA have set important precedents, but gaps remain, and global alignment is still needed—a topic explored in detail in Chapter 7.

At the same time, technology itself is evolving to support privacy-conscious practices. Innovations such as encryption, blockchain-based networks, and AI-driven privacy tools are reshaping how data is collected, stored, and used. Social media companies face increasing scrutiny, requiring them to adopt ethical and transparent practices in order to maintain user trust.

Users themselves also play a critical role in this emerging landscape. Digital literacy, awareness of privacy risks, and collective advocacy are essential for holding companies accountable and making informed choices about personal data. The rise of user-led privacy initiatives demonstrates that individuals are beginning to demand more than passive protection—they are asserting agency over the digital environments they inhabit.

In this hyper-connected world, privacy is no longer a passive expectation but an active responsibility. Understanding how social media operates, the scale of data collection, and the choices available to protect personal information is vital for individuals, organizations, and policymakers alike. While legislation and corporate policies are critical to safeguarding privacy, individual users also play an essential role in shaping the digital environment.

Protecting personal information requires active engagement: regularly reviewing privacy settings, using encryption tools, and being mindful of what is shared online can all reduce exposure to unwanted data collection.

Beyond personal safeguards, individuals can advocate for ethical technology use by supporting organizations and initiatives that promote transparency and digital rights. Engaging in conversations about privacy ethics, corporate accountability, and the societal impact of digital surveillance further challenges the status quo and encourages a culture in which privacy is valued and respected. Individual action—combined with regulatory frameworks and responsible corporate behavior—is a key driver for a more privacy-conscious digital ecosystem.

As we move forward into the next chapter, we turn our attention to the mechanisms that most compromise our privacy in the age of social media: the systems of data collection, processing, and monetization that operate beneath the surface.

References

Albury, K., Burgess, J., Light, B., Race, K., & Wilken, R. (2017). Data cultures of mobile dating and hook-up apps: Emerging issues for critical social science research. Big Data & Society, 4(2) https://doi.org/10.1177/2053951717720950

Andrejevic, M. (2022). *Automated media.* Routledge.

Couldry, N., & Mejias, U. A. (2019). *The costs of connection: How data is colonizing human life and appropriating it for capitalism.* Stanford University Press.

Crawford, K., & Paglen, T. (2021). Excavating AI: The politics of images in machine learning training sets. *AI & Society, 36*, 127–144. https://link.springer.com/article/10.1007/s00146-021-01162-8

European Union. (2023). *Regulation (EU) 2024/1689 of the European Parliament and of the Council of 14 June 2023 laying down harmonised rules on artificial intelligence (Artificial Intelligence Act)*. Official Journal of the European Union.

Orlowski, J. (Director). (2020). *The Social Dilemma* [Film]. Netflix

Solove, D. J. (2011). Why privacy matters even if you have 'nothing to hide'. Chronicle of Higher Education, 15. https://www.chronicle.com/article/why-privacy-matters-even-if-you-have-nothing-to-hide/

Tufekci, Z. (2022). *Twitter and tear gas: The power and fragility of networked protest.* Yale University Press. https://yalebooks.yale.edu/book/9780300234176/twitter-and-tear-gas/

Zuboff, S. (2020). *The age of surveillance capitalism: The fight for a human future at the new frontier of power.* Profile Books.

3 The Mechanics of Data Collection

This chapter explores the intricate mechanisms behind how social media platforms and connected technologies extract value from user behavior. From cookies and tracking pixels to biometric data and emotion detection, data collection has evolved into a sophisticated, invisible infrastructure. Each click, pause, or scroll becomes a data point feeding algorithms that can predict, persuade, and profit. Often framed as personalization or convenience, these processes operate through a complex web of permissions, defaults, and opaque terms of service. Even anonymized data, once thought to be safe, can be reassembled to reveal personal identities.

Everyday interactions fuel a powerful surveillance system, challenging the notion that privacy is simply a matter of user choice. As users, we need to ask ourselves: what are we really giving away and who benefits most?

Seeing What We Don't See

We live in a world where convenience has become inseparable from connectivity. Social media now frames how we communicate, share, entertain, grieve, celebrate, and even protest. These platforms have seamlessly woven themselves into our daily lives, offering personalization, social bonding, and entertainment at the tap of a screen. Yet, beneath this simplicity lies a complex, finely tuned infrastructure whose primary function is not to connect, but to collect.

Most users are familiar with the visible side of social media: the content, the interface, the reactions. What remains largely invisible, however, is the systematic and pervasive data collection happening behind the scenes. This data is not limited to what users post. It includes what they type and delete, how long they hover over content, what device they use, which notifications they click, and even the timing of their silences. In short, users are seen in ways they do not see themselves.

A Mirror We Cannot Look Into

When we log into a platform, we see our feed. The platform, in contrast, sees everything: what we ignore, what we pause on, what we search but don't click, what we watch late at night, who we message and who we don't reply to. We might think we are in control, curating our presence through careful posts and filtered

DOI: 10.4324/9781003654322-4

selfies, but the real story is one that the platforms track, predict, and monetize being written silently in the background.

In earlier eras, surveillance was a visible act—security cameras, phone taps, patrols. In contrast, today's digital surveillance is largely invisible, embedded in design. It does not rely on force, but on infrastructure. It works not by invading our space, but by becoming the space itself. This invisibility is what makes it so powerful and so easy to ignore.

The Illusion of Visibility

Part of the challenge lies in a fundamental design choice: platforms are made to appear user-centric. The interface is friendly, responsive, even empowering. Settings are customizable. Notifications are personalized. Feeds are tailored to 'what you want to see'. It feels like the user is in charge.

This feeling is reinforced through language. Platforms speak of "sharing," "engagement," and "connection." But they rarely speak of "collection," "extraction," or "profiling." The reality is that every touchpoint is an opportunity to capture data, and every feature is a mechanism of observation.

Consider a single photo upload. To the user, it's a memory shared. To the platform, it's:

- A timestamp (when it was taken and posted)
- A location (where it happened, based on GPS metadata)
- A facial recognition input (who is in it)
- A style preference (what colors, filters, subjects)
- A social graph update (who reacts and how quickly)
- A behavioral signal (what kind of content you are likely to post next)

Multiply this by billions of interactions per day, and you begin to see the scale of the machinery for a system built not just to observe, but to learn.

Participation as Surveillance

Perhaps the most profound shift of the digital age is that participation itself is surveillance. To be online is to be watched not necessarily by people, but by systems. To post, like, search, or linger is to be measured. And to opt out of these actions often only changes *how* one is tracked, not whether one is tracked at all.

There are many types of social media users, from frequent posters to those who mainly scroll, watch, or listen; even those who don't post much are still generating data, including location signals, device IDs, browser fingerprints, app usage logs, and behavioral metadata. The system doesn't need us to speak. It listens to our silence just as effectively.

Importantly, this surveillance is not limited to any single platform. Through cross-site tracking, third-party cookies, and shared ad networks, users are monitored across much of their digital activity. Actions on one platform—like a TikTok search or scrolling through Instagram—can indirectly influence the ads and recommendations you see elsewhere. Privacy does not begin and end with a single app; it is shaped by the digital ecosystem as a whole.

Data as Raw Material

In this ecosystem, data is not the byproduct of social media, it is its core product. Every like, follow, pause, or swipe becomes a data point. These points are then:

1. Collected (logged through sensors, APIs, and trackers)
2. Processed (fed into algorithms for pattern recognition)
3. Profiled (used to build predictive models about users)
4. Monetized (sold, shared, or used to target ads/content)

It is tempting to think of this as a fair trade. Users get "free access" to a platform in exchange for their data. But this is a false equivalence. The user is not just paying with their data, they are powering a system designed to extract maximum value from their behavior, often in ways they are not aware of, cannot control, and cannot meaningfully contest.

Moreover, the value of this data increases not linearly, but exponentially, when aggregated and analyzed at scale. A single user's scrolling habits may not seem valuable. But when combined with millions of others, they fuel entire industries: targeted advertising, behavioral prediction, emotion detection, content curation, and more.

Designing for Extraction

What makes this form of surveillance especially potent is that it is not accidental, it is designed.

The very architecture of platforms encourages:

- Continuous engagement (e.g., infinite scroll, autoplay)
- Rapid interaction (e.g., likes, emojis, swipe responses)
- Data generation (e.g., polls, story views, tagging)

Each design choice is calibrated not just for user experience, but for data yield. New features are often tested not only for aesthetics, but for their ability to capture attention and trigger behavioral loops.

Notifications, for instance, are designed to bring users back. But each "return" is also an opportunity to update behavioral profiles. A new filter or sticker may seem fun, but its real function may be to gather new kinds of user data (e.g., facial recognition inputs or mood signals).

Social media users are not just engaging with a platform—they are interacting with systems optimized for data extraction.

The Vanishing Point of Consent

Given the scale and opacity of this system, the idea of user consent becomes deeply problematic. As we have already noted, most users agree to Terms of Service without reading them. Those who try often find them dense, legalistic, or vague. And even those who manage to understand what they're consenting to may not fully grasp what is technically possible with the data they give away.

Worse, consent is often framed as a one-time event: click "I Agree" and move on. But data collection is ongoing, dynamic, and often hidden in plain sight. Users might believe they've limited access through privacy settings, but tracking continues through metadata, integrations, and background processes.

The result is what this book later describes as the "consent illusion," a ritual that gives the appearance of control, while disguising a deeper reality of systemic surveillance.

Why It Matters

Some may argue: if you've done nothing wrong, you have nothing to hide. But this line of thinking almost misses the point. The issue is not hiding, it's having space to be human without performance, without prediction, without commodification.

When every action is tracked, analyzed, and stored, the freedom to experiment, reflect, or even forget is diminished. Identity becomes fixed by algorithm. Desire becomes shaped by data. And the self becomes just another input in a feedback loop optimized for engagement.

Moreover, this data is not used solely for advertising. It can also be used to influence:

- Financial services, via credit risk assessments using signals from online behavior
- Hiring and other employment decisions, where profiling may be informed by an individual's digital presence
- Content visibility, determining what is prioritized or suppressed within newsfeeds

These downstream consequences make it clear: data collection is not a neutral act. It is a force that shapes opportunity, perception, and power. This chapter begins with a simple premise: we do not see what sees us. As we explore the mechanics of data collection, we will uncover the technologies, practices, and infrastructures that make this possible.

> It's important to note that while previously data has been used for political influence, in October 2025, Meta stopped running political, electoral, and social issue ads across its platforms in the European Union—this was in response to the EU's Transparency and Targeting of Political Advertising

(TTPA) regulation, which requires stricter disclosures and consent for political ad targeting.

From Click to Capture—What Gets Collected

Most people don't remember the exact moment they began to trade their privacy. It wasn't a grand decision or a dramatic surrender. It was something quieter, maybe a photo upload, a terms-of-service checkbox, or a "continue with Google" login. It felt simple. Harmless, even. And perhaps that's the most astonishing thing about digital surveillance: how effortlessly it blends into daily life.

This section asks a seemingly basic question—what, exactly, is being collected? The answer, however, is anything but basic. Because data collection doesn't begin and end with what we share. It extends far beyond the visible, reaching into every corner of our digital interactions, even the ones we don't notice.

What You Know You're Sharing

Let's begin with the obvious. When you sign up for a social media platform, you usually provide:

- Your name
- Email or phone number
- Profile photo
- Gender
- Date of birth
- Location

This is called voluntarily submitted data information, which you consciously provide. Over time, this grows to include:

- Posts
- Likes and reactions
- Comments
- Shared media (photos, videos, reels, stories)
- Check-ins and tags

This is what most people think of when they hear "personal data." And platforms do give you some control over this type of information. Within account settings, and when posting, you can choose what to share, who sees it, and who can comment. Posts can be edited, and deleted. But this is only surface level.

Figure 3.1 shows the multi-layered nature of data collection, where passive and ambient behaviors—generated through routine, often unnoticed interactions—feed into sophisticated profiling systems. It shows how a simple interaction can be broken into multiple streams of analyzable data.

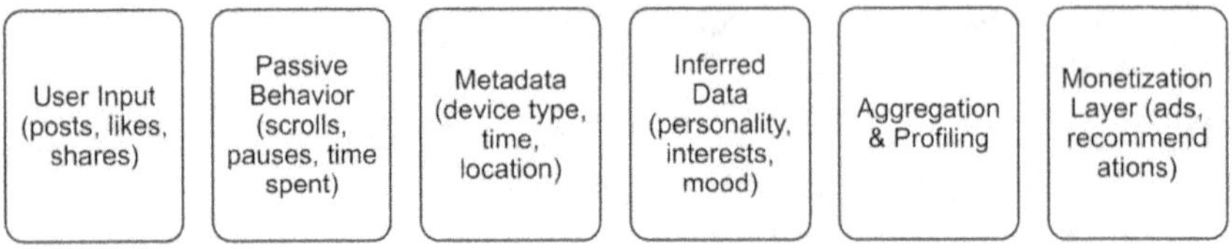

Figure 3.1 Layers of Data Collection on Social Media Platforms.

What You Don't Realize You're Sharing

Beyond your conscious choices, every interaction on a platform generates behavioral data. These are patterns extracted not from what you say but from how you behave.

For example:

- How long you view a post
- What time of day you're most active
- How fast you scroll
- Which emojis you use regularly

This is where data begins to watch you back. It quietly maps your interests, emotions, and attention not based on your posts, but also on your pauses. For instance, if you linger on videos of dogs, even without liking or commenting, your feed will subtly begin to include more of them.

This kind of tracking is what makes platforms feel intuitive like they "get" you. But this intuition comes at a cost. Because the more the system learns about what engages you, the more it optimizes itself to hold you there.

Metadata: The Digital Breadcrumbs

If posts are the main content, then metadata is the context. And context, it turns out, is incredibly revealing.

Metadata includes:

- Time and date of activity
- Geolocation data
- Device and browser information
- Language and keyboard usage
- IP address and network connections

Even if you never post anything on social media, your device still generates metadata every time you open an app, scroll through a feed, or tap a notification.

Former National Security Agency intelligence contractor and whistleblower Edward Snowden once said, "Metadata is extraordinarily intrusive. As an analyst, I would prefer to be looking at metadata than looking at content." That's because metadata shows patterns, the who, when, and where of our lives which can often be more telling than what we actually say.

Inferred Data: The You They Build

Here's where it gets more personal. Platforms don't just collect what you give or generate what you do, they also infer what you haven't told them.

Using machine learning algorithms, social media platforms can estimate:

- Your political beliefs
- Your sexual orientation
- Your income level
- Whether you're pregnant
- Whether you're likely to change jobs
- Whether you're experiencing stress or anxiety

These inferences aren't based on a single data point. They emerge from patterns across your behavior, often in comparison with millions of other users. This is how targeted advertising becomes so eerily accurate: it isn't reading your mind; it's reading your data twin's mind—someone just like you, statistically speaking.

The Body as Data: Biometric and Sensor Inputs

With the rise of mobile and wearable technology, platforms now collect a wide range of biometric and sensor data. This includes facial recognition from photos, voice tone from voice notes or videos, gait and posture from accelerometer readings, and heart rate or step counts from fitness integrations. TikTok, Instagram, and Snapchat use facial landmark data for filters and augmented reality effects. Though this may seem harmless, turning your face into a puppy or swapping genders, it involves real-time scanning and analysis of facial structure, proportions, and expressions.

Once collected, this kind of data becomes part of a highly sensitive dataset—one that, unlike a password, cannot be changed if compromised—and can be used in ways users may not fully anticipate, from improving app functionality to targeting ads, monitoring health, or training artificial intelligence (AI).

Even Silence Is Captured

You might think that not posting, not liking, or simply being passive means you're safe from data collection. Unfortunately, even inaction can be highly informative. Not responding to a message may signal disinterest or an emotional shift, skipping certain content can influence what is deprioritized in your feed, and regularly turning on "Do Not Disturb" at specific times can reveal patterns in your sleep.

As researcher Zeynep Tufekci argues, the system doesn't need you to speak; it just needs you to act—and even nonaction counts as action in the eyes of machine learning.

Why It Matters

Understanding what gets collected isn't just about paranoia or control. It's about recognizing that your online self is being interpreted, scored, and monetized sometimes more than your offline self ever is.

Your "digital twin," an aggregated version of *you* created by data, can be used to:

- Serve you content that shapes your worldview
- Target ads that predict your desires
- Influence recommendations about news, jobs, and people
- Make decisions that affect your real-life opportunities

This is not neutral. The version of *you* that the system sees may become more real to institutions, advertisers, and algorithms than the version you show to friends or family. And that version is being shaped by data you may not even know you've given away.

What gets collected is not just your photos or posts—it's your rhythms, your moods, your silences, your subtle hesitations. The clicks you forget about, the videos you half-watch, the ads you don't click but still pause on—all of it matters.

Modern data collection doesn't rely on asking questions—it relies on watching closely enough to predict the answers. And as we'll see in the next section, the tools used to collect all of this data aren't hidden behind walls, they're embedded in the very code of how platforms function.

Tools of the Trade—Technologies Behind Data Harvesting

For many users, the internet feels intuitive—tap, swipe, scroll, and move on. But every seemingly simple interaction is layered with invisible complexity. Behind the smooth interfaces and fast-loading feeds lies a network of surveillance technologies designed not just to deliver content, but to observe, record, and learn. These tools aren't abstract or futuristic. They are embedded in the very code that powers the platforms we use daily.

One of the most common data harvesting tools is the humble cookie. Originally intended to improve user experience by remembering settings or login sessions, cookies have since evolved into powerful tracking mechanisms. While first-party cookies are set by the site you're directly interacting with, third-party cookies set by advertisers or embedded trackers follow you across sites, building detailed behavioral profiles. Visiting a travel blog could silently notify an advertising network, which might then display flight offers when you're browsing an unrelated news site. Even when you're not logged into a platform, cookies can tie your activity to an overarching online identity.

Another subtle but powerful tracking method is the use of pixels. Tracking pixels are tiny, often invisible, image files embedded in web pages, emails, or advertisements. When a user opens a message or lands on a page, the pixel quietly pings a server logging data such as the time of access, device used, and IP address.

Companies like Meta and LinkedIn offer tracking pixel services that allow businesses to monitor when someone views a product on their website—even if that person never clicks "buy". Email marketing tools use similar pixels to tell senders whether you opened their message, when, and sometimes where you were when you did.

Perhaps even more difficult to detect, in comparison to cookies and tracking pixels, is a technique known as browser fingerprinting. This method doesn't need external trackers; it simply reads the unique configuration of your device and browser. Screen resolution, installed fonts, time zone, device type, and language preferences may seem like small, impersonal details—but together, they form a surprisingly distinctive fingerprint—a set of characteristics that can distinguish you from others online. This means that even if you block cookies, your identity can still be inferred based on your device's "signature." Fingerprinting techniques are often used in combination with other trackers, further strengthening the profile that platforms and data brokers build around you.

Mobile apps, in particular, have their own tracking arsenal. When you download an app, it often requests permissions to access your location, microphone, contacts, camera, or motion sensors. Many of these requests seem justified ("This app needs access to your photos to upload a profile picture"), but once granted, the access often sits silently in the background. Some apps collect location data even when the app isn't open. Others monitor which other apps you have installed, how often you use them, and how your device moves through space. In some cases, even accelerometer and gyroscope data have been used to infer walking patterns, emotional state, or whether you're alone.

For platforms that allow social login using a single sign-on (SSO)—"Log in with Facebook" or "Sign in with Google"—a different kind of data harvesting occurs. These logins offer convenience, but they also create deep integration between platforms and services. Every time a user logs into a third-party site using a social account, data flows between the two services. That integration may include basic identity details like name and email address, but often extends to friends lists, browsing history, or behavioral data. This means that your activity on one site can feed into the profile that another platform maintains about you even if you're not actively using it.

Even search engines and keyboards aren't off the hook. Autocomplete suggestions, search history, voice inputs, and typing patterns all become part of a behavioral dataset. Some virtual keyboards track what you type to improve predictions, but this also means they can record passwords, sensitive messages, or private notes unless explicitly designed with privacy in mind. Smart assistants like Siri, Alexa, or Google Assistant operate through voice inputs, which means their microphones are always passively listening for wake words. While they only start recording after detecting the activation phrase, this still means they're listening more often than many users realize.

Then there's geolocation data, which is often collected passively. A photo taken on a smartphone might include GPS coordinates in its metadata. A weather app might access your precise location even when not in use. Wi-Fi signals, Bluetooth beacons, and cell tower triangulation can all contribute to tracking a user's physical movement—even indoors. Combined over time, these signals reveal routines, favorite places, workplace habits, and more. Social media platforms can use this information to personalize content, suggest nearby events or friends, target ads based on location, and even infer lifestyle patterns, such as commuting habits or frequent visits to certain types of venues.

Beyond hardware and software, platforms also embed data collection into advertising technologies. Ad networks combine behavioral, demographic, and contextual data to serve highly targeted content. Programmatic advertising, which automates the buying and selling of ad space through real-time auctions, operates in milliseconds to decide which ad to show each user. At that moment, hundreds of data points—from browsing history to inferred interests—may be used to determine which ad is most likely to capture your attention. Most users are unaware this exchange is happening, and in most cases they don't need to be; the process operates invisibly behind the scenes. While regulations require platforms to provide some disclosures or opt-out options, these laws only offer partial visibility into a system that functions at lightning speed.

All of these tools cookies, pixels, fingerprinting, permissions, logins, sensors, and real-time auctions are not isolated features. They are part of a multi-layered surveillance system where every piece of data reinforces the next. It's not just that platforms know what you do, they know how you do it, how often, how fast, with what device, and under what conditions. And crucially, they also know how your behavior compares to millions of others, enabling them to make predictions, personalize feeds, and sell targeted access to your attention.

The challenge isn't just technical—it's philosophical. The more seamless the user experience becomes, the more invisible data collection is. We rarely question the cost of this convenience—the trade-offs in our privacy, autonomy, and personal data—because the interaction feels natural. This hidden complexity is what makes data harvesting so powerful. It's not one tool or one company; it's the convergence of design, infrastructure, and habit, all working together to ensure that your behavior is always producing value for someone else.

The Algorithmic Assembly Line

If data is the raw material of the digital world, platforms act like sophisticated digital factories. Your clicks, swipes, pauses, searches, and posts enter the system and are processed through machine learning models, sentiment analyzers, engagement predictors, and content classifiers. Unlike traditional machines, which transform tangible materials—wood, metal, or grain—through visible assembly lines, these algorithms operate on invisible behavioral inputs, running in a closed loop of signals and feedback. The output is a dynamic, personalized platform experience—curated not just to your interests, but to what is most likely to keep you engaged, returning, and, ultimately, generating revenue for the platform.

Most users never see the assembly line; they only experience the end product, a carefully shaped and often addictive digital environment. Figure 3.2 explains

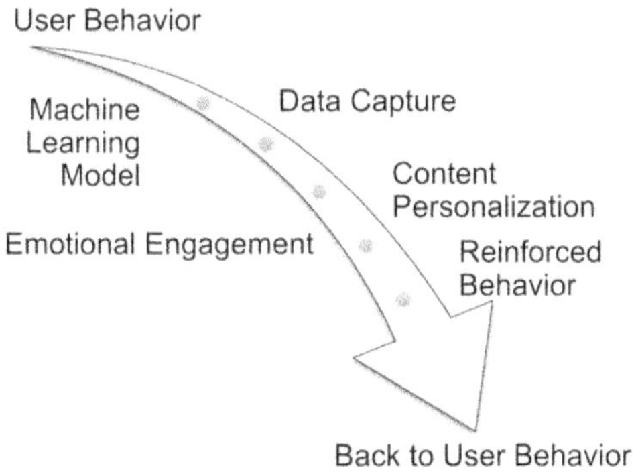

Figure 3.2 The Algorithmic Feedback Loop.

how algorithmic systems feed on user behavior to refine content curation, creating a self-reinforcing loop of engagement, profiling, and retention.

The first step in this algorithmic assembly line is data aggregation. Every bit of information you produce, no matter how small, is bundled and stored. It includes things you explicitly do (such as liking a post), things you implicitly do (such as hovering over a comment), and things you don't do at all (such as not responding to a message). The system doesn't just track actions. It tracks inaction, timing, frequency, and sequence. These patterns are often more revealing than the content itself. For instance, someone who scrolls rapidly late at night is engaging differently than someone who lingers mid-afternoon on a single post.

Once data is collected, it's sent into processing models. At this stage, machine learning algorithms start finding patterns not based on identity alone, but by comparing your behavior to others. You become part of a cohort, or what's often referred to as a "lookalike audience." These aren't your friends, necessarily. They are people who behave similarly to you: they browse the same way, engage with similar content, use the app at similar times, and interact with similar ads. This is the heart of predictive modelling. If "someone like you" clicks on a particular product or watches a specific kind of video, there's a high chance you might too. Increasingly, AI now automates much of this work, continuously analyzing behavior and adjusting what you see in real time.

Personalization is the next link in the chain. Social media feeds are no longer chronological—they are algorithmic, ranked, and filtered to prioritize what is most likely to keep you engaged. The algorithm is optimized for retention.

The feedback loop is a crucial part of this system. When you engage with what's shown—watching, reacting, sharing—it reinforces the system's assumptions about your preferences. When you don't engage, the algorithm adjusts. Over time, this creates a self-reinforcing cycle. You see what the system thinks you'll like, and your behavior trains the system to keep showing you more of the same. This is how filter bubbles and echo chambers form not necessarily by design, but as a side effect of optimization. The more predictable your behavior becomes, the more efficiently you can be targeted for content, ads, or influence.

This system does not require your identity. It doesn't need your name or address. It just needs your behavior: your clicks, patterns, and rhythms. And yet, the conclusions drawn from this behavior can be incredibly intimate. They can estimate your mood, your insecurities, your health, your finances, and even your relationships. In a sense, these algorithms see you not as you are, but as a constantly shifting set of probabilities. You are not a person, you are a prediction. And that prediction is worth money.

It's worth noting that not all algorithms are equal. Many are designed with guardrails, such as fairness checks, human oversight, or content moderation policies. Others operate with minimal transparency, driven primarily by performance metrics like engagement or revenue. The more opaque a system—that is, the less visible or understandable its internal logic—the harder it becomes to see why decisions are made or to challenge them. These systems are often called "black boxes" because you can see what goes in and what comes out, but the inner workings remain hidden, even to the platforms themselves. Complex models learn from massive datasets and produce outcomes through patterns rather than explicit rules, raising profound ethical concerns around accountability, fairness, and trust.

The algorithmic assembly line has real-world consequences. It shapes which news stories go viral, amplifies hate speech and misinformation, and influences political discourse, public opinion, mental health, and social norms. Because these systems are largely invisible, users may not realize how profoundly their online experience is being shaped until the effects spill into everyday life.

Perhaps what makes this system so powerful is that it feels personal, even though it is entirely data-driven. The posts you see feel tailored to you, the ads seem timely, and the recommendations seem as if they just "get" you. But all of it is built on probabilities, not relationships. The system doesn't need to know you personally—only someone "like you"—and that is enough to drive engagement and influence behavior.

As we move forward, we'll examine what happens when all of this data, the raw material and the algorithmic output, is passed beyond the platform. Because for all the control platforms seem to have, they're only part of the ecosystem. Behind them also stands a network of data brokers, advertisers, and third-party aggregator entities that deal in profiles, scores, and segments, shaping realities far outside your screen.

Data Brokers and the Shadow Market

Most people understand that social media platforms collect their data. Fewer realize that the information gathered doesn't just stay within the walls of the platforms such as Meta, LinkedIn, or TikTok. Instead, it often ends up in the hands of data brokers—companies that don't offer services or content to the public, but exist solely to buy, aggregate, analyze, and sell data.

These companies are the shadow market of surveillance capitalism, where our lives are broken down into datasets, sold in silence, and reassembled for profit.

The Rise of the Data Broker Industry

The concept of data brokers isn't new. For decades, credit agencies and marketing firms have gathered consumer information such as purchasing habits, home ownership, and employment history. What has changed is the scale, speed, and granularity of this process in the digital age.

Recent industry research shows that the global data broker market has grown significantly in recent years and is now worth well into the hundreds of billions of dollars. One estimate put the market at around US$277.4 billion in 2024, with projections suggesting it could reach over US$512 billion by the early 2030s as demand for personalized data insights increases across advertising, analytics, and business decision-making.

Today's data brokers don't just buy mailing lists or census reports—they purchase real-time location data, browser histories, in-app behavior, and even emotionally tagged content from social media platforms. Much of this activity occurs through legal gray zones, hidden partnerships, and layers of subcontracting. Some brokers also acquire data through unauthorized scraping or other methods that may violate platform policies or local laws. While regulations such as the U.S. Fair Credit Reporting Act, California's CCPA, and the EU's GDPR provide some oversight, enforcement is uneven, leaving large portions of the industry operating with limited transparency.

Figure 3.3 shows how data from multiple sources flows into broker systems, where it is processed and segmented by audience criteria before being repackaged into detailed profiles —usually beyond what users realize from agreeing to the lengthy platform terms of service.

How Data Brokers Work

At its core, the business model of a data broker is simple: collect as much data as possible, from as many sources as possible, and sell access to that data in as many configurations as clients demand.

Data brokers source information from:

- Social media platforms, either directly (via partnerships) or indirectly (via cookies, pixels, or SDKs)

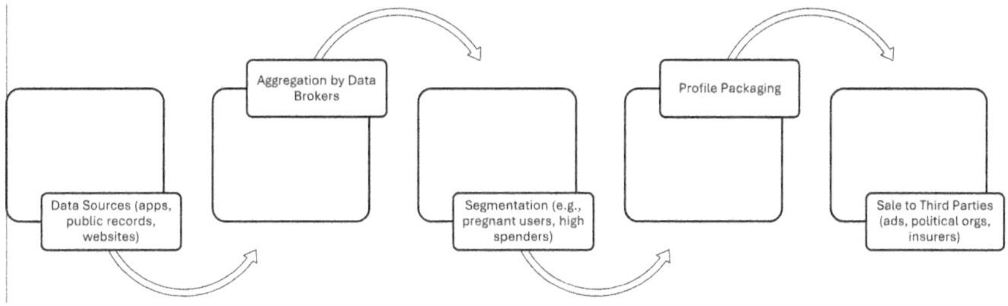

Figure 3.3 Data Broker Pipeline.

- Public records (voter rolls, court documents, property deeds)
- Retailers and e-commerce sites
- Mobile apps, especially free games, weather apps, or QR code scanners
- Credit card processors and loyalty programs
- Web trackers and third-party cookies

Once collected, data is aggregated, meaning it's compiled and cross-referenced. If a user's email from a shopping site matches their email on a fitness app and their Facebook profile, a more complete portrait begins to form. Data can then be segmented into groups that would be of interest to potential buyers. These might include categories like "Tech Savvy Millennials," "Expectant Mothers," "Rural Budget-Conscious Consumers," or "High-Risk Insurance Candidates".

Finally, this classified data can be sold or licensed to a wide range of buyers, including advertisers and marketing firms, financial institutions, insurance companies, real estate agencies, political campaigns, employers conducting background checks, and government entities or law enforcement.

The types of data sold in the broker ecosystem are astonishingly detailed. They include:

- Demographics: age, gender, race, income, marital status
- Contact information: phone numbers, emails, home addresses
- Health indicators: pregnancy status, chronic conditions, prescription use
- Financial traits: credit score range, mortgage status, income bracket
- Online behavior: website visits, search terms, time spent on page
- Shopping preferences: brands, frequency, basket size
- Location history: GPS movements, routine routes, visited businesses
- Social media activity: engagement patterns, sentiment, group affiliations
- Personality traits and interests: extraversion, risk-aversion, political alignment

The power of data brokers lies not in any single piece of information but in the ability to cross-link everything. A phone number becomes the gateway to a consumer's home, habits, mood, movements, and more.

The Emotional Toll of Being Profiled

Beyond technical and ethical concerns, data brokerage carries a deeply human cost. Technically, these systems rely on opaque algorithms that categorize, score, and predict behavior in ways few can understand. Ethically, the processes often operate with minimal transparency, formal consent that isn't fully informed, and little accountability for biased or discriminatory outcomes. Decisions about who sees what content, who is offered certain financial products, or how pricing is tailored can be completely hidden from users yet profoundly affect their lives.

Research shows that being constantly profiled can trigger feelings of unease, reduce perceived autonomy, and even reshape behavior and social perception.

Being reduced to a data profile—scored, categorized, and traded—can feel somewhat depersonalizing because it simplifies human behavior into signals that computers can interpret. These "profiles" shape the experiences and choices you encounter online, subtly influencing how you navigate digital spaces and even how you see yourself. In this way, the shadow market doesn't just affect commerce—it quietly shapes your digital identity and everyday online life.

Resistance, Regulation, and the Path Forward

Change is possible, but it requires visibility. Efforts like the Mozilla Foundation's Privacy Not Included project, the Data Detox Kit, and advocacy groups like the Electronic Frontier Foundation have helped expose the practices of data brokers. Some European watchdogs have fined brokers for failing to comply with GDPR, and proposed U.S. legislation such as the American Data Privacy Protection Act (ADPPA) seeks to create a federal framework for accountability.

But regulation alone is not enough. Users must also be empowered with digital literacy, ethical alternatives, and clear choices. Platforms can no longer rely on passive consent buried in legalese, and users should be able to see and understand how their data is collected, combined, and shared by third-party brokers.

The Illusion of "Anonymous" Data

The term "anonymous" carries a comforting weight. It suggests invisibility, protection, and freedom. For users and organizations navigating digital spaces, the idea that data can be collected "anonymously" offers a kind of reassurance: "Sure, they may track me, but at least they don't know who I am."

Platforms and data companies often lean into this language promising that collected data is "de-identified," "aggregated," or "non-personally identifiable." But in practice, these reassurances are largely an illusion.

In a world of massive datasets, powerful algorithms, and constant cross-referencing, anonymity is no longer the protective shield we imagine. Data that has been stripped of names or direct identifiers can still tell a remarkably detailed story, and one that can be traced back to individuals with alarming accuracy. Figure 3.4 shows how anonymous data can be reidentified by cross-referencing datasets, highlighting the fragility of current anonymization techniques in the age of big data.

Reidentification: More Common Than You Think

Reidentification is the process of linking anonymous data back to an individual. It sounds like a technical feat, but it's surprisingly easy, especially when datasets are rich in behavioral, geographic, or demographic detail. In fact, several landmark studies have shown just how fragile anonymization really is.

In 2000, computer scientist Latanya Sweeney famously demonstrated that 87% of the U.S. population could be uniquely identified using just three data points:

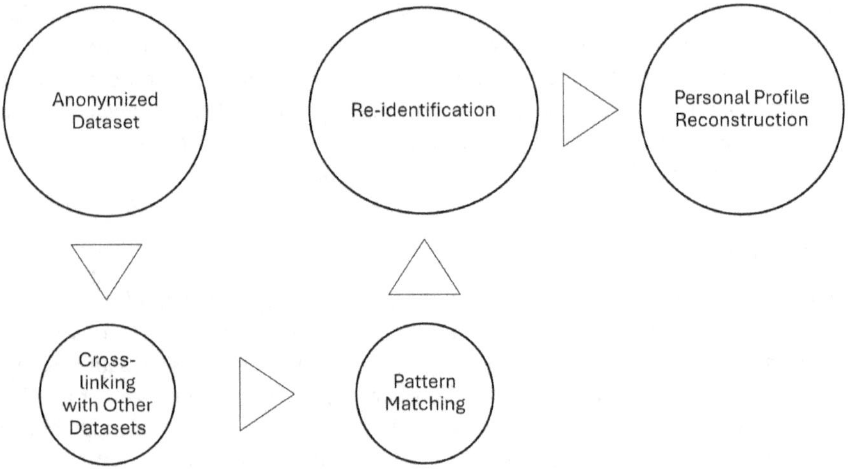

Figure 3.4 The De-Anonymization Process.

zip code, gender, and date of birth. Using these, she successfully reidentified the medical records of the Governor of Massachusetts from an "anonymous" health dataset. This foundational study shattered the myth that removing names and social security numbers was enough to protect privacy.

More recently, a 2025 research paper analyzing a large set of anonymized mobility data found that existing privacy techniques were insufficient to prevent reidentification. By using population density, temporal patterns, and structural correlations in users' location trajectories, researchers were able to reidentify real individuals from the supposedly anonymized dataset, showing that standard anonymization methods leave enough structure for identification.

Anonymization is not a guarantee of privacy.

What Makes Data "Identifiable"

We tend to think of identity in terms of names, emails, or ID numbers. But identity can also be inferred through patterns. Your daily commute, favorite coffee shop, shopping habits, bedtime browsing routine, or the way you type on a keyboard—all of these create your unique behavioral fingerprint.

Consider location data. A dataset might claim to be anonymized by omitting names or precise coordinates. But if someone's phone regularly appears at a specific address at 11 p.m. and then at an office park at 8 a.m., it's not hard to guess where they live and work. Cross-reference this with public property records or LinkedIn profiles, and identification becomes easy.

Even online behavior such as the combination of device type, browser version, screen size, and installed fonts can be used to create a browser fingerprint that uniquely identifies users across sites, even without cookies.

These subtle signals are what make reidentification so powerful and dangerous. Data doesn't need to say your name to tell your story.

Cross-Linking and the Power of Datasets in Combination

One of the most overlooked risks to anonymity is the cross-linking of datasets. A single dataset may appear safe when isolated. But when combined with another, say, a fitness tracking app merged with a dating profile, or a public voter registry with a shopping database, the combined insight can reveal far more than intended.

This is exactly what happened in the 2015 Cambridge Analytica scandal. While the data collected through a third-party app was supposedly anonymized, it was cross-linked with Facebook's internal data and public information to create detailed psychological profiles. These were then used to target voters with tailored political content during major election campaigns.

Sometimes, companies claim that they don't collect individual data at all and that they only use "aggregated" information. This typically means data is summarized at a group level: average age, regional trends, or general patterns. But even aggregated data can be deconstructed if group sizes are small or segmentation is too specific. For example, imagine a report that says "70% of users aged 25–29 in a specific postcode area clicked on ads for baby products last month." If only a few people in that demographic exist in that area, the aggregation may be mathematically meaningless; it's close enough to real identities to pose a risk.

Moreover, when aggregated datasets are sliced repeatedly (by age, gender, behavior, or location), they often reveal subsets that are small enough to isolate individuals, especially when linked to outside sources.

So while aggregation may obscure identity temporarily, it does not eliminate the risk of exposure.

The Commercial Incentive to Push the Boundaries

Companies perhaps have little incentive to keep data truly anonymous especially when reidentification creates more valuable datasets. Behavioral profiles, predictive models, and targeted advertising all rely on granularity. The more specific the data, the more profitable it becomes.

That's why many so-called anonymized datasets are designed to be reidentifiable when needed—either internally (by platforms) or externally (by partners and data buyers). This quiet undermining of anonymity is rarely disclosed to users, and often protected by vague language in privacy policies, for example: "we may share aggregated or de-identified data with partners for research and analytics."

But "de-identified" should not be equated with "safe". While it adds a layer of protection, staying aware of what data you share is still important. You can take practical steps to reduce exposure, such as reviewing app permissions, using privacy-focused browsers like Brave or Firefox, installing tracker blockers like uBlock Origin or Privacy Badger, enabling two-factor authentication, and using secure messaging apps such as Signal. These measures won't make you invisible, but they give you more control over your data and help limit what can be linked back to you.

Anonymity as a Moving Target

Another concerning aspect of the anonymity illusion is that what is considered anonymous today may not be anonymous tomorrow. Advances in AI, facial recognition, voice synthesis, and behavioral modeling continue to erode the effectiveness of de-identification techniques.

For instance, researchers have shown that synthetic voices like those used in podcasts, online videos, or phone recordings can now be linked to real identities through AI-powered voiceprints. Similarly, photos shared online, even without names, can be matched to existing databases using facial recognition algorithms. A post on Reddit or a comment on a forum might seem disconnected from your identity, but if you use similar writing patterns or expressions elsewhere, natural language processing can connect the dots.

The Ethical and Legal Vacuum

Despite the growing risks, there is a significant regulatory and ethical gap surrounding anonymized data. Many privacy laws, including GDPR and CCPA, offer fewer protections once data is considered fully anonymized.

This creates a loophole: as long as a company treats data as anonymized, it can be shared, sold, or analyzed with far fewer restrictions—even when reidentification remains possible. In practice, this has enabled a large, largely unregulated market of quasi-anonymous data, traded under the guise of privacy preservation. The result is that detailed behavioral or demographic profiles can be built, influencing what ads people see, which content they are recommended, and even how services or offers are targeted to them—again, all without their knowledge or consent.

In Chapter 7, we will look more closely at how regulation is responding to the realities of modern data collection and profiling.

Data Collection by Design, Not Accident

It's tempting to believe that data collection is just the price of using digital tools that it's incidental, perhaps even accidental. A necessary trade-off for convenience. A side effect of innovation. But as we've seen throughout this chapter, this belief is not just mistaken, it's misleading.

Data collection is not a byproduct of social media platforms and digital services, it *is* the business model. It is built in, baked into the architecture, and often invisible by design.

Every interaction in the digital world, however minor, is optimized to generate data. And that data is not stored for safekeeping; it is analyzed, segmented, sold, and repurposed to influence what we see, how we feel, what we buy, and how we behave. Platforms are not neutral spaces. They are carefully crafted systems that prioritize engagement, prediction, and monetization. The user experience, as smooth and customizable as it may seem, is shaped to serve these deeper goals.

This chapter has peeled back the layers of that system. We've explored the vast spectrum of data types that are captured not just what we post, but what we hesitate to type, what we hover over, how fast we scroll, and when we go silent.

We've looked at the tools that gather this data: cookies, pixels, browser fingerprints, and app permissions. We've examined how that data is processed, how it flows through algorithmic engines, how it is bundled into predictive profiles, and eventually sold or traded in markets most people never see.

And we've examined the infrastructures that allow this system to thrive: the shadow economy of data brokers, the illusion of anonymity, and the regulatory gray zones that allow companies to extract deeply personal information without meaningful consent or accountability. Together, these systems form an ecosystem where privacy is optional, surveillance is ambient, and choice is often limited.

What makes all of this especially powerful and difficult to resist is that it's wrapped in convenience. We don't feel the data being collected. We don't see the brokers who buy it. We aren't shown the profiles that predict us. The system is seamless by design. Frictionless. Invisible. And perhaps of most concern, normalized.

This normalization is one of the defining features of surveillance in the digital age and to dismiss concern as overreaction. Yet this quiet acceptance stands in stark contrast to the original vision of the web as a space for creativity, collaboration, and human connection. As Tim Berners-Lee himself warned, systems designed to empower people have increasingly given way to large, impersonal infrastructures that observe, predict, and manipulate behavior at scale.

It is this shift that makes resistance feel futile and digital literacy seem irrelevant. This chapter was written to challenge that inertia, and to argue that awareness is not a luxury, but a responsibility.

Because while data collection has become invisible, its consequences are not. They appear in the form of algorithmic bias, polarized news feeds, predatory advertising, compromised autonomy, and rising mental fatigue. They show up in the ways we change our behavior when we know we're being watched. They can influence hiring decisions, insurance rates, dating experiences, political opinions, and even personal identity. When we are observed constantly, we perform constantly. And when we perform constantly, we begin to lose track of who we are when no one is watching even if, in reality, no one ever stops.

Importantly, this is not a call to reject all technology. We know that social media has genuine benefits: they connect, entertain, inform, and empower. The problem isn't the tool, it's how the tool is designed, used, governed, and monetized.

We need several shifts. We need better regulation laws that reflect the realities of data inference, anonymization risks, and behavioral manipulation. We need media and educational systems that prioritize digital literacy as a foundational skill, not a technical niche. And perhaps most importantly, we need a cultural shift that rejects the idea that everything must be optimized, predicted, and monetized.

The systems described in this chapter are not inevitable. They are products of choice—corporate, political, and societal. And that means they can be challenged, reimagined, and redesigned. But doing so begins with understanding.

As we transition to the next chapter, we move from the mechanics of data extraction to the social, psychological, and political consequences of life under algorithmic surveillance. What does it mean to grow up under constant observation? To curate a public self for unseen audiences? To exist in a world where your emotions are data points and your silence is a signal?

These are the questions we must now confront as everyday realities.

References

Boyd, d. (2010). Social network sites as networked publics: Affordances, dynamics, and implications. In Z. Papacharissi (Ed.), *A networked self: Identity, community, and culture on social network sites* (pp. 39–58). Routledge.

Citron, D. K., & Pasquale, F. (2014). The scored society: Due process for automated predictions. *Washington Law Review, 89*(1), 1–33.

Grand View Research. (2025). *Data broker market size, share & trends analysis report, 2025–2033.* Retrieved from https://www.grandviewresearch.com/industry-analysis/data-broker-market-report

Kosinski, M., Stillwell, D., & Graepel, T. (2013). Private traits and attributes are predictable from digital records of human behavior. *Proceedings of the National Academy of Sciences of the United States of America, 110*(15), 5802–5805. https://doi.org/10.1073/pnas.1218772110

Mishra, A. K., Cunche, M., & Arcolezi, H. H. (2025). *Breaking anonymity at scale: Re-identifying the trajectories of 100K real users in Japan* (preprint). arXiv. https://arxiv.org/abs/2506.05611

Nissenbaum, H. (2010). *Privacy in context: Technology, policy, and the integrity of social life.* Stanford University Press.

Solove, D. J. (2006). A taxonomy of privacy. *University of Pennsylvania Law Review, 154*(3), 477–564.

Sweeney, L. (2000). *Simple demographics often identify people uniquely* (Data Privacy Working Paper 3). Carnegie Mellon University, Data Privacy Lab. https://dataprivacylab.org/projects/identifiability/paper1.pdf

Tufekci, Z. (2015). Algorithmic harms beyond Facebook and Google: Emergent challenges of computational agency. *Colorado Technology Law Journal, 13,* 203–218.

Westin, A. F. (1967). *Privacy and freedom.* Atheneum.

Zhang, D., Strycharz, J., & Boerman, S. (2025). *Google knows me too well! Coping with perceived surveillance in an algorithmic profiling context.* Computers in Human Behavior.

Zuboff, S. (2019). *The age of surveillance capitalism: The fight for a human future at the new frontier of power.* PublicAffairs.

4 The Concept of Privacy in a Digital World

In the digital age, privacy is no longer about hiding information; it's about controlling what is seen, shared, and interpreted. As users navigate platforms designed for visibility, the boundaries between public and private have become increasingly blurred. Social media encourages openness, yet—as we are discovering—beneath every post lies a trail of data both visible and invisible collected, analyzed, and monetized.

This chapter redefines what privacy means in a world of constant connectivity. It explores how traditional notions of personal space, consent, and confidentiality have shifted, and why understanding privacy today is essential not only for protection, but for autonomy, accountability, and psychological well-being—for both individuals and organizations.

Rethinking Privacy in a Public Age

In a time dominated by social media, the concept of privacy has undergone a quiet but profound transformation. What was once associated with solitude, secrecy, and the ability to control boundaries around information has evolved into something far more complex and fragile.

The digital world has redefined what it means to be seen, to be known, and ultimately, to be left alone.

Privacy today is no longer a binary condition something one either has or doesn't have. Instead, it exists on a spectrum, shaped by context, platform architecture, and user behavior. Every post, comment, or interaction contributes to an ever-expanding portrait—not just of individuals, but also of organizations—often curated intentionally, but increasingly interpreted and recombined by algorithms for marketing, profiling, and operational decision-making.

In this new reality, users are not just sharing voluntarily; they are being observed continuously. Privacy settings may hide information from other users, but they rarely shield it from the platform itself. Even passive behavior such as scrolling, hovering, or pausing leaves a digital trace. What you don't say, but silently react to, is still data.

This chapter invites a reexamination of what privacy means in today's hyperconnected world. It challenges the myth that privacy is only for those with

DOI: 10.4324/9781003654322-5

something to hide and argues instead that privacy is a prerequisite for freedom, identity development, and psychological well-being.

As we navigate the boundaries between public and private, it becomes increasingly clear: privacy is not about secrecy, it is about control.

The New Public–Private Spectrum

In pre-digital society, the boundary between public and private was relatively straightforward. The home was a private space; the workplace or street was public. Conversations had clear audiences, and privacy breaches were visible and physical, for example, someone listening through a door or opening a confidential letter.

Today, those boundaries have dissolved into a spectrum of visibility, where moments once considered private are now routinely shared with strangers, corporations, and algorithms.

Social media has not only changed what we share, it has transformed *how* we think about sharing.

Platforms are designed to encourage visibility, rewarding users with attention, affirmation, and algorithmic reach when they disclose. The private becomes public by design, often subtly and without explicit consent. A photo meant for close friends might be reshared, screenshot, or pushed into the feeds of unknown viewers. An update posted in frustration might be picked up by a viral thread. In this world, virality can be accidental, and visibility is no longer optional.

This shift has led to what scholars call "context collapse" the merging of multiple audiences into a single, indistinguishable mass. Where once we tailored our words to specific people (family, colleagues, friends), now we must speak to all of them at once. A joke that resonates with friends might offend a professional audience. A political opinion shared casually might be scrutinized by a future employer. Social media collapses these contexts into one giant stage, where the boundaries between intention and interpretation blur.

Moreover, many platforms do not offer fine-grained audience controls or if they do, they are difficult to navigate. Users often believe their posts are private because they are visible only to a selected group, but even private content is subject to data harvesting, algorithmic analysis, and potential redistribution through backend systems. Even deleted content may persist in backup servers, accessible to the platform long after the user assumes it's gone.

Importantly, the public–private spectrum is not just technical, it is psychological. The *feeling* of privacy can be deceptive. Privacy is no longer a matter of whether information is hidden; it's a question of who sees it, when, and under what circumstances.

The implications of this are far-reaching. As users struggle to manage their identities across overlapping social circles, they may begin to self-censor, perform curated versions of themselves, or disengage entirely. The pressure to remain visible while maintaining control is emotionally taxing and ultimately unsustainable. Businesses face parallel challenges: brand presence, digital reputation, and corporate identity are constantly interpreted and reshaped by algorithms and public perception. Missteps or inconsistent messaging can be amplified, eroding trust, impacting customer relationships, and influencing strategic decisions in ways that are often difficult to anticipate.

To navigate the new public–private spectrum, users need more than privacy settings; they need a new kind of privacy literacy. This includes understanding that visibility is not binary, that context matters as much as content, and that control over one's digital self must be actively maintained, not passively assumed.

Types of Digital Privacy

Digital privacy cannot be understood through a single lens. Rather, it consists of multiple overlapping dimensions that influence how users interact with platforms, how they are observed, and how their information is interpreted. Figure 4.1 visualizes privacy as a multi-dimensional concept, helping distinguish between different types of threats and controls. It outlines four core types of digital privacy—informational, social, behavioral, and algorithmic.

Informational Privacy

Informational privacy refers to the ability of individuals to control the collection, storage, and distribution of their personal data. On social media, this includes details such as names, email addresses, and locations. Platforms gather this information both explicitly through forms and profiles and implicitly by tracking user interactions.

Informational privacy is often compromised not through breaches, but through routine platform operations. Platforms store and analyze user data to power features, personalize content, and enable targeted advertising; advertisers typically access only aggregated or anonymized signals rather than raw personal data. Loss of informational privacy means that even seemingly insignificant details can be combined to reveal deeply personal insights.

Social Privacy

Social privacy focuses on controlling visibility and access within social circles. This includes managing who sees posts, stories, photos, and comments. It is about

Figure 4.1 The Four Dimensions of Digital Privacy.

audience control, choosing what to share and with whom. Social privacy becomes challenging when content intended for one group—such as friends, family, or colleagues—can also be seen by others, or when the platform's default settings prioritize public visibility.

The boundaries between groups on social media are often unclear. Content meant for a close friend may be visible to a colleague or stranger, either through resharing or through platform recommendation algorithms. When platforms collapse these contexts, users lose the ability to communicate differently to different groups. This results in self-censorship or the adoption of a curated digital persona.

Behavioral Privacy

Behavioral privacy concerns how platforms monitor and interpret user activity. Unlike informational privacy, which focuses on what users provide, behavioral privacy focuses on what users do when they click, how long they view content, which videos they pause on, and how they navigate the interface.

This behavior is collected continuously, even when users are not actively engaging. Platforms analyze these patterns to infer preferences, emotions, and habits. This creates a feedback loop where inferred behaviors are used to shape the content that users see, often without their knowledge or consent. Loss of behavioral privacy leads to users being tracked, profiled, and targeted in increasingly personal ways.

Algorithmic Privacy

Algorithmic privacy relates to how user-related data is used to make decisions and predictions through automated systems. Social media platforms employ algorithms to decide what content appears in a feed, which ads are displayed, and how users are categorized or ranked. These decisions are often invisible to users and cannot easily be reviewed or challenged.

Digital privacy is not just about what is visible to others it is about how platforms interpret, process, and act upon user data. Each of these four types—informational, social, behavioral, and algorithmic—represents a different layer of vulnerability. Understanding them is the first step toward building digital resilience and regaining control in an environment where exposure is the norm.

Metadata—The Invisible You

When people think about digital privacy, they often focus on the content they share status updates, photos, videos, and messages. But in the world of social media, what you say is only part of the story. Equally, if not more, revealing is what you don't say—the silent trail of data generated as you scroll, click, pause, or simply exist on a platform. This invisible trail is known as metadata, and it plays a central role in undermining user privacy.

Metadata is often described as "data about data". It includes information such as the time a post was made, the device used to make it, the geolocation, the duration of engagement with a piece of content, and the identity of people tagged or mentioned. It can also include subtle behavioral cues like how quickly you respond to a message, how long you hover over a video, or the order in which you view stories. Though metadata does not always contain direct content, it reveals patterns, behaviors, and relationships with striking accuracy.

On social media platforms, metadata is constantly generated even when users are not posting anything. Every interaction leaves a digital fingerprint that platforms can collect, store, and analyze in real time. For example, a user might not upload a photo, but their location can be tracked through GPS tags. They might not "like" a post, but if they spend extra time reading it, that interest is captured and added to their profile.

This is where metadata becomes particularly powerful. Because it is often invisible to the user, it escapes the scrutiny that might come with more obvious forms of data collection. Users may feel they are protecting their privacy by limiting what they post or keeping their accounts private. But the platform is still watching—measuring time spent on content, analyzing device activity, and detecting browsing patterns.

Metadata also has a unique advantage: it scales effortlessly. Because it is automatically generated and easily standardized, it can be aggregated across millions of users to create predictive models and behavioral profiles. It is the foundation of the many algorithms that decide what content users see.

The consequences of this silent surveillance are significant. It shifts control away from the user, as decisions are made based on patterns they may not even realize they've formed. It also fuels asymmetry platforms and advertisers know far more about users than users know about themselves.

What makes metadata particularly troubling is that it often feels harmless. Users don't necessarily feel "watched" when they scroll or when their device switches between Wi-Fi and mobile data. But those actions produce metadata just the same. And in the hands of powerful systems, even passive data can become an instrument of profiling, prediction, and manipulation.

Understanding metadata is essential for understanding modern digital privacy. In many ways, it is the most accurate portrait of who we are online not because we created it, but because it reflects how we behave when we think no one is watching.

Context Collapse and Loss of Control

As discussed earlier, context collapse is one of the most subtle yet impactful challenges to privacy in the digital world. The merging of previously distinct social boundaries reduces our ability to manage different audiences, limiting control over how we are perceived online. While the concept may sound academic, its consequences are experienced every day, particularly on social media platforms where personal, professional and public identities increasingly overlap.

In the offline world, people routinely navigate between multiple social contexts: we might speak differently to a colleague than to a friend, dress one way at a formal event and another way at home, and share different aspects of ourselves with family than we do with professional contacts. Each setting provides a distinct audience, a set of shared expectations, and a level of privacy. These contextual boundaries help us manage our identities fluidly and appropriately.

Social media, however, disrupts these boundaries. Platforms often collapse our multiple social spheres into a single, undefined audience. A post shared on Facebook might be seen by college friends, work contacts, distant relatives, and acquaintances all at once.

This merging of audiences strips users of the ability to tailor their self-presentation. The result is not just embarrassment or awkwardness, it's a deeper loss of social control, where users no longer know who is watching, how they're being interpreted, or what the consequences might be. The freedom to express oneself differently in different contexts is severely diminished.

What makes context collapse especially concerning is how it violates the expectation of contextual integrity. In traditional settings, people implicitly understand the social norms of a particular context: what is appropriate to say, what is considered private, and who is allowed to see/hear what. When these norms are ignored or overridden intentionally or not privacy is breached, not because information was made public, but because it moved between contexts without consent.

For example, sharing a personal anecdote in a small WhatsApp group of friends might feel safe, even intimate. But if one member copies and shares that message to another group or worse, posts it publicly it breaks the context in which the original sharing occurred. The content hasn't changed, but its meaning has, because the audience has changed. This is context collapse in action.

Social media platforms are structured in ways that make such breaches routine. Even when users attempt to manage their audiences through privacy settings, custom friend lists, or "close friends", stories, platform design choices, resharing functions, algorithmic visibility, and accidental misclicks can override those efforts.

Platform Design and the Default to Public

One reason context collapse is so pervasive is because many social media platforms are designed with a "default-to-public" architecture. Visibility is often encouraged, if not required, for engagement, discoverability, and algorithmic reach. Platform likes, comments, followers, and algorithmic boosts are tied to openness and public sharing, not to privacy or control.

Even platforms that offer granular privacy controls rarely make them intuitive. Users must often navigate multiple layers of settings to restrict visibility, and many don't realize how content visibility changes when they tag someone, or reshare a post, for example.

Some platforms have limited audience segmentation tools altogether. A single post reaches all followers unless a user maintains a private or "locked" account. The ability to tailor messaging to different social circles so central to human communication is therefore difficult to replicate online. Reddit takes a different approach by organizing interaction around topic-based communities rather than personal networks. This can reduce some forms of social audience overlap, but posts remain publicly visible, persistent, and subject to platform-level observation and reuse.

Notably, Google+ (now sunset) was explicitly designed to address this problem through "Circles", allowing users to share content with clearly defined social groups. While the platform ultimately failed for other reasons, its design acknowledged a core tension of social media: the difficulty of replicating the way humans naturally adjust what they say depending on who they are speaking to. When platforms collapse these contexts by default, the ability to communicate differently to different social circles becomes harder to sustain online.

Context collapse erodes one of the most fundamental pillars of privacy: the ability to share selectively. It can reduce users' agency, heighten social anxiety, and transform personal expression into a performance for an invisible crowd.

In this collapsed landscape, control is replaced by constant calculation, and spontaneity gives way to careful risk management. Research on social media behavior shows that when audiences are unclear or overlapping, users monitor and adjust their content strategically, weighing how different social groups might interpret it. This self-presentation can lead to withholding, editing, or curating posts, reflecting a shift from natural expression to ongoing impression management and heightened digital self-monitoring. As social media continues to mediate nearly every domain of life—from personal relationships to professional branding—the ability to rebuild contextual boundaries will be essential to preserving authenticity, well-being, and privacy in the digital world.

The Consent Illusion

Consent is often held up as the foundation of digital privacy, the act that legitimizes data collection, content sharing, and algorithmic profiling. Every time a user signs up for a platform, downloads an app, or adjusts their settings, they are asked to consent. The message is clear: if you agree, you are in control.

But this idealized view of consent masks a more troubling reality. In practice, digital consent is largely an illusion shaped by design choices, psychological nudges, and legal formalities that obscure more than they reveal. While users technically "agree" to share data, the conditions under which they do so rarely meet the standards of informed, voluntary, and meaningful consent. This disconnect has become one of the central privacy challenges of the social media age.

Figure 4.2 illustrates the consent funnel through which users are progressively nudged toward data sharing during routine digital interactions. What begins as a simple app sign-up or website visit quickly introduces cookie banners, pop-ups, and lengthy terms of service that are rarely read in full. Rather than enabling meaningful choice, these interfaces are often designed around opt-in by default, using dark patterns that prioritize speed and convenience over informed decision-making. As users click "Accept" to proceed, consent becomes passive rather than

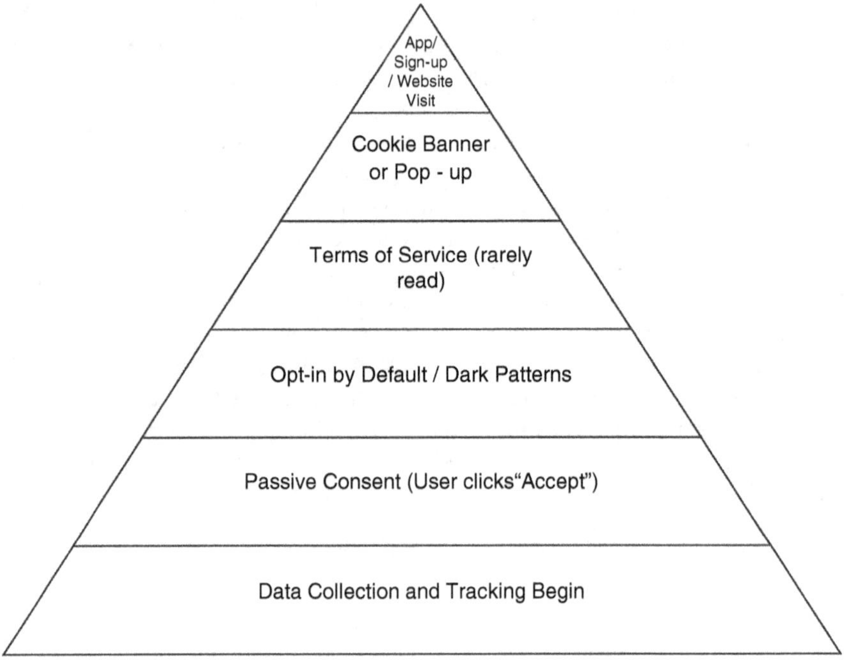

Figure 4.2 The Consent Funnel: How Users Are Nudged to Agree.

deliberate, signaling compliance without genuine understanding. At the base of the funnel, data collection and tracking commence, often extending beyond the immediate service to include third-party analytics and advertising networks. The figure highlights how consent is not a single informed decision but a layered process shaped by interface design, time pressure, and information overload—raising important questions about whether such consent can truly be considered voluntary or informed.

Across multiple aspects of platform interaction, consent is widely assumed to grant control, transparency, and reversibility. In practice, however, user agency is often limited, partial, or illusory. While many users report skimming terms and conditions, the complexity and length of these documents make meaningful understanding unlikely within the time typically spent reading them. Similarly, actions such as disabling cookies or revoking app permissions are commonly interpreted as comprehensive opt-outs, yet tracking frequently continues through alternative technical mechanisms such as device identifiers, metadata, or inferred behavioral profiles.

Table 4.1 highlights the dissonance between perceived and actual user control, emphasizing how consent is often symbolic rather than functional. It exposes a persistent gap between how users perceive digital consent and how data practices operate in reality.

Table 4.1 Users' Perception vs. Reality of Digital Consent

Aspect of Consent	*What Users Believe*	*What Actually Happens*	*Source*
Reading terms & conditions	36% say they "glance through" or "skim"	Average reading time: 46 seconds	Pew Research Center (2019)
Opting out of tracking	72% think turning off cookies stops all tracking	Tracking persists through device/ browser IDs	Mozilla Foundation (2021)
Data deletion	68% think deleting a post removes all traces	Data often retained in backups/server logs	GDPR Transparency Reports (2020)
Control over ads	61% believe they can control ad targeting	Algorithms use metadata and inferred traits	Zuboff, *Surveillance Capitalism* (2019)
Revoking app permissions	54% believe revoking access stops data flow	Apps may continue passive tracking	AppCensus Privacy Audit (2022)

The table also highlights misconceptions around data deletion and advertising control. Users often believe that deleting content or adjusting ad settings removes their data or influence over targeting, whereas platforms may retain information for operational, analytical, or commercial purposes. These discrepancies reveal how consent mechanisms are designed to signal compliance rather than enable genuine control. Rather than empowering users, consent becomes a procedural checkbox that legitimizes ongoing data extraction, reinforcing the argument that digital consent is increasingly symbolic rather than functionally protective.

The Overload of Permissions and Complexity

The first problem with digital consent is sheer volume. Every app, platform, website, or tool requires its own set of permissions and disclosures, from cookie banners and pop-ups to multipage privacy policies and software updates.

This is compounded by complexity: these documents are long, legalistic, and often opaque, burying key details about data sharing, retention, profiling, and artificial intelligence-driven inference in ways that make it almost impossible for users to fully understand what they are agreeing to.

For most users, the only way to access the service is to accept it quickly, and often without reading. The act of giving consent has become a reflex, not a considered decision. Platforms know this: consent prompts are designed to be easy to accept and difficult to decline. The "Agree" button is bright and easy to find; the "Manage Settings" option is often buried in layers of submenus.

Over time, users experience what researchers call "consent fatigue". They are so frequently asked to approve terms and policies that the process becomes meaningless. Consent becomes habitual, passive, and automatic—undermining the very principle it was meant to protect.

Where privacy controls exist, they often place an unfair burden on the user. Individuals are expected to act as their own data managers, constantly reviewing permissions, reading policy updates, and adjusting settings. This shifts responsibility from the platform to the individual, creating a system where privacy becomes a privilege for the technically savvy or obsessively vigilant.

Therefore, for most users, the choice becomes binary: accept everything or leave. And leaving is rarely a realistic option. Social media is so deeply integrated into modern life used for professional networking, event coordination, news consumption, and daily communication. Rejecting terms often means opting out of the digital world altogether, which is not a realistic choice for most people, either personally or professionally.

The Design of Consent Interfaces

Beyond legal language, the very interfaces used to request consent are often manipulative by design. Known as "dark patterns", these are interface strategies that steer users toward a particular outcome, usually acceptance.

Examples include:

- Pre-ticked checkboxes
- Confusing double negatives (e.g., "Don't not allow tracking")
- Emotional prompts (e.g., "You'll miss out!")
- Interface asymmetry (e.g., bold "Accept All" button vs. small "Settings" link)

These tactics exploit cognitive biases, encouraging users to choose convenience over caution. In doing so, they create the illusion of choice while nudging users toward greater data exposure. The result is a form of coerced consent, where users agree not because they want to, but because it is the path of least resistance.

To note: many of these practices are now considered legally questionable: under GDPR, CPRA/CCPA, and the EU Digital Services Act, consent obtained through manipulative or opaque interfaces may not be valid, and regulators can require platforms to redesign interfaces to ensure fairness and transparency.

Chapter 5 will explore how psychology shapes these interactions, showing how design, cognitive biases, and behavioral patterns influence the choices users make about their privacy.

Consent and Power Imbalance

At its core, the challenges of digital consent stem from a fundamental imbalance of power between users and platforms. Users are expected to give informed, voluntary consent to systems they cannot fully understand, governed by policies they cannot negotiate, within ecosystems they cannot opt out of.

In ethical terms, consent should be:

1. Informed—the user knows what they are agreeing to
2. Voluntary—the user has a real choice, without coercion

3 Specific—the agreement is clear and limited in scope
4 Reversible—the user can change their mind at any time

Digital consent, in its current form, fails on all four counts. It is not informed, because policies are too complex. It is not voluntary, because refusal often means exclusion. It is not specific, because consent covers broad and vague uses. And it is not reversible, because withdrawing consent is difficult or impossible.

Rethinking Consent

To move forward, consent must be reimagined as more than a legal checkbox. It must be restructured as a process—continuous, clear, and user-centric.

This means:

- Designing consent flows that prioritize clarity over complexity
- Offering real alternatives to data sharing without denying access
- Enabling consent revocation that is as easy as acceptance
- Shifting toward data minimization by default, that is, collect only what is necessary
- Building trust-based relationships where users are treated as partners, not products

The consent illusion is one of the most persistent and damaging myths of the digital age. It enables surveillance, justifies exploitation, and shifts responsibility away from those with power. Users are led to believe they are in control, when in fact they are navigating systems designed to minimize their agency.

True privacy cannot be built on illusion. It must be grounded in transparency, accountability, and respect for the rights of individuals and organizations. Until platforms treat consent as a shared ethical commitment not just a legal requirement the digital landscape will continue to prioritize convenience over conscience, and compliance over choice.

Contextual Integrity and Ethical Boundaries

As we've explored throughout this chapter, privacy in the digital world is far from straightforward. It transcends technical configurations or legal definitions. It lives in subtle negotiations between what is shared and what is held back, between who we are and who sees us, between what is appropriate in one moment but invasive in another.

To make sense of these shifting dimensions, the concept of contextual integrity offers a compelling framework. It reframes privacy not as secrecy or isolation, but as the preservation of appropriate information flows that respect social context, roles, and expectations. In doing so, it opens a more realistic path to understanding how privacy works in everyday digital life.

Coined by philosopher and information ethicist Helen Nissenbaum, contextual integrity challenges the common idea that privacy is simply about keeping information secret or under personal control. Instead, it suggests that privacy is maintained when information flows appropriately, according to the social norms of a given context.

For example, it is not necessarily a violation of privacy for a patient to share medical details with a doctor. But it would be inappropriate for the doctor to share those details with a pharmaceutical company, or a colleague at a party, even if no laws were broken. The breach here is not about secrecy but about crossing a contextual boundary.

This idea becomes even more critical in the digital world, where data flows are automatic, often invisible, and frequently detached from their original social setting. Contextual integrity helps us assess not only who has access to our data, but whether that access is ethically appropriate within the context in which the information was initially shared.

The Four Parameters of Contextual Integrity

According to Nissenbaum, information flow is contextually appropriate when it aligns with the following four parameters:

1. Context—The specific social setting or environment (e.g., workplace, family, health clinic)
2. Actors—The entities involved in the information exchange (e.g., sender, recipient, subject)
3. Attributes—The type of information being shared (e.g., financial data, opinions, emotions)
4. Transmission Principles—The norms or expectations governing how that information is shared (e.g., confidentiality, reciprocity, consent)

A violation of privacy occurs when any of these parameters are breached or misaligned. For instance, sharing a friend's photo from a private group chat on a public platform may involve the same actors and attributes but breaks the transmission principle expected in the original setting. The harm, in this case, is social and emotional, not necessarily legal or technical.

Why Contextual Integrity Matters in the Social Media Age

In the digital age, context collapses easily. A message meant for close friends gets screenshot and circulated. A harmless search term triggers algorithmic recommendations across platforms. A user's data is repackaged and sold to third-party advertisers, who operate entirely outside the original interaction.

These breaches often go unnoticed not because they are invisible, but because they have been normalized. Platforms operate under an implicit model of data as property: once shared, it can be moved, copied, or monetized with minimal resistance. But from a contextual integrity perspective, this approach is ethically problematic. It ignores the meaning and intent behind information sharing. It breaks the social contract that users assume, even if they don't read the small print.

Take, for instance, a student sharing mental health struggles on a university peer support forum, as illustrated in Figure 4.3. If the platform or moderators decide to use that data to generate user profiles, or integrate it into a machine learning model to identify "at-risk" students without consent, it creates a fundamental mismatch between contextual expectation and actual data use. The information may still be anonymized, but the trust embedded in the original context is violated.

The adoption of real-name policies—platform rules that require users to register and participate under their legal or officially verified names rather than pseudonyms or aliases—illustrates this tension clearly. While presented as a measure to promote transparency or reduce abuse, these policies can put certain users at risk. For people in politically sensitive regions, members of LGBTQ+ communities, or survivors of domestic violence, for example, the ability to use a pseudonym is not deceit—it is protection.

Targeted advertising and emotional profiling represent another form of contextual integrity breach. Platforms that analyze posts for emotional tone or mood to serve "relevant" ads treat personal expression as behavioral currency. When a user shares experiences of personal milestones or family events, they do so in a social context, not as a signal for commercial exploitation. Leveraging these attributes for ad targeting reframes deeply personal expression as a resource to be monetized, stripping it of its intended emotional and social meaning.

Finally, the use of facial recognition on public posts illustrates how technology can erode both actor expectations and transmission principles. Even when photos are publicly visible, users do not necessarily consent to biometric analysis or automated surveillance. The deployment of facial recognition software shows how individuals can be identified and tracked at scale without their knowledge or permission, raising profound privacy concerns.

Each of these examples highlights the same ethical flaw: failing to respect the original context in which information was shared.

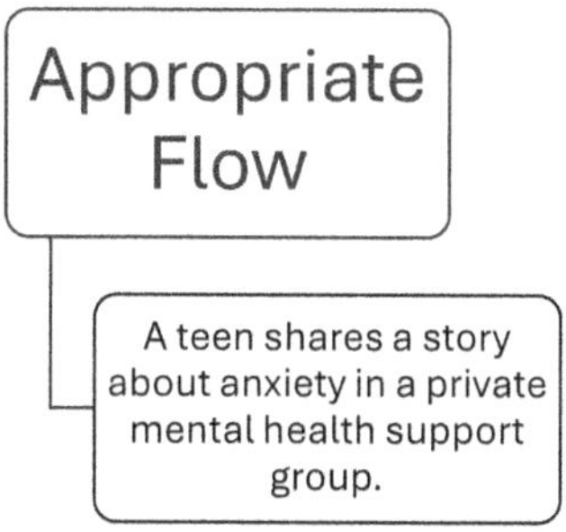

Figure 4.3 Contextual Integrity in Practice: When Sharing Becomes a Breach.

Empowering Users and Ethical Platform Governance

While platform-level responsibility is essential, users also benefit when they are empowered to manage context on their own terms. Some platforms have introduced features to support this, such as Facebook's multiple-profile functionality, which allows users to maintain distinct identities for different social circles. Other context-specific sharing tools, such as the ability to designate different audiences for different posts, auto-expiring content that reflects temporal boundaries like stories or disappearing messages, and privacy labels or contextual warnings that help users assess visibility before sharing, all support this goal. Informed consent cues, including tooltips or visual prompts, can remind users of potential data flows. These tools should not be treated as optional extras—they provide the infrastructure necessary for digital autonomy, particularly for those navigating multiple roles, identities, and social circles.

Contextual integrity can also guide broader platform governance. Moderation practices, for example, should distinguish between public and private content contexts, while data-sharing policies should align with the original intent behind data submission.

Platforms can support contextual integrity not only through design features but also through clear accountability mechanisms. One key measure is transparency reporting, where companies disclose how data is collected, used, and shared. Transparency reports could specify not just what data was accessed, but in what context and under which transmission principles.

Clear ethical boundaries help users feel respected and foster long-term trust, making governance not only a matter of design but also of accountability and values.

It is important to acknowledge that applying contextual integrity is not without challenges. Contexts can be ambiguous, overlapping, or emergent, making it difficult to define what is "appropriate". User expectations are dynamic and shaped by platform and social norms, so what seems acceptable may already be influenced by prior design choices.

In addition, the theory is difficult to automate, raising questions about implementation at scale within algorithmic systems. These critiques are valid, but rather than seeing them as limitations, they highlight the need for ongoing dialogue, human-in-the-loop systems, and user-centered design processes that prioritize interpretation over inflexibility.

As we prepare to conclude this chapter, contextual integrity offers a timely reminder: digital privacy is not just about protecting data it's about honoring the contexts that give our expressions meaning.

In the next and final section of this chapter, we turn to users themselves who are navigating these blurred boundaries every day. From quiet refusals to intentional resistance, we explore how individuals are reclaiming their right to privacy, even in systems designed to take it away.

Users on the Frontlines—Narratives of Resistance

While governments draft legislation and the platforms set design policies, it is often individuals and organizations who carry the responsibility of navigating, resisting, and shaping the digital privacy landscape. The actions of these individuals and organizations—such as journalists adopting encrypted communication or companies implementing stronger data protection practices—may not always be visible or coordinated, but they represent a quiet, persistent movement toward reclaiming control over identity and autonomy online.

If we shift the lens away from systems and frameworks to focus on the people who live with the consequences of privacy erosion every day—and who, in their own ways, push back—we see a different perspective. Their actions may not always be visible or coordinated, but their experiences and choices are essential. Digital privacy, while shaped by policies and platforms, whether for themselves or on behalf of an organization.

Everyday Acts of Digital Resistance

Not all resistance is loud or collective. For many users, resistance shows up in small, intentional acts that quietly assert agency in an otherwise extractive system, including anonymity tools and use of privacy settings to limit visibility. For example:

- A parent creates a private account to share family photos only with close relatives
- A student uses a pseudonym account to express political views safely
- A young professional disables read receipts, hides their online status, or deletes old posts to avoid being misunderstood
- A user refuses to accept unnecessary permissions, choosing a less convenient app in favor of better privacy
- A creator moves to decentralized platforms, sacrificing reach for control

These choices may seem minor, but they are deeply meaningful. They signal a refusal to conform entirely to platform logic—a decision to prioritize self-protection over seamless participation. Importantly, these acts are often not about complete withdrawal or paranoia. Instead, they represent a growing awareness that engagement can, and should, be on the user's terms.

Digital Minimalism and Intentional Sharing

Another notable form of resistance is the rise of digital minimalism—a philosophy and lifestyle that encourages conscious, value-driven use of technology. Digital minimalists are not anti-social media, but they reject the notion that constant connectivity is necessary or healthy. They regularly audit and clean their digital presence, limit app usage through screen-time boundaries, opt for text-based communication over performative posting, and share selectively with clear intentions.

For these users, privacy is not only about what is hidden, but also what is preserved: attention, mental space, and authentic connection. By taking control over when, how, and with whom they interact online, digital minimalists resist the pressures of the attention economy, reduce exposure to algorithmic manipulation, and reclaim agency over their digital lives. For organizations and brands, this trend signals a shift in how audiences engage—focusing less on quantity of interactions and more on the quality of engagement. In this way, digital minimalism demonstrates that both individuals and organizations can assert intentionality in a system designed to maximize activity and data generation.

Counter-Surveillance and Conscious Disengagement

Some users take resistance a step further—actively working to reduce their digital footprint through the use of encrypted tools. This includes using:

- Encrypted messaging apps, for example, Signal, ProtonMail
- VPNs and browser extensions to block tracking
- Privacy-focused search engines like DuckDuckGo

Others go further still: deleting social media accounts altogether, refusing cookies across all sites, or shifting to analog tools for tasks like journaling, scheduling, or communication.

For these users, resistance is both practical and symbolic—a way of opting out of an ecosystem they no longer trust. Though this may come with trade-offs in convenience or visibility, the gain is a sense of freedom—being online without being constantly watched. For platforms, these behaviors signal a challenge to engagement-driven business models, highlighting the need to rethink how value, attention, and trust are generated in a landscape where some users may actively limit their data exposure.

The Power of Saying No

Perhaps the most powerful narrative emerging from users today is not one of rebellion or escape—but of quiet realignment. A recognition that while social media is embedded in modern life, its influence can be questioned, and reshaped.

In a digital landscape that constantly nudges users to post more, share more, and be more visible, simply saying "no" becomes an act of resistance.

- No, I won't allow this app to access my contacts
- No, I won't tag my location
- No, I won't post pictures of my children—I'll wait until they are old enough to provide their own consent
- No, I'll restrict sharing to private groups instead of posting publicly

These refusals may be quiet, even invisible to others—but they are powerful. They reclaim space, protect mental and emotional well-being, and preserve boundaries between different social contexts. They also remind us that consent, when it is genuine, includes the freedom to withhold—and that control over one's digital life can be exercised in small, deliberate ways every day.

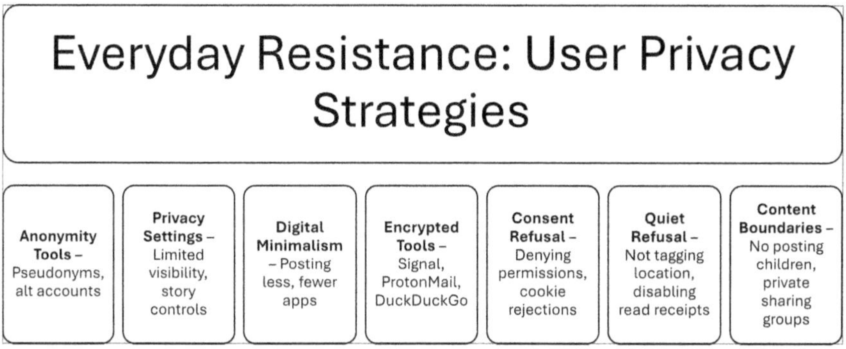

Figure 4.4 User Resistance Toolkit.

Figure 4.4 summarizes the inventory of everyday tactics users employ to maintain control over their digital lives.

Privacy as a Personal and Collective Practice

As this chapter has shown, privacy in the digital world is not just about data—it is about context and choice. While the structures around us—platforms, algorithms, policies—shape the rules of engagement, users also find creative, intentional ways to navigate them.

Whether through minimalism, anonymity, encryption, or silence, users are not giving up. They are adapting. They are learning. They are quietly reclaiming control, even in spaces designed to erode it. In doing so, they demonstrate that privacy is not dead. It is simply being rewritten—every day, by the people determined to define their own boundaries.

In the next chapter, we dive into the psychology of privacy, exploring how human cognition, emotion, and social behavior shape the ways we experience, manage, and protect our personal information.

References

de Montjoye, Y.-A., Radaelli, L., Singh, V. K., & Pentland, A. (2015). Unique in the shopping mall: On the reidentifiability of credit card metadata. *Science, 347*(6221), 536–539. https://doi.org/10.1126/science.1256297

Facebook. (2014). Experimental evidence of massive-scale emotional contagion through social networks. *Proceedings of the National Academy of Sciences, 111*(24), 8788–8790. https://doi.org/10.1073/pnas.1320040111

Federal Trade Commission. (2014). *Data brokers: A call for transparency and accountability.* https://www.ftc.gov/reports/data-brokers-call-transparency-accountability-report-federal-trade-commission-may-2014

Harding, L. (2014). The Snowden files: The inside story of the world's most wanted man. Vintage

Kosinski, M., Stillwell, D., & Graepel, T. (2013). Private traits and attributes are predictable from digital records of human behavior. *Proceedings of the National Academy of Sciences, 110*(15), 5802–5805. https://doi.org/10.1073/pnas.1218772110

Mozilla Foundation. (2021). *Privacy not included: App tracking report.* https://foundation.mozilla.org/en/privacynotincluded/

Mozilla Foundation. (2022). *Privacy not included: Mental health and prayer apps.* https://foundation.mozilla.org/en/privacynotincluded/

Narayanan, A., & Shmatikov, V. (2008). Robust de-anonymization of large sparse datasets. *In 2008 IEEE Symposium on Security and Privacy* (pp. 111–125). *https://ieeexplore.ieee.org/document/4531148*

Pew Research Center. (2019). *Americans and privacy: Concerned, confused and feeling lack of control over their personal information.* https://www.pewresearch.org/internet/2019/11/15/americans-and-privacy-concerned-confused-and-feeling-lack-of-control-over-their-personal-information/

Rocher, L., Hendrickx, J. M., & de Montjoye, Y.-A. (2019). Estimating the success of re-identifications in incomplete datasets using generative models. *Nature Communications, 10*(1), Article 3069. https://doi.org/10.1038/s41467-019-10933-3

Schneier, B. (2015). *Data and Goliath: The hidden battles to collect your data and control your world.* W. W. Norton & Company.

Sherman, J. (2021). Data brokers and sensitive data on us individuals. Duke University Sanford Cyber Policy Program, 9. https://techpolicy.sanford.duke.edu/report-data-brokers-and-sensitive-data-on-u-s-individuals/

Sweeney, L. (2000). *Simple demographics often identify people uniquely* (Data Privacy Working Paper No. 3). Carnegie Mellon University. https://dataprivacylab.org/projects/identifiability/index.html

Tufekci, Z. (2015). Algorithmic harms beyond Facebook and Google: Emergent challenges of computational agency. *Colorado Technology Law Journal, 13*, 203–218. https://scholar.law.colorado.edu/ctlj/vol13/iss2/4

Van der Nagel, E., & Frith, J. (2015). Anonymity, pseudonymity, and the agency of online identity: Examining the social practices of r/Gonewild. First Monday. https://doi.org/10.5210/fm.v20i3.5615

Vitak, J. (2012). The impact of context collapse and privacy on social network site disclosures. *Journal of Broadcasting & Electronic Media, 56*(4), 451–470. https://doi.org/10.1080/08838151.2012.732140

Wachter, S., Mittelstadt, B., & Floridi, L. (2017). Why a right to explanation of automated decision-making does not exist in the General Data Protection Regulation. *International Data Privacy Law, 7*(2), 76–99. https://doi.org/10.1093/idpl/ipx005

5 The Psychology of Privacy

Privacy in the age of social media is fundamentally shaped by psychology—not just how users feel about it, but how platforms design for it, how cognition processes information flows, and how trust is built or eroded through interface choices.

This chapter examines the psychological mechanisms underlying privacy behavior on social media platforms, focusing on design patterns, cognitive biases, and the structural features that influence user decision-making.

The Psychology of Consent and Decision Architecture

Social media platforms leverage well-established principles of psychology to shape user privacy choices. The most significant of these is the power of defaults. Research in behavioral economics demonstrates that default options carry enormous weight in decision-making: users tend to accept preselected settings regardless of whether they align with their actual preferences.

Platforms consistently set defaults that maximize data collection and visibility. Privacy-protective options exist, but they require active effort to locate and enable. This design choice is not accidental—it reflects an understanding that most users will follow the path of least resistance, particularly when faced with complex or time-consuming alternatives.

The psychological principle at work here is cognitive load. When users encounter lengthy privacy settings with dozens of toggles, checkboxes, and nested menus, decision fatigue sets in. The complexity itself becomes a barrier to informed choice. Users confronted with overwhelming options often default to the platform's preferred settings simply to complete the onboarding process and access the service.

Dark Patterns and Behavioral Manipulation

Dark patterns are design choices that subtly influence user behavior in ways that benefit the platform rather than the user. These patterns exploit cognitive biases and psychological vulnerabilities to guide users toward choices they might not otherwise make.

DOI: 10.4324/9781003654322-6

On social media platforms, dark patterns frequently appear in privacy-related contexts.

Common examples of dark patterns include:

- Misleading language: privacy-reducing options labeled with positive framing ("Stay connected with friends!") while privacy-protective choices carry negative framing ("Limit your experience")
- Forced action: requiring users to accept certain permissions to access basic functionality, even when those permissions are not technically necessary
- Obstruction: making it significantly easier to enable data sharing than to disable it, through asymmetric design of opt-in versus opt-out processes
- Nagging: repeatedly prompting users to reconsider privacy-protective choices through persistent notifications and reminders
- Confirmshaming: using guilt-inducing language in opt-out options (e.g., "Are you sure you want to miss out on personalized content?")

The Psychology of Digital Nudging

Digital nudging refers to the strategic use of interface design to influence user behavior without restricting choice. While nudging can be used ethically—for example, promoting healthier defaults—social media platforms often employ it to increase engagement and data collection at the expense of user privacy.

This operates through several psychological principles:

- Anchoring effects: initial privacy settings establish a reference point that shapes subsequent decisions. If users begin with highly permissive defaults, they're less likely to restrict access later, even when presented with the option.
- Social proof: platforms display information suggesting that "most users" have certain settings enabled, leveraging the human tendency to conform to perceived norms. This can pressure users into accepting less privacy-protective options.
- Scarcity and urgency: limited-time offers or urgent language ("Complete your profile now!") trigger psychological responses that reduce careful consideration of privacy implications.

Over time, these techniques train users to consent passively, engage compulsively, and relinquish privacy unconsciously.

The Psychological Architecture of Surveillance Capitalism

Social media companies transform extracted data into what Shoshana Zuboff terms "prediction products"—models that anticipate how users will behave, what they will click, buy, share, or avoid. These predictions are then sold to advertisers, political campaigns, or any party willing to pay for influence.

What makes this market different from traditional advertising is its granularity and psychological precision. Companies aren't just placing ads; they're bidding on emotional states, cognitive biases, and contextual moments. A user scrolling late at night after a breakup might be more likely pay attention to ads for dating apps, therapy services, or luxury goods—capitalizing on emotional vulnerability.

This represents a shift from advertising to influence, marking a turning point in social media's role. Platforms no longer simply reflect human behavior; they shape it.

Instrumentarian Power and Autonomy

Surveillance capitalism exerts what Zuboff calls "instrumentarian power"—the power to modify, steer, and automate behavior without awareness. On social media, this manifests through:

- Algorithmic content delivery: reinforcing confirmation bias—the tendency to seek out, interpret, and remember information that confirms existing beliefs—and emotional reactivity
- Nudging design: push notifications, badge rewards, and curated feeds
- Behavioral conditioning: creating habits around checking, scrolling, and engaging

These mechanisms reduce user autonomy not by restricting choice, but by engineering the illusion of choice. Users believe they are freely choosing what to consume, when in reality their behaviors are guided by systems designed to maximize time on platform and ad exposure.

Measuring the Impact: Platform Design Features

Platform design features are not neutral—they actively shape user behavior, emotional responses, and data profiles.

This recognition has influenced proposals to restrict access for under-16s, with many focusing not on social media as a whole but on specific platform features associated with potential harms, such as algorithmic recommendation systems, infinite scrolling, direct messaging, targeted advertising, and engagement-driven design patterns.

Infinite scroll keeps users engaged by removing natural stopping cues, creating a sense of endless content. Each new post or video acts as a potential source of novelty and gratification, which can lead to prolonged sessions and compulsive browsing. From a privacy perspective, every scroll provides platforms with more behavioral data to refine recommendations and target advertising.

Push notifications deliver intermittent alerts that tap into dopamine-driven anticipation. Users receive small, unpredictable rewards—messages, likes, or mentions—that prompt immediate engagement. While convenient, they also encourage habitual checking, and each interaction generates granular tracking data, revealing patterns of attention, activity, and emotional responsiveness.

Emoji use may seem casual or playful, but it is rich in behavioral information. Platforms track which emojis are used, in which contexts, and with whom. This data contributes to emotional and sentiment profiles: frequent late-night laughing emojis may indicate escapism, while crying emojis across different moods can suggest complexity or performative behavior. These signals influence feed curation, ad targeting, and engagement predictions.

Typing indicators—the little bubbles or dots that show someone is composing a message—create a sense of social presence and immediacy. They trigger anticipation and subtle social pressure to respond quickly, reinforcing attention and engagement. Platforms can also capture these micro-interactions to infer conversational style, responsiveness, and behavioral patterns.

Autoplay videos automatically play content as users scroll, exploiting our preference for passive consumption and reducing friction to engage with more media. Every pause, skip, or replay is tracked to infer interests, preferences, and emotional reactions.

Together, these features exemplify how emotional design and behavioral cues are embedded into platform architecture. The resulting data is not just about clicks and views—it forms the backbone of a sophisticated surveillance and predictive system that subtly guides user behavior while shaping personal digital profiles.

Table 5.1 summarizes the main design features, the psychological principles they leverage, and their privacy consequences.

Attention as a Psychological Resource

Perhaps the most contested resource in the digital age is human attention. Platforms compete not just for time, but for presence—for uninterrupted, emotionally engaged focus. This competition has given rise to what design ethicists call the "race to the bottom of the brainstem"—where platforms may be able to exploit psychological vulnerabilities to keep users engaged.

Notifications are not merely reminders; they're interruptions designed to reorient focus. Autoplay reduces decision-making barriers and increases screen time. Infinite scroll removes natural stopping cues that help users disengage.

Table 5.1 Platform Design Features, Psychological Effects, and Privacy Consequences

Feature	*Psychological Principle*	*Intended Effect*	*Privacy Consequence*
Infinite scroll	Removal of stopping cues	Extended session time	Compulsive use
Push notifications	Intermittent reinforcement	Reengagement	Continuous behavioral tracking
Reaction emojis	Emotional anchoring	Expressive feedback	Emotional state profiling
Typing indicators	Social presence bias	Anticipation	Real-time activity monitoring
Autoplay videos	Reduced cognitive effort	Seamless consumption	Content preference inference

These features leverage fundamental aspects of human psychology:

- Variable reward schedules: unpredictable content quality creates psychological patterns similar to gambling, where the possibility of discovering something interesting maintains engagement.
- Loss aversion: exploits the psychological principle that losses feel more significant than equivalent gains.
- Commitment and consistency: having already invested time in scrolling, users experience psychological pressure to continue rather than "waste" their previous investment.

These features are not inherently bad—but when they are engineered without regard for user well-being, they can become exploitative. Drawing the line means recognizing attention as a finite, precious resource, and taking back control of how, when, and why we give it.

Tactics for reclaiming attention include:

- Turning off nonessential notifications
- Using time-limiting tools or digital well-being apps
- Intentionally scheduling social media use instead of using it reactively
- Practicing "intentional engagement"—consciously deciding why you're logging on and what you hope to achieve

Recognising concerns about the impact of engagement-driven design, social media platforms have introduced a range of attention-management features for younger users, including screen-time reminders, daily limits, sleep modes, and notification controls. For example, Instagram's Teen Accounts include daily time limits and sleep mode features designed to encourage healthier usage patterns, while TikTok has introduced screen-time controls, notification muting schedules, and sleep reminders. However, these interventions place responsibility partly on users and families, while the underlying engagement-driven business models and design features intended to capture and retain attention remain central to many social media platforms.

The Erosion of Privacy Expectations

Over time, the practices of surveillance capitalism have become so embedded in the social media experience that many users no longer question them. Features once viewed as intrusive—such as personalized ads or automated suggestions—are now expected.

This psychological shift occurs through several mechanisms:

- Habituation: repeated exposure to privacy-invasive practices reduces their salience. What initially feels intrusive becomes routine.
- Reciprocity: platforms frame data collection as an exchange ("We provide free services; you provide data"), activating psychological principles of reciprocity that make refusal feel antisocial.

- Sunk cost: users who have invested years of content, connections, and memories in a platform experience psychological resistance to leaving, even when privacy concerns arise.

Trust, Transparency, and Platform Credibility

Trust in social media platforms represents a psychological paradox. Despite widespread awareness of data breaches and privacy scandals – such as those shared in Chapter 8 – billions of users continue to engage daily. This apparent contradiction reflects several psychological theories:

- Trust as default: humans are psychologically predisposed to trust, particularly when the alternative (constant vigilance) is cognitively exhausting. Platforms exploit this by designing interfaces that appear trustworthy, even when underlying practices are opaque.
- Compartmentalization: users mentally separate their awareness of systemic problems from their individual experience. "Yes, Facebook has privacy issues, but my personal risk feels low" represents this cognitive splitting.
- Learned helplessness: when users repeatedly encounter privacy violations with few consequences or available alternatives, they may develop a sense that resistance is futile, leading to passive acceptance.

Transparency as Performance

Many platforms have introduced transparency initiatives—privacy centers, data download tools, and clearer consent language. While these represent improvements, they often function more as trust signals than substantive reforms.

Psychologically, the presence of transparency mechanisms reduces concern even when users don't actively engage with them. The mere existence of a privacy dashboard creates the impression of accountability, whether or not the underlying data practices have changed.

This phenomenon, known as "privacy theater", parallels security theater in physical spaces: visible measures that provide psychological comfort without proportional protection.

The Role of Cognitive Biases

Cognitive biases are mental shortcuts or tendencies that can shape the way we interpret information, often without conscious awareness. On social media, these biases influence how users perceive platform trustworthiness and make decisions about privacy. Further examples of cognitive biases include:

- Optimism bias: users tend to believe negative outcomes (data breaches, harassment) are more likely to affect others than themselves, reducing precautionary behavior.
- Present bias: immediate benefits (social connection, entertainment) are psychologically weighted more heavily than future risks (data misuse, privacy loss), encouraging engagement despite known concerns.

- Availability heuristic: high-profile scandals are memorable but may be dismissed as exceptional rather than systemic, particularly as time passes and media attention shifts.

Understanding these biases is crucial for interpreting why users often overlook privacy risks or engage with platforms in ways that might compromise their personal information.

Context Collapse and Audience Management

Context collapse—the flattening of multiple audiences into a single context—presents a unique challenge. In offline life, we naturally moderate our self-presentation based on social context: we behave differently with family, colleagues, and friends. Social media platforms disrupt this by combining all audiences into one undifferentiated feed.

This creates cognitive dissonance. Users must reconcile competing self-presentations (professional, personal, familial) within a single platform, leading to several psychological responses:

- Strategic ambiguity: posting content that is deliberately vague or neutral enough to be acceptable across contexts, reducing authenticity.
- Self-silencing: avoiding topics or perspectives that might be controversial in any context, limiting expression.
- Platform segregation: maintaining multiple accounts or using different platforms for different aspects of identity, increasing cognitive load.

Visibility and Impression Management

The persistent visibility of social media creates what sociologist Erving Goffman would recognize as perpetual "front stage" performance. Users are constantly aware of potential audiences, leading to heightened impression management—the psychological work of curating how one appears to others.

This is not inherently negative; self-presentation is a normal aspect of social interaction. However, the scale and persistence of digital visibility intensifies this process. Users cannot easily distinguish between moments of "performance" and moments of "authentic self", potentially affecting identity formation and self-concept over time.

The Psychology of Data Value

Users engage in what researchers call "privacy calculus"—a mental cost-benefit analysis weighing privacy risks against platform benefits. This calculation is influenced by several psychological factors:

- Immediate versus delayed consequences: platform benefits (connection, entertainment) are immediate and tangible, while privacy risks often feel abstract and distant.

- Information asymmetry: users lack complete information about how their data is used, making accurate risk assessment impossible. This uncertainty typically biases toward underestimating risk.
- Social influence: if peers use platforms despite privacy concerns, social proof suggests the risks are acceptable.

The Personalization Trade-off

Platforms frame data collection as necessary for personalization, positioning it as a benefit rather than an extraction. Psychologically, this reframing is effective because:

- Personalization provides immediate, visible value (relevant content, targeted ads)
- The connection between data collection and personalization feels intuitive
- Refusing personalization may be framed as choosing an inferior experience

This creates a psychological bind: users who value personalization must accept extensive data collection, while those who prioritize privacy must sacrifice convenience and relevance.

Table 5.2 compares two common user profiles: those who have adapted to evolving platform norms versus those who adhere to legacy privacy expectations, highlighting their behaviors, skills, and vulnerabilities across key dimensions of digital engagement.

Contextual Integrity as a Psychological Framework

Helen Nissenbaum's concept of contextual integrity offers a psychologically grounded approach to understanding privacy. Rather than defining privacy as secrecy or control, contextual integrity recognizes that privacy concerns arise when information flows violate contextual norms—the shared expectations about what information is appropriate in specific contexts.

This framework aligns with psychological research on social norms and expectations. Users don't object to all information sharing; they object to sharing

Table 5.2 Comparative Characteristics of Pragmatic and Privacy-Conscious Social Media Users

Dimension	*Pragmatic Users (Normalized Surveillance)*	*Privacy-Conscious Users (Legacy Privacy Norms)*
Trust in platforms	Pragmatic (normalized surveillance)	Skeptical, values legacy privacy
Platform navigation skills	High	Varies (often low for new tools)
Privacy settings	Strategic but inconsistent	Often limited, sometimes misinformed
Engagement	High (via algorithmic feeds)	Often limited
Vulnerability to manipulation	High (via algorithmic feeds)	High (via scams, fake content)

that feels contextually inappropriate. A photo shared in a private group chat feels different from the same photo appearing in a public algorithmic feed, even if the same people might eventually see it.

Trust Through Appropriate Information Flow

From this perspective, platforms can build trust not by collecting less data, but by ensuring information flows match user expectations. This requires:

- Context-specific defaults: different settings for different types of content and audiences
- Transparent flow mapping: clear communication about where information travels and who accesses it
- User agency over contexts: meaningful control over how different audiences interact with content

When platforms disrupt contextual integrity—sharing work information in social contexts, or making private communications visible to broader audiences—they can trigger psychological responses of violation and betrayal, eroding trust far more effectively than abstract privacy policies.

The psychology of privacy on social media is not fixed; it is actively constructed through design choices, interface patterns, and platform architectures. Users' privacy attitudes and behaviors reflect not just individual preferences but the psychological affordances and constraints of the systems they inhabit.

Understanding these psychological mechanisms is essential for:

- Regulators: crafting policies that address the behavioral realities of platform design, not just technical capabilities
- Designers: creating interfaces that respect cognitive limitations and support genuine informed consent
- Users: recognizing that privacy challenges are structural, not personal failures
- Researchers: investigating the long-term psychological effects of living in persistently surveillant environments

Privacy in the digital age is a question of psychological architecture—how platforms shape cognition, influence decision-making, and structure the possibilities for trust, autonomy, and appropriate information flow. Recognizing this positions privacy not as an abstract right to be protected, but as a lived psychological experience to be designed with intention and care.

Generational Perspectives on Digital Privacy: Natives, Immigrants, and the Psychology of Use

While age alone does not determine behavior online; generational experiences with technology can shape how individuals perceive, value, and protect their personal information. The distinction between digital natives and digital immigrants—terms popularized by educator Marc Prensky —offers a useful lens to examine how different populations navigate the social media landscape, interpret privacy norms, and respond to surveillance.

Digital Immigrants: Cautious, Curious, and Often Confused

Digital immigrants—typically older Gen Xers and Baby Boomers—experienced childhoods largely in analog contexts and adapted to digital tools as adults. Their approach to social media often reflects legacy habits, skepticism, and caution. Platforms were initially adopted for specific purposes—email for work, Facebook for reconnecting with friends—and only later expanded into broader social use.

This cohort often struggles with the opacity of platform design. Complex privacy settings, hidden data permissions, and algorithmic feeds can confuse even attentive users. Many assume that visible measures, such as private profiles, fully protect them, unaware of background tracking or predictive analytics. Yet digital immigrants also display strengths: they tend to value privacy as a fundamental right, are more alert to breaches, and are receptive to tools like ad blockers, password managers, and careful data-sharing practices.

Their slower adoption and cautious approach can create vulnerabilities, however, particularly to misinformation, phishing, and scams. The combination of high privacy concerns and lower digital literacy requires targeted guidance to navigate modern social media safely.

Digital Natives: Adaptable, Connected, and Desensitized

Digital natives—generally millennials and Gen Z—grew up with the internet, mobile devices, and social media as integral parts of daily life. Fluent in the "language" of digital interaction, they navigate apps, algorithms, and platform features with ease. For these users, the digital world is not just a tool but an extension of self. Platforms such as Instagram, Snapchat, TikTok, and YouTube shape their social relationships, self-expression, and expectations around sharing.

This familiarity often breeds a degree of desensitization to surveillance. While digital natives are aware that data is tracked, many accept it as the cost of participation, with common sentiments like "I have nothing to hide" or "they already know everything". Yet this acceptance does not equate to ignorance. Many digital natives actively manage their online presence: using "Finstas" (secondary Instagram accounts), disappearing messages, or encrypted apps to control visibility.

Despite this fluency, they remain vulnerable to subtle forms of manipulation. Algorithmic content shaping, behavioral targeting, and persuasive design can operate beneath conscious awareness, making hyper-visibility feel intuitive rather than engineered. Without strong privacy education, even highly competent users risk exposure and manipulation in invisible ways.

Cultural Reflections on Youth, Digital Life, and Privacy

Popular culture can illuminate psychological and social dynamics that traditional research sometimes overlooks, and *Adolescence*—a 2025 Netflix limited series—has sparked widespread conversation about the interplay between teenagers, digital spaces, and identity. The drama follows a 13-year-old boy at the center of a traumatic event and uses this narrative to explore how online environments can influence youth behavior, emotional development, and social relationships.

Commentators and psychologists alike have observed that the series highlights the blurred boundaries between online and offline life, the pressures of belonging in digital communities, and how digital cultures can amplify risk, isolation, and harmful ideologies. In doing so, *Adolescence* offers a vivid lens on how social media and online subcultures can shape psychological development and underscore the importance of open communication, digital literacy, and emotional support as young people navigate complex digital landscapes.

Generational Strengths and Weaknesses

Both demographics exhibit distinct strengths and vulnerabilities when navigating digital platforms, as shown in Table 5.3.

While these categories are not absolute—some younger users adopt cautious practices, some older users become proficient—the distinction helps highlight trends, gaps, and areas for intervention.

Social Implications of Divergent Expectations

Generational differences can create friction within digital communities, particularly around consent, visibility, and acceptable behavior. A digital native may tag a friend in a public post without considering privacy, while a digital immigrant might perceive this as a boundary violation. Younger users often favor ephemeral communication, while older users expect permanence and clarity. Disparities also appear in attitudes toward digital legacy: older users prioritize digital wills and

Table 5.3 Strength and Weaknesses of Digital Natives vs. Digital Immigrants

	Digital Natives	*Digital Immigrants*
Strengths	Platform fluency, multi-platform awareness, rapid adoption of new tools, peer-driven privacy strategies	Appreciation of privacy as a right, critical thinking informed by analog experiences, trust in legal/regulatory frameworks
Weaknesses	Desensitization to surveillance, normalization of algorithmic control, dependency on platforms	Susceptibility to scams, confusion around app settings, slower adaptation to evolving digital norms

Table 5.4 Digital Native vs. Digital Immigrant Privacy Behaviors

Behavior/Trait	*Digital Natives*	*Digital Immigrants*
Use of encrypted messaging	Moderate (e.g., WhatsApp, Signal)	Low to moderate
Trust in platforms	Pragmatic (normalized surveillance)	Skeptical, values legacy privacy
Platform navigation skills	High	Varies (often low for new tools)
Privacy settings engagement	Strategic but inconsistent	Often limited, sometimes misinformed
Vulnerability to manipulation	High (via algorithmic feeds)	High (via scams, fake content)

account management after death, whereas younger users often assume platforms manage such concerns automatically.

Two Audiences, One Digital World

Digital natives and digital immigrants now inhabit the same ecosystem. Understanding their divergent perspectives is essential, as highlighted in Table 5.4, for designing inclusive technologies, crafting effective policies, and cultivating a culture where privacy is a shared responsibility. Across generations, the ultimate challenge is the same: reclaiming agency in a world where behaviors are tracked, shaped, and monetized. All users deserve transparency, control, and dignity in their digital lives.

Cultural Perspectives on Privacy

Privacy is often treated in policy and platform design as a universal principle—something that can be defined once and applied everywhere. In practice, however, privacy is a culturally shaped concept, influenced by social norms, political structures, historical experiences of surveillance, religious traditions, and collective attitudes toward visibility, authority, and individual autonomy. What feels intrusive in one cultural context may feel routine or even protective in another. What one society considers deeply personal, another may regard as inherently communal.

The rise of global social media has brought these differing privacy worldviews into constant contact. Platforms designed in one cultural context now mediate social interaction across many others, collapsing local norms into shared digital spaces. As a result, assumptions about what users expect, tolerate, or resist around data collection, visibility, and monitoring are increasingly misaligned with lived experience.

This section examines how privacy is understood, valued, and negotiated across cultures, and why recognizing these differences is essential not only for effective regulation but for the psychological safety, trust, and dignity of users.

Without a culturally informed understanding of privacy, even well-intentioned technologies risk misunderstanding the people they are designed to serve.

The Western Lens: Privacy as Individual Autonomy

In many Western democracies particularly in North America and parts of Europe privacy is often framed as a right to individual autonomy. It is closely tied to liberal values of freedom, self-determination, and personal space. The emphasis here is on choice and control: individuals should have the right to decide what to disclose, to whom, and under what conditions.

This view of privacy underpins many of the legal frameworks governing data protection in the West. The European Union's General Data Protection Regulation, for instance, is based on the idea that individuals have the right to control their personal data. It mandates transparency, informed consent, the right to be forgotten, and strict limitations on data processing.

In the United States, while federal privacy laws are more fragmented, there is still a strong cultural expectation that personal data is a form of property, something that should not be accessed or sold without permission. Privacy in this context is often associated with the home, the body, and digital devices, all of which are viewed as extensions of the self.

This worldview has influenced how platforms conceptualize privacy tools: settings panels, consent checkboxes, and data download options are designed to give users "control". But this individualistic framing does not always translate effectively in more collectivist or state-centric cultural contexts.

Eastern Contexts: Privacy as Relational and Situational

In contrast, many Asian societies take a relational and situational approach to privacy. In countries including Japan, China, India, and South Korea, privacy is often less about asserting individual rights and more about maintaining social harmony, managing reputation, and respecting interpersonal boundaries within defined relationships. Table 5.5 emphasizes how privacy is culturally contextual, with differing fears, behaviors, and trust levels around visibility and data sharing.

Table 5.5 Comparative Privacy Attitudes Across Regions

Region/ Country	*Top Privacy Concern*	*Common Digital Behavior*	*Trust in Platforms*	*Source*
EU (e.g., Germany)	Data sharing with third parties	Frequent privacy setting changes	Low	Eurobarometer (2021)
USA	Corporate data misuse	Ad-blockers, incognito browsing	Moderate	Pew Research Center (2020)
India	Family or social reputation	Multiple accounts, status control	High (for large platforms)	Oxford Internet Institute (2021)
China	Government monitoring	Heavily platform-dependent communication	High (in domestic platforms)	Citizen Lab Reports (2022)
Japan	Contextual appropriateness	Pseudonyms, content moderation by user	Low	NICT Japan Survey (2020)

In Japan, for example, the concept of *uchi–soto* (inside–outside) shapes much of social life. People behave differently depending on whether someone is part of their in-group or out-group, and privacy is understood not as secrecy, but as contextual appropriateness.

Personal matters may be shared within close circles, but not beyond. Digital expression often follows these norms: anonymous accounts, pseudonyms, and subtle visual cues are used to maintain distance while still participating socially.

In India, privacy norms are strongly influenced by family structures, community life, and religious traditions. Physical proximity and shared spaces are common, but there is also a deep sense of boundary within the home or within one's phone. People may live communally yet guard their mobile devices with intense privacy. Trust is often more relevant than legal guarantees: individuals are more concerned with how their own network might judge or misuse their data than with abstract concerns about state or corporate surveillance.

In China, privacy is shaped by the dynamics between individual, society, and state. While Chinese users have historically been more accepting of platform tracking, especially in exchange for convenience and social connectivity, there is a rising awareness around data use, algorithmic control, and online visibility. However, privacy discourse is still largely framed in terms of trust in institutions, rather than individual rights. This makes Western privacy models, with their emphasis on self-sovereignty, less intuitive in Chinese digital environments.

Religious and Moral Dimensions of Privacy

Cultural attitudes toward privacy are also deeply influenced by religious and moral teachings. In Islamic cultures, for example, privacy is rooted in religious obligations to protect dignity, modesty, and family sanctity. The concept of *awrah* what should remain concealed applies to both physical and informational spaces. In many Muslim-majority countries, this leads to an emphasis on gendered privacy norms, filtered images, private groups, and codes of online behavior that preserve religious values.

Similarly, in many Christian and Jewish traditions, privacy is tied to moral accountability, spiritual introspection, and the right to a personal conscience. In these contexts, privacy supports the idea of a private relationship with God, a space where individuals can reflect, repent, and grow without public scrutiny.

These values influence not just what people share, but how they judge others for sharing or not sharing certain things. A post that might be considered liberating self-expression in one cultural setting might be viewed as inappropriate or shameful in another.

Global Platforms, Local Norms: A Tension in Design

The design of most major social media platforms originates from Western tech hubs particularly Silicon Valley. As such, platform defaults often reflect Western assumptions about transparency, individualism, and openness. Features like real-name policies, public profiles, timeline visibility, and location sharing are intended to foster authenticity and connection but may clash with local norms around discretion, anonymity, or modesty.

For example, Facebook's early insistence on "real identity" made it difficult for users in countries with strict speech laws or conservative cultures to participate safely. TikTok's algorithmic feed exposes users to massive, unpredictable audiences great for virality, but challenging for users in contexts where visibility can carry social risk. WhatsApp's group features have raised privacy concerns in communities where phone numbers are tied to caste, religion, or gender.

These examples highlight a persistent design mismatch between global functionality and local expectations. What's seen as a feature in one place may be perceived as a threat in another. And when platforms apply uniform rules to diverse users, they risk reinforcing digital inequalities and misunderstanding cultural needs.

Cross-Cultural Misunderstandings and Social Tensions

The blending of digital cultures has also led to misunderstandings not just between users and platforms, but between users themselves. A comment that's lighthearted in one cultural context may be offensive in another. A level of openness that's admired in one place may be read as reckless elsewhere. Misinterpretation can lead to online harassment, cultural stereotyping, or the alienation of users who feel that their norms are not respected.

Moreover, diasporic communities often navigate multiple privacy cultures at once. A second-generation immigrant in the UK might use Instagram differently from their relatives back home or their peers in school. They may post stories for friends but hide content from family. They may maintain different profiles for different languages, faith groups, or social codes. For them, privacy is not static, it's dynamic, multilingual, and emotionally layered.

These hybrid identities challenge the idea that privacy is something that can be managed through one-size-fits-all settings. They reveal the need for more adaptive and culturally sensitive tools, ones that recognize how people switch codes, audiences, and boundaries across time and context.

Toward Culturally Respectful Privacy Design

In an ideal world, platforms would incorporate cultural privacy differences at every level of design from default settings and visibility tools to content moderation and policy enforcement. This doesn't mean creating entirely separate platforms for each culture, but rather designing with cultural pluralism in mind.

Some suggestions include:

- Offering flexible visibility settings that support context-specific sharing
- Supporting pseudonymous participation where real-name policies may be harmful
- Localizing privacy education resources in ways that reflect community concerns

- Designing for trust, not just control, especially in collectivist cultures
- Partnering with regional experts and user communities to understand lived realities

Importantly, platforms must go beyond translation or token localization. Cultural respect means rethinking design philosophy, not just interface language. It means recognizing that privacy is not merely about preventing harm, but also about preserving dignity, autonomy, and social belonging on users' own terms.

A Shared Value, Differently Expressed

Privacy is not a Western invention. Nor is it a fixed universal. It is a shared human need expressed, practised, and protected in different ways across time and culture. While the digital age has introduced new challenges to privacy, it has also opened up new conversations about what privacy means to different people, in different places, and under different circumstances.

To build a more inclusive digital future, we must move beyond assuming what privacy *should* look like, and instead listen to how people experience it in practice. By embracing cultural diversity in privacy norms, platforms can foster spaces that are not only safer, but also more empathetic, responsive, and reflective of the world they serve.

This chapter has explored how privacy is experienced, perceived, and negotiated in the digital age. From how platform design shapes emotional and behavioral responses, generational differences between digital natives and immigrants, to cultural variations in expectations of personal information, privacy emerges as a deeply psychological phenomenon.

Users are not passive data points—they interpret, adapt, and respond to surveillance architectures in ways shaped by identity, context, and cognition. This chapter highlights the tensions between autonomy, attention, and potential manipulation, emphasizing that privacy is both an individual right and a collective concern, influenced by social norms, and technological design.

The next chapter examines the business of social media, revealing how profit motives, advertising models, and data-driven monetization intersect with—and often conflict with—the human need for privacy. By tracing the economic incentives that underpin platform decisions, we can better understand why privacy challenges persist and how business models might evolve to align profitability with ethical stewardship of user data.

References

Bennett, S., Maton, K., & Kervin, L. (2008). The 'digital natives' debate: A critical review of the evidence. *British Journal of Educational Technology, 39*(5), 775–786. https://doi.org/10.1111/j.1467-8535.2007.00793.x

Bowden-Green, T., & Wise, L. (2026). *Marketing and psychology: Understanding customer behaviour with the ABC approach.* Routledge.

Dhingra, N., Gorn, Z., Kener, A., & Dana, J. (2012). The default pull: An experimental demonstration of subtle default effects on preferences. *Judgment and Decision Making, 7*(1), 69–76. https://doi.org/10.1017/S1930297500001844

Instagram. (n.d.). Supporting your child's Teen Account. Instagram Help Centre. https://help.instagram.com/1555818391956130

Hofstede, G. (2001). *Culture's consequences: Comparing values, behaviors, institutions, and organizations across nations* (2nd ed.). Sage.

Matias, J. N., & Marquez, D. (2023). A thematic analysis of dark patterns in social networking services. *ACM Digital Library*. https://dl.acm.org/doi/10.1145/3544548.3580695

Meta. (2021, December 7). New teen safety features and "Take a Break" on Instagram. Meta Newsroom. https://about.fb.com/news/2021/12/new-teen-safety-tools-on-instagram/

Netflix. (2025). *Adolescence* [TV series]. Netflix. https://www.netflix.com/title/81756069

Nissenbaum, H. (2010). *Privacy in context: Technology, policy, and the integrity of social life*. Stanford University Press.

Prensky, M. (2001). Digital natives, digital immigrants. *On the Horizon, 9*(5), 1–6. https://doi.org/10.1108/10748120110424816

Obar, J. A., & Oeldorf-Hirsch, A. (2020). The biggest lie on the internet: Ignoring the privacy policies and terms of service policies of social networking services. *Information, Communication & Society, 23*(1), 128–147. https://doi.org/10.1080/1369118X.2018.1486870

TikTok. (2023, March 1). New features for teens and families on TikTok. TikTok Newsroom. https://newsroom.tiktok.com/en-us/new-features-for-teens-and-families-on-tiktok

Zuboff, S. (2020). *The age of surveillance capitalism: The fight for a human future at the new frontier of power.* Profile Books.

6 The Business of Social Media—Balancing Profit and Privacy

As we have explored in this book, social media has evolved from a way to connect friends and family into a driving force of the global economy. Today, behind every post, like, and scroll lies a complex infrastructure designed not just to connect people, but to collect and monetize their attention. And, at the heart of this ecosystem is personal data. The modern social media business model thrives on it, turning human behavior into highly valuable advertising real estate.

This transformation didn't happen by accident. As platforms matured, they discovered that what users shared—knowingly or otherwise—could be analyzed, segmented, and packaged for advertisers with extraordinary precision. The more time people spent online, the more data they generated, and the more attractive these platforms became to brands seeking targeted access to specific audiences.

But this success story is accompanied by discomfort. As users become more aware of how their data is collected and used, questions of ethics, privacy, and corporate responsibility have moved to the forefront. In some cases, the consequences have been more than theoretical: data misuse, and large-scale breaches have raised legitimate concerns about how platforms monetize their audiences.

This chapter explores the business side of social media—how platforms monetize user data, the tools and tactics involved, and the moral dilemmas that arise when commercial gain collides with individual privacy. It also considers how businesses using social media must strike their own balance between targeting and trust, and how legal frameworks are beginning to shape a more accountable future.

How Social Media Companies Make Money

When asked during his testimony before the U.S. Senate Commerce and Judiciary Committees in April 2018 how Facebook sustains a business model that doesn't charge users, Mark Zuckerberg simply replied, "Senator, we run ads". He explained that advertising revenue is the primary source of funding, with user information enabling advertisers to target audiences more effectively, while users can access the platform for free.

Social media platforms are, at their core, media companies. While they may provide services like messaging, content sharing, or professional networking, the revenue model behind nearly all major platforms is built on advertising. In 2024,

DOI: 10.4324/9781003654322-7

Meta, the parent company of Facebook and Instagram, derived nearly 98% of its revenue from advertising. Similarly, platforms like LinkedIn, TikTok, and X rely heavily on ad sales to fund their operations and grow their user bases.

> In addition to advertising revenue, social media platforms generate income through developer APIs, which allow third-party apps to integrate with their services for a fee, and through subscription models that offer premium features, enhanced analytics, or ad-free experiences to paying users.

To understand the core model, it's helpful to consider how digital advertising works. Traditional advertising—on television, in print, or on billboards—targets broad demographics. A fashion brand might place an ad in a women's magazine, hoping to reach readers likely to buy their clothes. But social media platforms offer something much more powerful: precision.

By collecting data on users' behaviors, interests, connections, and even emotions, platforms can build detailed profiles that allow advertisers to reach exactly the kind of person they want to influence. This level of specificity is unmatched in traditional media, and is a goldmine for advertisers, who can pay to access audiences based on incredibly specific characteristics. A skincare brand, for instance, might target users aged 18–24 who recently searched for "acne treatment", likes beauty influencers, and follows dermatologists.

The infrastructure that supports this is vast. Platforms track users' activity on and off their own sites through cookies, tracking pixels, and Software Development Kit (SDKs) embedded in third-party apps. They monitor likes, comments, follows, video watch times, shopping habits, location data, and even the time-of-day people are most likely to engage. This data is fed into algorithms that determine what content and ads to show—and when.

This process operates in real time. When a user opens an app or refreshes a feed, a silent auction takes place in milliseconds. Advertisers bid to show their ad to that specific user, and the winner's content appears. The more relevant the ad, the more likely the user is to click or engage—making the data that fuels this system incredibly valuable.

The result is a business model that rewards platforms for maximizing time spent and engagement. The longer users stay online, the more ads they see, and the more data they generate. That's why the design of these platforms is not neutral. Features like infinite scrolling, notifications, algorithmically curated feeds, and autoplay video are carefully engineered to capture attention and keep it.

TikTok is a prime example of this model at scale. Its recommendation engine is one of the most sophisticated in the world, relying heavily on machine learning to surface content based on micro-signals of user interest. TikTok collects information such as how long a user lingers on a video, what they skip, what they save, and what they share. This constant feedback loop powers an experience that feels deeply personalized—and incredibly addictive.

LinkedIn, while focused on professional use, also benefits from a similar logic. The platform gathers employment history, skills, interests, connections, and content preferences. This makes it invaluable not only to recruiters, but to business-to-business advertisers targeting decision-makers by industry, role, or seniority level. For example, a software company selling cloud security services can place its ads in front of chief information security officers in the finance sector—a level of precision that traditional media would struggle to offer.

But when does personalization become surveillance? How aware are users of the depth and extent of this data collection? And can a platform that relies on data-driven advertising ever truly prioritize privacy?

These questions are not academic. In 2021, Apple introduced App Tracking Transparency (ATT), a feature requiring iOS apps to ask users for permission before tracking their activity across other apps and websites. This change led to a significant decline in tracking consent, with analytics showing that for apps displaying the ATT prompt, only around one-quarter of users opt in. As a result, major platforms like Meta have had to rethink their ad targeting models and adapt to a landscape where cross-app tracking is far less pervasive.

The Ethics of Data Monetization

Social media platforms operate under a business model that is, by design, highly profitable. The product is free to users, but not without cost. As we explored in Chapter 3, that cost is paid in data, which is aggregated, analyzed, and sold through access to targeted advertising. This exchange—free content in return for surveillance—raises complex ethical questions about transparency, choice, and power in the digital economy.

At the heart of the ethical debate is the understanding that users are not the customer, they are the commodity. Advertisers are the paying clients, and platforms compete fiercely for their budgets by offering increasingly sophisticated targeting capabilities. While this system enables precision marketing, it also encourages platforms to design features that maximize user data.

The ethical challenge becomes particularly sharp when considering the methods used to harvest attention. Platforms optimize for engagement because engagement drives revenue. But engagement is not neutral. Outrage, controversy, and sensationalism often outperform reasoned debate or factual reporting. As we explored in Chapter 5, this creates an environment in which disinformation can thrive, polarization deepens, and addictive design features—like infinite scroll or autoplay—prolong exposure.

And, as we have already mentioned, there's also the problem of consent. While users technically "agree" to terms of service and privacy policies, these agreements are rarely informed and undermine the argument that users are making a free and informed choice to share their data.

Meanwhile, businesses advertising on social platforms often have limited insight into how their campaigns are actually delivered. A company may target "eco-conscious millennial parents in urban areas", but it cannot see the internal signals, inferred attributes, or optimization processes the platform uses to build that audience or decide which users ultimately see the ad. This gap between the advertiser's intent and the platform's execution creates uncertainty and limits accountability for both targeting outcomes and ad placement.

What makes the ethical dilemma so complex is that data monetization is not inherently malicious. Used responsibly, data can improve customer experiences, tailor support, and power innovation. Many users appreciate relevant content and timely recommendations. Advertisers value the efficiency of precision marketing. But ethical use requires oversight, clarity, and a commitment to protecting individuals from harm.

In response, new frameworks are emerging. Ethical tech design, algorithmic audits, and privacy-enhancing technologies (PETs) are gaining traction among platform developers and regulators alike. Initiatives like the *IEEE's Global Initiative on Ethics of Autonomous and Intelligent Systems*, and the Centre for Humane Technology's campaigns for more responsible platform design, are pushing the conversation forward.

Business Models under Scrutiny

The business model of social media is built on a simple but powerful exchange: free access to services in return for user data. This data is then used to fuel targeted advertising—the lifeblood of the social media economy. For more than a decade, this arrangement has been the foundation of exponential growth and unprecedented profitability across the tech sector. But as public awareness of privacy issues grows, and as regulatory and legal frameworks tighten, this model is facing a level of scrutiny that challenges its long-term sustainability.

The most profitable social media companies—Meta, TikTok, X, and LinkedIn—rely heavily on personalized advertising. This is made possible by harvesting vast amounts of behavioral data: what users click on, how long they pause on a post, their location, social networks, device usage, and more. Machine learning algorithms then use this data to create detailed profiles, allowing advertisers to reach micro-targeted audiences with surgical precision.

On the surface, this can seem like a win-win. Users see ads that are relevant to their interests, and businesses maximize their return on ad spend. But beneath this efficiency lies a more complicated ethical landscape. The business model incentivizes platforms to keep users engaged at all costs—leading to design choices that prioritize time on site, even if that means pushing polarizing, misleading, or emotionally manipulative content.

At the same time, advertisers are increasingly questioning whether platforms can ensure brand safety. Incidents of ads appearing alongside misinformation, hate speech, or user-generated scams have triggered a new wave of concern. There have been multiple high-profile incidents of ads appearing next to extremist or harmful content, prompting companies like Hyundai and IBM to pause or stop advertising on X, for example, while they seek assurances about where their messaging appears. Broader industry surveys suggest trust in advertising environments has fallen sharply, with only a small fraction of marketers saying the platform provides brand safety, leading many brands to cut or reassess their spending and pushing platforms to confront the limits of their moderation and transparency systems.

In this climate, clearly platform business models are needing to evolve. X, under Elon Musk's leadership, introduced their subscription service that offers verification and other benefits in exchange for a monthly fee, signaling a potential pivot away from reliance on ad revenue.

Meta has a similar paid verification service, offering benefits including increased reach and improved support. These models are still experimental and have yet to replace the scale or profitability of advertising, but they signal a growing recognition that the current system may not be viable forever.

LinkedIn, in contrast, has long operated a dual-revenue model, combining advertising with premium subscriptions and recruitment services. This diversification has insulated it somewhat from the privacy backlash, although it, too, has had to respond to scrutiny around fake profiles and data scraping. Microsoft, LinkedIn's parent company, has invested in data governance tools and AI-driven moderation to protect the platform's professional integrity.

Another avenue of change is in the use of differential privacy and on-device processing, which allow platforms to use aggregate data insights without storing or exposing individual records. Apple and Google have pioneered these approaches, and social media platforms are slowly beginning to experiment with similar technologies. These innovations aim to preserve the utility of data without compromising personal privacy—offering a potential path forward that doesn't require abandoning advertising altogether.

Still, the fundamental question remains: can platforms reconcile the business of monetizing attention with the principles of ethical data stewardship?

Shareholder pressure demands growth and monetization; public pressure demands protection and restraint.

Critically, the debate about business models is not just about platform architecture—it's about societal values. What are we willing to exchange for convenience and connection? Who should control the data that shapes our experiences and identities?

User Trust and the Privacy-First Movement

Trust is the cornerstone of any relationship—especially one as intimate and data-dependent as the one between a social media platform and its users. For much of the last two decades, that trust has been eroded by repeated scandals, opaque practices, and an ever-expanding appetite for personal information. In recent years, however, a new shift has emerged: the rise of the privacy-first movement. It's a response, both cultural and commercial, to growing user dissatisfaction with surveillance capitalism and a demand for greater transparency, control, and respect in how data is handled.

This movement didn't emerge in a vacuum. It was born from a series of high-profile breaches, whistleblower revelations, and policy failures that highlighted how deeply enmeshed our digital lives had become with corporate interests. Incidents that we will explore in the next chapter, such as the Cambridge Analytica scandal in 2018, which revealed the misuse of Facebook data for political profiling, shocked many users into a new awareness of their own vulnerability online. It also marked the start of a broader conversation about data ethics in the public domain.

In response, many tech companies have begun to reframe their public image around privacy. Apple's "Privacy. That's iPhone." campaign launched in 2019 was a masterclass in repositioning: a multi-billion-dollar brand aligning itself with data minimization and user control. While Apple isn't a social media platform, its stance has exerted significant pressure on the digital advertising ecosystem by limiting third-party tracking on iOS devices—a move that reshaped how platforms gather behavioral data and deliver ads.

Social media companies are adapting. Meta now offers a range of privacy tools and ad preference settings, and has rolled out messaging features with end-to-end encryption (though this, too, has sparked concerns around online safety and law enforcement access). TikTok, following scrutiny over its data handling practices, introduced a Transparency Center to allow closer examination of its data practices and moderation policies. LinkedIn too has added tools to help users manage visibility and connections more easily, aiming to reduce impersonation and scams.

Recent global research shows that a growing number of consumers are not only concerned about how their data is used, but are taking concrete steps to protect it. In Cisco's 2024 Consumer Privacy Survey, a majority of respondents reported awareness of privacy laws in their countries and said this awareness increased their confidence in protecting personal data. Younger adults, in particular, were more likely than older adults to update privacy settings, use protective tools, or switch service providers based on data policies, indicating an increasingly active approach to managing privacy in the digital age.

Crucially, the business world is also taking notice. Companies that rely on social media to reach customers are increasingly aware that association with poor privacy practices can damage reputation and erode customer loyalty. The Cisco 2025 Data Privacy Benchmark Study shows that privacy has evolved from a regulatory requirement to a core component of organizational strategy and trust. Organizations increasingly recognize that protecting data ethically and transparently is critical to maintaining customer confidence, especially as AI-driven services expand. They also see value in strong privacy programs—not just for compliance, but as a way to differentiate themselves, enhance reputation, and manage risk. Investment in privacy infrastructure, ethical AI frameworks, and data governance is widely viewed as beneficial, reflecting a shift toward proactive, trust-centered approaches rather than reactive, compliance-driven practices.

Ethical Innovation: Can Profit and Privacy Coexist?

The tension between profit and privacy is not just a strategic concern—it is a defining challenge for the digital age. Social media platforms have long championed innovation, but for many years, innovation meant growth: more users, more engagement, more ad revenue. Today, innovation must also mean responsibility.

Platforms that offer advertising have had to rethink the mechanics of targeting. While traditional third-party tracking is under pressure, interest-based advertising, contextual targeting, and strategies built on first-party data are gaining prominence. Rather than relying on external cookies or cross-site tracking, platforms are increasingly leveraging the data users provide voluntarily—such as likes, follows, search terms, and time spent on content—within their own ecosystems. AI and machine learning play a central role in this shift, helping platforms infer patterns, cluster audiences, and predict interests from first-party signals and contextual cues, even when detailed tracking is limited. At the same time, some detailed targeting criteria have been reduced, reflecting both policy and regulatory responses to privacy concerns.

TikTok, a platform born into a more privacy-conscious era, has attempted to frame itself as a curator of culture rather than a data vacuum. Its "For You" feed is opaque, but the company has made moves toward transparency, including opening European transparency centers and committing to allow researchers access to elements of its algorithm. However, such efforts are often met with skepticism—especially given TikTok's ties to ByteDance and the geopolitical anxieties surrounding its operations in China, and past U.S. efforts to ban the app over national security concerns. In late 2025, a majority-American joint venture agreement resolved these issues, allowing TikTok to continue operating in the United States.

Ethical innovation also involves giving users more agency. Social media platforms are offering more granular privacy settings, including controls over who sees content, how long data is retained, and how algorithms personalize feeds. Instagram has introduced "quiet mode", TikTok allows users to reset their For You feed, and LinkedIn enables users to limit profile visibility and manage ad preferences with relative ease, for example. The actions we are listing are not exhaustive; there are many, but there are also still gaps.

The ethical dilemmas here are not hypothetical. Consider the choice to delay a privacy update because it could reduce ad revenue, or to design a user interface that makes opting out of tracking more difficult. These are business decisions, but they are also moral ones. As regulation increases and public expectations rise, ethical leadership will become a crucial competitive edge.

Importantly, ethical innovation is not about abandoning profit—it's about redefining how profit is pursued. In the long term, businesses that protect privacy and respect user agency are more likely to earn trust, attract loyal audiences, and avoid reputational or legal fallout. This is particularly true as digital natives—young consumers who expect ethical standards as a baseline—become the dominant force in the market.

Education plays a key role here. Understanding the business models behind social media is essential for navigating the industry, whether as users, marketers, entrepreneurs, or policymakers. Ethical fluency—the ability to think critically about trade-offs, incentives, and long-term consequences—should be considered a core digital skill.

There are early signs that the industry is beginning to internalize these lessons. Meta has invested in ethics review boards. X owner Elon Musk has touted free speech, though critics also argue this has led to underinvestment in trust and safety. LinkedIn continues to focus on professional integrity, and TikTok has opened data centers in Europe to address sovereignty concerns. These are not perfect steps, often driven as much by external pressure as by internal conviction—but they are steps nonetheless.

Ultimately, the future of social media depends not on whether platforms can make money, but on how they choose to do so. As Tim Berners-Lee has long cautioned, the web was intended as a tool for creativity and collaboration, not manipulation or surveillance. Innovation and profit are not inherently at odds with privacy and ethics, but aligning them requires leadership, transparency, and a willingness to make difficult choices—especially when those choices don't yield immediate financial gain. The companies that take this path won't just survive; they'll help restore the web's original promise and set the standard for the digital economy of tomorrow.

Changing User Expectations and the Value of Trust

A decade ago, convenience trumped caution. Users signed up to social media platforms in droves, rarely pausing to question what would be done with their data. The terms and conditions were long, the privacy settings obscure, and the consequences of digital exposure still largely unknown. But the climate has changed—and so too have the expectations.

Today's users are more aware, more demanding, and more vocal. A growing body of mainstream media coverage, documentaries such as *The Social Dilemma* (2020), and *The Great Hack* (2019), as well as recent books like Nick Clegg's *How to Save the Internet* (2025), Carole Cadwalladr's *The Age of Influence* (2020), and Sarah Wynn-Williams' *Careless People* (2025), have exposed the mechanics of social media, advertising, and data exploitation. These works have brought the conversation about privacy, surveillance, and ethical platform design to a broader audience, helping to fuel public scrutiny and debate.

This evolution has reshaped user attitudes. Increasingly, people want transparency over how their data is used, control over what is collected, and assurances that their online presence is not being monetized irresponsibly.

Trust has become the new currency. When it's earned, it leads to loyalty, advocacy, and long-term engagement. When it's lost, it can trigger user backlash, regulatory scrutiny, and reputational damage. Platforms that fail to meet modern privacy expectations risk more than just fines—they risk irrelevance.

For instance, WhatsApp's 2021 attempt to update its privacy policy sparked widespread criticism and user migration to alternatives like Signal and Telegram. The issue wasn't necessarily the change itself, but the perceived lack of clarity and control. Users want to feel informed and empowered. When trust is broken, many now know they have options.

Younger audiences are especially attuned to these issues. Gen Z, having grown up in a digital-first world, demonstrates a nuanced relationship with social media: they are avid users, yet critically aware of how platforms operate. Research shows that this cohort expects privacy and safety features by default, actively manages who sees their content, and is more likely than older generations to switch platforms if ethical concerns arise. They are willing to share some personal data for convenience or improved experiences, but only when transparency and choice are clear, reflecting a sophisticated understanding of digital agency.

This has created a new imperative for platforms: trust is no longer a "nice to have"—it's a precondition for sustained relevance. Platforms must now view trust not just through a legal lens (compliance with GDPR, CCPA, or other frameworks), but as a design principle, a product differentiator, and a moral obligation.

Earning trust begins with transparency. This includes clear communication around how data is used, accessible privacy settings, and easily navigable terms of service. Companies like Apple have set a high bar in this regard, publishing regular privacy reports and introducing visual cues—like the App Store's "privacy nutrition labels"—to make data practices more understandable at a glance.

Social media platforms are attempting to follow suit, with varying degrees of success. Meta introduced its Privacy Center to provide users with more control over their information. LinkedIn offers detailed ad settings and publishes transparency reports highlighting government data requests. TikTok and X also provide insights into moderation practices and data access, although the depth and frequency of these disclosures vary, and critics argue that the content is often too high level to be meaningful.

Recommendations for a More Ethical Future

If the first wave of social media growth was driven by speed and scale, the next must be shaped by intentionality. The digital economy has matured; users are savvier, regulators are more assertive, and public discourse has shifted. The question is no longer whether platforms should take privacy seriously—it's how they will embed ethical practices into the heart of their business models. Profit and privacy do not have to exist in opposition, but their alignment requires more than surface-level tweaks. It demands a rethinking of priorities, a recalibration of incentives, and a shared responsibility between platforms, policymakers, businesses, and users.

For social media platforms, the first recommendation is structural transparency. This doesn't mean flooding users with data dumps or annual reports full of legalese. It means communicating clearly, consistently, and accessibly. Users deserve to know what's being collected, why, and how it's used. Transparency should be a design principle—baked into user journeys, not hidden behind clicks and toggles. Clear dashboards, consent prompts, and contextual explanations help users make informed choices. These tools are not barriers to business; they're pathways to trust.

Second, platforms must rethink their data practices. The model of maximal data collection—hoarding every click, view, and swipe—belongs to a less accountable era. Instead, the focus should shift to data minimization, meaningful consent, and purpose limitation. Platforms need to justify why data is collected and ensure it is only used for what users agree to. AI and machine learning don't need an ocean of personal data to be effective. Ethical data science, based on anonymization, aggregate insights, and contextual relevance, is not just possible—it's preferable.

Third, there must be internal accountability. Platforms should have independent ethics boards, cross-functional privacy teams, and mechanisms to evaluate not just what a feature can do, but what it should do. Design decisions—from algorithmic tweaks to interface changes—should be reviewed for their impact on autonomy, equity, and safety. Importantly, these reviews must be given real power. Ethics should not be advisory—it should be operational.

For businesses using social media as part of their marketing strategy, the onus is on ethical engagement—making deliberate choices about targeting, placement, and data use, rather than relying uncritically on whatever the platform makes possible. Consent-based marketing, transparent data collection, and meaningful value exchange should guide customer interactions. They should also take responsibility for the platforms they partner with, choosing to spend their advertising budgets with companies whose values reflect their own. This is not just risk management—it's brand alignment.

Marketers can lead the way by embracing privacy as a creative challenge rather than a constraint. Can we design campaigns that are personalized but not invasive? Can we build loyalty without behavioral surveillance? Can we earn attention through relevance and resonance, not relentless tracking? These are the strategic questions that define a new era of responsible advertising.

Policymakers and regulators, meanwhile, must keep pace with the complexity of the digital landscape. It's no longer sufficient to respond only after harm has occurred. Regulation must be anticipatory, tech-literate, and global in ambition. Frameworks like the EU's Digital Services Act and the UK's Online Safety Act are steps in the right direction, but enforcement must be robust, and implementation must avoid being captured by corporate interests. Regulators must also consider the cumulative impact of design choices—not just content, but structure. Nudging platforms toward ethical defaults—shorter data retention, opt-in tracking, friction around data sharing—can make a measurable difference at scale.

Finally, users themselves have power. Collective demand for privacy, accountability, and fairness is already reshaping the ecosystem. User migration, platform switching, and rising support for privacy-first tools signal a cultural shift. While no individual action will transform the system, millions of small acts—reading settings, refusing permissions, choosing ethical brands—create market pressure.

The business of social media is evolving. Platforms that align commercial success with ethical commitment will not just survive the next wave of regulation or reputational crisis. They will lead.

Social media thrives on data, but at what cost?

This chapter examined the uneasy balance between profit and privacy—how platforms monetize attention and behavior, and what that means for users, businesses, and society. As public concern grows and regulation tightens, the industry stands at a crossroads. Ethical data use is no longer a fringe concern; it's central to trust, longevity, and legitimacy.

The future of social media lies not in harvesting more, but in doing better—with transparency, respect, and responsibility guiding the business model.

References

Adgate, B. (2025, December 19). *TikTok signs Trump-backed deal to avoid US ban*. The Guardian. https://www.theguardian.com/technology/2025/dec/18/tiktok-signs-deal-us-entity-sale

Anti-Defamation League, Avaaz, Decode Democracy, Mozilla Foundation, & New America's Open Technology Institute. (2021, September 1). *Trained for deception: How artificial intelligence fuels online disinformation* [Report]. Mozilla Foundation. https://www.mozillafoundation.org/en/campaigns/trained-for-deception-how-artificial-intelligence-fuels-online-disinformation/

Apple. (n.d.). *Privacy nutrition labels*. Apple. https://www.apple.com/uk/privacy/labels/

Bailey, J., & Chai, F. (Directors). (2019). *The Great Hack* [Film]. Netflix.

Center for Humane Technology. (n.d.). *A better future with technology is possible*. https://www.humanetech.com/

Cisco. (2024, March 27). *New Cisco survey shows strong relationship between privacy awareness and trust in AI*. Cisco Investor Relations. https://investor.cisco.com/news/news-details/2024/New-Cisco-Survey-Shows-Strong-Relationship-Between-Privacy-Awareness-and-Trust-in-AI/?utm_source=chatgpt.com

Cisco. (2025). *Cisco 2025 Data Privacy Benchmark Study*. Cisco. https://www.cisco.com/c/en/us/about/trust-center/data-privacy-benchmark-study.html

Clegg, N. (2025). *How to save the internet: The threat to global connection in the age of AI and political conflict*. The Bodley Head.

euronews. (2018, April 11). *Zuckerberg defends Facebook to US Senators*. EURACTIV. https://www.euronews.com/business/2018/04/11/zuckerberg-defends-facebook-to-us-senators

IEEE Standards Association. (n.d.). *The IEEE Global Initiative 2.0 on Ethics of Autonomous and Intelligent Systems*. IEEE. https://standards.ieee.org/industry-connections/ec/autonomous-systems/

Kantar. (2024). *Media Reactions report: Marketers' trust in ads on X drops to historic low*. https://www.kantar.com/Press-Center/More-marketers-to-pull-back-on-X-ad-spend-than-ever-before

Lundell, D. (2021, May 20). *iOS 14 opt-in rate: Behind the numbers*. Flurry Analytics. https://www.flurry.com/blog/ios14-opt-in-rate

Orlowski, J. (Director). (2020). *The Social Dilemma* [Film]. Netflix.

Statista. (n.d.). *Annual revenue of Facebook*. https://www.statista.com/statistics/268604/annual-revenue-of-facebook/

Tech Policy Press. (2025). *As privacy policy heats up, lawmakers should heed Gen Z's preferences*. https://www.techpolicy.press/as-privacy-policy-heats-up-lawmakers-should-heed-gen-zs-preferences

Wynn-Williams, S. (2025). *Careless people: A cautionary tale of power, greed, and lost idealism*. Pan Macmillan.

7 Privacy Laws and the Global Landscape of Regulation

This chapter explores the legal frameworks designed to protect personal data in the age of social media. It provides a comparative overview of major global privacy regulations such as the General Data Protection Regulation (GDPR) in the European Union (EU) and its UK equivalent, the California Consumer Privacy Act (CCPA) in the United States, and similar frameworks emerging in Asia-Pacific, Latin America, and Africa. It examines how these laws define personal data, what rights they grant to users, and how businesses, including social media platforms, must adapt their operations to remain compliant.

We also highlight gaps in enforcement, gray zones around anonymized or inferred data, and the complex reality of cross-border data flows. In addition, it considers how cultural interpretations of privacy shape both regulatory design and public expectations, showing that privacy norms vary across societies and influence how legal protections are understood and implemented. Examples illustrate how regulation has evolved in response to data breaches and public backlash. Together, these issues reveal both the strengths and limitations of existing legal protections, and why meaningful digital privacy cannot be achieved through policy alone.

A Global Mandate for Privacy

The right to privacy has long been enshrined in international human rights doctrine, but in the digital age, this right is tested daily, clicked away in consent boxes, buried under lengthy policies, or traded for access to services. As individuals increasingly live, work, and express themselves online, privacy is no longer a personal issue; it's a global concern, one that governments, corporations, and civil societies are grappling with across jurisdictions and cultural contexts.

The growth of social media platforms, targeted advertising, and algorithmic profiling has outpaced traditional notions of privacy protection. In response, a patchwork of regulatory frameworks has emerged across the world, each with its own definitions, requirements, and degrees of enforcement. From the GDPR in the EU and United Kingdom to emerging data protection laws in Brazil, India, and Kenya, privacy legislation has shifted from niche legal territory to a central issue of digital governance.

DOI: 10.4324/9781003654322-8

But this landscape is far from uniform. While some regions offer users sweeping rights over their personal data, others lag behind either due to lack of political will, infrastructural limitations, or economic dependencies on data-driven industries. Some nations approach privacy from a civil liberties lens, while others frame it within national security or digital sovereignty narratives. As a result, the rules of digital privacy are shaped not just by law, but by geography, economics, and ideology—creating the biggest challenge for individual users, organizations, and the social media platforms in trying to navigate an inconsistent and rapidly evolving landscape.

By exploring these shifts, beginning with the global rise in privacy regulation, and moving through comparative case studies, we reveal the diversity and inconsistency of legal protections around the world. It interrogates not only what these laws say, but what they leave unsaid: the gaps between regulation and enforcement, the loopholes around anonymized and inferred data, and the challenges posed by borderless technologies in a world of bounded jurisdictions.

In the following sections, we will look at the evolution of privacy law, from early data protection frameworks to today's complex, reactive systems. We'll then unpack key pillars of legislation such as consent, data minimization, the right to be forgotten, and algorithmic transparency while highlighting how different countries interpret and implement these principles. Finally, we'll explore why legal safeguards, though essential, are only part of the puzzle in securing digital dignity and autonomy.

> A note on legal guidance: This book provides an overview of privacy regulations and related issues for informational purposes only. The authors are not legally trained, and the content should not be interpreted as legal advice. Readers should consult a qualified legal professional in their own country or jurisdiction for guidance specific to their circumstances.

The Evolution of Privacy Regulation

The journey of privacy law is a story of acceleration, as shown in Table 7.1. What began as a niche concern in legal circles, protecting individuals from unwarranted intrusion, has evolved into a central pillar of modern digital governance. This transformation was not linear, nor universally applied. It has emerged, shaped by historical context, geopolitical events, technological shifts, and public backlash against corporate and state surveillance. Understanding this trajectory helps reveal not only how we arrived at today's regulatory landscape, but also why no one single model fits all.

Early Foundations: Privacy as a Civil Right

The concept of privacy as a legal right can be traced back to the late 19th century. In 1890, Samuel D. Warren and Louis D. Brandeis published a landmark article in the *Harvard Law Review* titled "The Right to Privacy," which argued for legal protections against invasive journalism and the public exposure of private life.

Table 7.1 Milestones in the Evolution of Global Privacy Laws

Year	*Country/ Region*	*Regulation/ Framework*	*Supervisory Authority*	*Key Feature*	*Impact*
1973	Sweden	First Data Protection Law	Data Inspection Board (Datainspektionen)	Recognized risks of automated data processing	Precedent for Europe
1995	EU	Data Protection Directive	National DPAs (EU Member States)	Harmonized member states' data laws	Foundation for GDPR
1998	USA	COPPA	Federal Trade Commission (FTC)	Child data consent requirement	Sectoral, age-specific
2018	EU	GDPR	DPAs + European Data Protection Board (EDPB)	Extraterritorial reach, harsh penalties	Global benchmark
2023	India	DPDP Act	Data Protection Board of India	Consent-based with exemptions	First comprehensive Indian law

Though not related to digital data, their framing laid the groundwork for privacy to be seen as a personal and societal good, not merely a matter of secrecy.

By the mid-20th century, as bureaucracies grew and states began collecting large amounts of citizen data, concerns around data governance began to emerge. These concerns sharpened during the Cold War era, especially in Europe, where historical experiences with totalitarian regimes made privacy a sensitive political issue. This resulted in early laws that focused on limiting state power and ensuring fair data practices in government record-keeping.

The Birth of Modern Data Protection: 1970s–1990s

The first formal data protection law appeared in Sweden in 1973, soon followed by Germany and France. These early laws recognized that automated data processing posed new risks, requiring new kinds of safeguards.

In 1980, the Organisation for Economic Co-operation and Development (OECD) issued its *Guidelines on the Protection of Privacy and Transborder Flows of Personal Data*. Although nonbinding, these guidelines were highly influential in shaping international data protection practices. They introduced several key principles, including purpose limitation, which requires that personal data be collected for specified, explicit, and legitimate purposes and not further processed in ways incompatible with those purposes. The guidelines also emphasized data minimization, meaning that only the data necessary for achieving the intended purpose should be collected and retained, reducing the risk of unnecessary exposure of personal information. Additionally, the OECD highlighted the individual rights of access and correction, ensuring that individuals could review the data held about them and correct any inaccuracies, thereby reinforcing transparency and accountability in data handling.

These principles laid the foundation for what would later become international norms in data protection. The 1995 EU Data Protection Directive codified many of these ideas, establishing a framework across Europe that treated personal data as a fundamental right.

Meanwhile, the United States adopted a more sectoral and self-regulatory approach, passing specific laws such as:

- 1970—Fair Credit Reporting Act (FCRA) for financial data
- 1996—Health Insurance Portability and Accountability Act (HIPAA) for health data
- 1998—Children's Online Privacy Protection Act (COPPA) for children

The divergence in legal philosophies—Europe's rights-based approach, which prioritizes individuals' privacy as a fundamental right, versus America's market-driven model, which emphasizes economic growth and self-regulation—continues to shape global privacy politics today.

The contrast influences how countries regulate data collection, cross-border data flows, and corporate accountability. European regulations, such as the GDPR, often impose strict obligations on organizations and grant individuals broad control over their personal data. In contrast, U.S. laws tend to target specific sectors or types of information, allowing more flexibility for businesses but offering less comprehensive protections for individuals.

This fundamental difference drives ongoing debates over international data transfers, compliance requirements, and the balance between innovation and privacy.

Privacy Enforcement: Global Supervisory Authorities

While privacy regulations establish the legal principles governing data protection, their real-world impact depends heavily on enforcement. Across jurisdictions, supervisory authorities are responsible for interpreting legislation, investigating complaints, conducting audits, and imposing penalties. These bodies act as intermediaries between abstract legal rights and practical accountability, determining whether privacy protections remain aspirational or enforceable.

In the United Kingdom, for example, the Information Commissioner's Office (ICO) oversees compliance for the UK GDPR and the Data Protection Act 2018, with powers to issue fines, enforcement notices, and guidance. At the European level, national Data Protection Authorities (DPAs) coordinate through the European Data Protection Board (EDPB), enabling cross-border enforcement against multinational platforms. Elsewhere, enforcement models vary considerably: the United States relies on sectoral regulators such as the Federal Trade Commission (FTC), while newer regimes, including India's Digital Personal Data Protection (DPDP) Act, establish dedicated authorities with evolving mandates.

Understanding who enforces privacy law is essential, as enforcement capacity, independence, and political context often shape how rigorously user rights are protected in practice.

The Turning Point: Data Breaches and the Snowden Effect

The 2000s marked a turning point in public awareness of data privacy. A series of high-profile corporate data breaches—affecting millions of customers at companies such as Sony, Target, and Yahoo—exposed the sheer scale of corporate data vulnerability and highlighted how easily personal information could be misused or stolen. These incidents sparked growing concern among consumers, media, and policymakers, laying the groundwork for broader debates about data protection.

However, it was Edward Snowden's revelations in 2013 that truly jolted the global privacy discourse. By exposing mass surveillance programs conducted by the U.S. National Security Agency (NSA) and its international partners, Snowden revealed that governments were not only capable of unprecedented data collection but were actively participating in it. The disclosures showed that personal communications, metadata, and online activity could be monitored on a global scale, often without individuals' knowledge or consent.

For many, these revelations underscored that data privacy was not merely a consumer or corporate issue, but a geopolitical one. Governments were not passive regulators; they were active actors in data extraction, blurring the lines between national security, corporate interests, and individual rights. The fallout from Snowden's disclosures included public outcry, legislative scrutiny, legal challenges to surveillance practices, and a renewed urgency around regulatory reform. In many countries, the revelations catalyzed discussions that would eventually contribute to comprehensive privacy frameworks across the world.

The GDPR Era and its Global Ripple Effect

In 2018, GDPR raised the bar for privacy laws worldwide by introducing several key requirements, including the right to be forgotten, which allows individuals to request the deletion of their personal data; explicit, informed consent, ensuring that individuals clearly understand and agree to how their data is used; data portability, enabling individuals to transfer their data between service providers; data breach notification mandates, requiring organizations to promptly report breaches to regulators and affected individuals; and harsh penalties for noncompliance, which can reach up to 4% of annual global turnover or €20 million, whichever is higher.

What made GDPR particularly impactful was its extraterritorial scope. It applied not only to companies operating within the EU but also to any organization processing the personal data of EU citizens, regardless of where the company was based.

GDPR's influence inspired similar frameworks around the world, including:

- 2018: Brazil: Lei Geral de Proteção de Dados (LGPD)
- 2018/2020: California: California Consumer Privacy Act (CCPA) and California Privacy Rights Act (CPRA)

- 2021: China: Personal Information Protection Law (PIPL)
- 2023: India: DPDP Act (Digital Personal Data Protection Act)
- 2011: South Korea: Personal Information Protection Act (PIPA)

While these laws differ in scope and stringency, they all reflect a growing global consensus that privacy must be actively protected by design, rather than merely retrofitted or promised after the fact.

The Rise of Digital Sovereignty and Strategic Regulation

As data became central to both national economies and political power, many governments framed privacy law as a key component of digital sovereignty—the idea that a nation should control the collection, storage, and flow of data generated within its borders. This reflects the view that data is not just a commercial resource, but also a strategic asset with implications for economic competitiveness, national security, and political autonomy. By regulating how domestic and foreign entities handle data, governments aim to keep critical information under national jurisdiction, highlighting the link between privacy law and broader geopolitical priorities.

In China and India, for example, privacy regulation has sometimes been coupled with restrictions on cross-border data flows, mandating data localization or giving governments more direct oversight of digital infrastructure.

In democratic nations such as the United States, Germany, and Australia, the focus has remained more squarely on protecting user rights, but the growing tension between privacy, security, and innovation is ever-present. Concerns over the misuse of AI, facial recognition, and predictive analytics have added new layers to the regulatory conversation, sparking debates about algorithmic transparency, accountability, and fairness.

Comparing Global Privacy Frameworks

As digital technologies become deeply embedded in personal, economic, and political life, the need for robust privacy protection is no longer a regional concern but a global imperative.

Across the world, governments have introduced legal frameworks to define, protect, and manage personal data, yet these laws vary greatly in scope, enforcement, and intent, reflecting different cultural values, economic pressures, and geopolitical priorities. These themes are central to Nick Clegg's argument in *How to Save the Internet*, where the former President of Global Affairs at Meta (and ex-Deputy Prime Minister of the United Kingdom) warns that without global cooperation on digital governance, the open internet and the protections it could offer—including strong privacy regimes—are at risk of fragmentation and undermining by divergent national approaches.

This section offers a comparative lens on the world's major data protection frameworks, examining how they define personal data, handle consent, enforce compliance, and balance individual rights against state or commercial interests. It explores both rights-based and regulatory control models, offering insights into how countries conceptualize privacy in law, and how those laws function in practice.

The European Union's GDPR: The Global Gold Standard

The GDPR, implemented in 2018, is widely regarded as the most comprehensive privacy law in the world. Built on the premise that privacy is a fundamental human right, GDPR applies to all organizations that process the personal data of EU residents, regardless of the organization's location.

> To note: following the Brexit vote in 2020, the United Kingdom adopted its own version of GDPR, known as the UK GDPR, which mirrors the EU regulation but operates alongside the UK Data Protection Act 2018, ensuring that UK organizations continue to meet robust privacy standards while maintaining compatibility with EU rules for cross-border data transfers. The minor nuance is that UK GDPR is technically domesticated legislation post-Brexit, so references to the European Commission or EU institutions are replaced with UK authorities (e.g., the Information Commissioner's Office, ICO). Substantive rights and obligations under the UK GDPR remain nearly identical to those in the EU GDPR.

Key features of EU and UK GDPR include:

- Clear definitions of personal data and special categories (e.g., health, political beliefs)
- A high standard for consent: freely given, specific, informed, and unambiguous
- Strong data subject rights: access, rectification, erasure ('right to be forgotten'), portability, and objection
- Mandatory breach notification within 72 hours
- Data Protection Impact Assessments (DPIAs) for high-risk processing
- Significant fines (up to €20 million or 4% of global turnover)

While GDPR enforcement varies across member states, several landmark cases have demonstrated its power. You will find some examples of these in Chapter 8. GDPR's extraterritorial reach has forced international companies to adopt more privacy-conscious practices, influencing privacy legislation far beyond Europe's borders.

Complementing GDPR, the EU has also introduced the Digital Services Act (DSA) and the Digital Markets Act (DMA), which, while not primarily privacy laws, intersect with data protection concerns. The DSA increases transparency and accountability for online platforms, including requirements around recommender systems and targeted advertising, while the DMA addresses the market power of large 'gatekeeper' platforms, including how they handle user data in ways that affect competition.

Together, these acts extend GDPR's influence by shaping the broader digital ecosystem in which personal data is collected, processed, and monetized.

Advertising, Disinformation, and Platform Regulation in the EU

While much of the global regulatory focus has centered on personal data protection such as through the GDPR or CCPA, governments and supranational bodies are increasingly expanding their scope to address how platforms manage advertising, political influence, and information integrity.

A key initiative in this space is the EU's Transparency and Targeting of Political Advertising (TTPA) regulation, adopted in March 2024 and applicable in practice from October 2025. This legislation aims to bring accountability to the political ad ecosystem by requiring platforms, political parties, and third-party advertisers to clearly disclose the origin, funding, targeting criteria, and reach of paid political messages. In doing so, the TTPA seeks to limit opaque microtargeting practices that have been used to manipulate or segment voters based on behavioral profiles—a practice often enabled by large-scale personal data harvesting.

Complementing this, the EU Code of Practice on Disinformation (revised in 2022) represents a voluntary framework that urges platforms, advertisers, and content creators to take stronger action against the spread of false or misleading information. Signatories—including major platforms like Meta, Google, and TikTok, commit to demonetizing disinformation, improving ad transparency, and enhancing user tools for flagging misleading content. While not legally binding, the Code has evolved into a reference point for EU policy and forms a cornerstone of the broader DSA landscape.

These regulatory efforts underscore a growing awareness that data privacy cannot be meaningfully addressed in isolation. The same profiling and tracking systems that violate individual consent rights are also what power targeted political messaging and algorithmic amplification of misleading content. Privacy, advertising integrity, and information disorder are therefore intimately linked.

It is important here to note that privacy and platform governance are converging domains. Regulations like the TTPA and the Code of Practice on Disinformation reflect a shift from reactive data control to proactive systemic accountability where not only what data is collected, but how it is used to shape public discourse, becomes a matter of legal concern.

United Kingdom's Data (Use and Access) Act 2025: A Post-GDPR Realignment

Following its departure from the EU, the United Kingdom has begun reshaping its data governance landscape to reflect both national priorities and emerging technological trends. The Data (Use and Access) Act 2025 represents a significant post-GDPR pivot in UK data policy, aimed at fostering innovation while maintaining core privacy protections.

The Act introduces several key changes that reflect a more flexible, risk-based approach to data use, particularly for public sector collaboration and scientific research. It loosens certain data sharing restrictions to promote data-driven services, AI development, and responsible innovation, while still upholding principles of transparency, accountability, and user control. Importantly, it clarifies lawful bases for processing data in the context of public interest, fraud prevention, and service improvement, aligning more with a pragmatic, utility-focused model.

Among its notable features:

- Encourages data interoperability between public and private sectors
- Introduces a duty to consider data minimization and proportionality in high-impact systems
- Expands legal gateways for pseudonymized data to be reused for approved research and analysis
- Enhances individual access rights and complaint mechanisms through the ICO

Some critics argue that the Act may weaken some of the stronger consent and purpose limitation safeguards established under the EU's GDPR framework. Supporters, however, see it as a necessary evolution toward innovation-friendly regulation in a rapidly digitizing economy.

The Data (Use and Access) Act exemplifies the UK's attempt to balance economic competitiveness with public trust, carving a middle path between the EU's rights-driven regime and the United States' market-led approach. It also signals growing divergence from Brussels in how privacy, access, and AI regulation will evolve in a post-Brexit policy environment.

United States' CCPA/CPRA: A Consumer-Driven Model

Unlike the EU, the United States does not have a single, comprehensive federal privacy law. Instead, it operates under a patchwork of sector-specific laws (e.g., HIPAA for health data, COPPA for children's data, FCRA for credit data) and a growing number of state-level initiatives.

The most notable legislation is the CCPA, enacted in 2018, and its expansion via the CPRA, passed in 2020.

Key features of CCPA/CPRA include:

- Grants consumers the right to know, delete, and opt out of the sale of personal data
- Broad definition of "sale", including sharing for valuable consideration
- Establishes the CPPA for enforcement
- Adds data minimization and purpose limitation under CPRA
- Introduces "sensitive personal information" (e.g., race, religion, geolocation)

However, compared to the GDPR, CCPA and CPRA rely on weaker consent standards, operating largely on an opt-out rather than opt-in basis, which places more responsibility on individuals to protect their data. In addition, there is no broad private right of action for most violations, with enforcement largely restricted to regulators and limited to data breaches. Finally, protections around inferred data and algorithmic profiling remain relatively narrow, leaving gaps in how emerging data practices are regulated.

Other U.S. states, including Virginia, Colorado, Utah, and Connecticut, have passed their own privacy laws with varying levels of stringency. The lack of a unified federal law creates a fragmented regulatory environment, complicating compliance and weakening user protections.

China's PIPL: Privacy under State Oversight

China's PIPL, enacted in 2021, represents the country's first comprehensive data privacy law. While it adopts many GDPR-like elements, it does so within the framework of authoritarian governance and strong state control.

Key features of PIPL include:

- Consent as the primary legal basis for data processing
- Extra-territorial application to overseas companies handling Chinese citizens' data
- Data localization requirements for Critical Information Infrastructure Operators
- Strict cross-border data transfer conditions
- Strong individual rights (access, correction, deletion)

PIPL has several distinctive features that set it apart from Western privacy frameworks. It explicitly requires that personal data must not be processed in ways that could "harm national interests", embedding data protection within broader state priorities. The law also grants government agencies wide discretion to access, monitor, and regulate data practices. As a result, while PIPL strengthens consumer privacy protections, it simultaneously reinforces extensive state oversight of both individual users and organizations.

PIPL reflects China's growing role in shaping data governance norms, particularly in the Global South. Its model blends privacy protection with surveillance infrastructure, offering a markedly different paradigm from rights-based Western frameworks.

Brazil's LGPD: Inspired by GDPR, Shaped by Local Context

Brazil's LGPD came into effect in 2020 and draws heavily from the GDPR framework. It was designed to provide a unified data protection law applicable to both the public and private sectors.

Key features of LGPD include:

- Applies to any entity processing data in Brazil or of Brazilian citizens
- Defines ten legal bases for data processing (including consent, legal obligation, legitimate interest)
- Establishes data subject rights (access, correction, deletion, portability)
- Requires appointment of a Data Protection Officer in most cases
- Created the National Data Protection Authority (ANPD), providing transparent oversight and enforcement

- Adopts an inclusive approach across all sectors and provides clear mechanisms for cross-border data transfers.

Early enforcement of the LGPD has been cautious, reflecting both the novelty of the law and the evolving regulatory environment. Data literacy among users and businesses remains in development, and periods of political instability have at times undermined regulatory clarity. Despite these challenges, the LGPD has played a significant role in shaping privacy regulation across Latin America. It has inspired similar frameworks in countries such as Chile, Argentina, and Mexico, contributing to a growing regional momentum for comprehensive data protection and privacy reform.

India's DPDP Act: A Delayed but Strategic Move

India passed the DPDP Act in 2023 after several years of delays and consultations. While it is considered a significant milestone for the world's largest digital democracy, the Act has received mixed responses.

Key features of DPDP include:

- Defines personal data broadly and provides rights of access, correction, and grievance redress
- Establishes a Data Protection Board for oversight
- Mandates user consent for data processing, with exceptions
- Imposes obligations on data fiduciaries and processors
- Penalizes data breaches and noncompliance

The DPDP Act has faced a number of criticisms. Exemptions for government agencies are wide and loosely defined, and there are no strong provisions to ensure algorithmic transparency or limit profiling. In addition, the Data Protection Board is not fully independent, remaining subject to executive oversight, and the law allows consent to be bypassed in the name of the "public interest", Overall, the DPDP Act reflects a balancing act between enabling digital innovation and asserting sovereign control over data. Its practical impact will depend heavily on how implementation and enforcement unfold, as many details are still evolving.

These developments reflect an emerging consensus as shown in Table 7.2 that privacy protection is a global priority, even if the models differ widely.

Other Jurisdictions: Emerging and Evolving

Several other regions are developing or refining their privacy laws, including:

- Japan's Act on the Protection of Personal Information was amended in 2022 to align more closely with GDPR standards.
- Kenya, Nigeria, and South Africa have passed laws inspired by GDPR but face challenges in enforcement infrastructure.
- Australia is reforming its Privacy Act to expand individual rights and introduce penalties more aligned with international norms.

Table 7.2 Comparison of Key Global Privacy Laws

Country/ Region	*Law*	*Consent Standard*	*User Rights*	*Cross-Border Rules*	*Enforcement Power*
EU and UK	GDPR	Opt-in, informed	Strong	Restricted, with SCCs	Strong fines, active
USA (CA)	CCPA/ CPRA	Opt-out	Moderate	None federally	Limited, state-based
China	PIPL	Opt-in, strict	Strong but state-controlled	Localization required	Strong,government-driven
Brazil	LGPD	Mixed	Strong	Allowed with safeguards	Moderate, developing
India	DPDP	Opt-in with exceptions	Limited	Rules pending	Weak to moderate

Diverse Models, Common Gaps

Despite the diversity of privacy laws across the globe, as shown in Table 7.2, several themes and tensions persist:

1. Consent vs. Control—Many frameworks emphasize user consent, yet in practice, users often lack real choice or understanding.
2. Rights on Paper vs. Reality—Legal rights are not always enforceable due to weak institutions or political interference.
3. Corporate Compliance vs. Ethical Design—Regulations can compel minimum compliance but rarely inspire humane or ethical tech design.
4. State Exemptions—Most laws grant broad surveillance powers to governments, undermining the principle of universal protection.
5. Jurisdictional Fragmentation—In a borderless digital economy, data flows across regulatory boundaries, challenging enforcement.

As global citizens increasingly live online, the need for harmonized, transparent, and enforceable data protection frameworks becomes ever more urgent.

The following sections of this chapter will examine how these laws are enforced in practice, where they fall short, and how regulatory loopholes continue to be exploited.

Enforcement, Compliance, and the Reality Gap

Even the most well-crafted privacy laws are only as effective as their enforcement. On paper, frameworks like the GDPR, CCPA, PIPL, and LGPD offer powerful protections: clearly defined rights, high standards for consent, and harsh penalties for violators. But in practice, users often experience a very different reality, one where their data continues to be collected, tracked, profiled, and exploited with little visible consequence. This disconnect between law and lived experience is

Table 7.3 Comparison of Key Global Privacy Laws—Key Features

Feature	*GDPR (EU & UK)*	*CCPA/CPRA (USA)*	*PIPL (China)*	*LGPD (Brazil)*	*DPDP (India)*	*PIPA (South Korea)*
Legal basis for processing	Consent, legitimate interest, contract	Consumer opt-out	Consent, public interest	Multiple legal bases	Consent, legal obligation	Consent, statutory necessity
Enforcement agency	Data Protection Authorities (DPAs)	California Privacy Protection Agency	Cyberspace Administration of China (CAC) and state bodies	ANPD	Data Protection Board	Personal Information Protection Commission (PIPC)
Penalties	Up to 4% of global turnover	$7,500 per violation	Up to 50M yuan or 5% of turnover	Up to 2% of turnover	₹250 crore	Up to 3% of annual turnover
Cross-border transfer rules	SCCs, adequacy decisions	Limited	Strict, localization-heavy	Similar to GDPR	TBD	Adequacy, certification, consent
Individual rights	Broad (incl. right to be forgotten)	Moderate (opt-out focused)	Strong but state-overridden	Broad	Moderate	Broad (access, correction, deletion)

what we call the "reality gap", a space where rights exist but aren't fully realized, and where compliance is promised more than practiced.

We will now explore how this gap emerges, why enforcement remains inconsistent, and what happens when compliance becomes a check-box exercise rather than a commitment to ethical data stewardship. We will also examine the power imbalances between regulators and tech giants, the exploitation of legal gray zones, and the rise of "performative privacy", where companies appear compliant while undermining user rights behind the scenes.

The Enforcement Bottleneck: Capacity vs. Complexity

One of the biggest barriers to effective enforcement is institutional capacity as shown in Table 7.4. DPAs are tasked with monitoring compliance, investigating violations, and imposing sanctions. But many are chronically underfunded, understaffed, and technologically outpaced.

For example, Ireland's Data Protection Commission (DPC), responsible for regulating most of Big Tech in Europe due to some corporate HQs being based in Dublin, has faced criticism for delays, backlogs, and relatively lenient penalties. While GDPR grants DPAs strong powers, the volume and complexity of modern data ecosystems make real-time oversight nearly impossible without far more resources.

Even when regulators do act, the process is often slow. Investigations can take years, allowing noncompliant practices to continue in the meantime. Fines, when they do arrive, are often absorbed as a cost of doing business rather than a deterrent.

Regulatory Capture and Political Pressure

Another challenge to enforcement is regulatory capture, where agencies tasked with oversight become influenced, directly or indirectly, by the industries they regulate. In some cases, this is due to lobbying, political appointments, or economic dependency. For instance, governments may be reluctant to crack down on data practices that benefit national tech champions or attract foreign investment.

Table 7.4 Barriers to Effective Enforcement Across Jurisdictions

Barrier	*What It Means*	*Example*	*Impact*
Under-resourced regulators	Limited staff and tech capacity	Ireland DPC delays	Slows enforcement
Jurisdictional complexity	Cross-border enforcement challenges	Schrems II (EU–US)	Creates legal uncertainty
Corporate obstruction	Legal teams delay cases	Meta litigation	Regulatory fatigue
Fragmented frameworks	No federal law in the United States	CCPA vs. state gaps	Uneven protection
Consent fatigue	Users overwhelmed by choices	Cookie popups	User disengagement

This is especially pronounced in regions where data flows are tightly linked to economic development, such as parts of Southeast Asia and Africa. In such cases, regulators may prioritize digital growth over digital rights, delaying enforcement or crafting exceptions for politically connected firms.

Even in democratic states, enforcement is often entangled in geopolitical tensions. Decisions around cross-border data transfer, surveillance cooperation, or tech bans are shaped not just by privacy law, but by trade, security, and diplomacy.

The Compliance Theatre: Tick Boxes, Not Transformations

For many companies, especially large platforms, privacy compliance has become a matter of legal engineering, not ethical transformation.

This phenomenon, often referred to as "compliance theatre", involves:

- Updating privacy policies with complex legal jargon users won't read
- Adding opt-outs that are hidden or difficult to navigate
- Displaying cookie banners designed to nudge acceptance
- Performing "data minimization" while continuing profiling through indirect means

These measures allow companies to technically meet regulatory requirements while doing little to change how data is collected, processed, or monetized. Consent is frequently manufactured rather than meaningfully obtained, often using dark patterns that exploit behavioral psychology to guide user decisions.

In this environment, compliance can become a surface-level performance, often driven by legal risk mitigation rather than a genuine commitment to user privacy.

Asymmetric Enforcement: The Big Tech Paradox

One of the ironies of modern privacy enforcement is that while laws were often introduced in response to the power of "Big Tech", enforcement is typically harder against these organizations, than against smaller firms.

Tech giants such as Meta, Google, Amazon, and TikTok possess significant structural advantages that complicate regulatory oversight. They maintain vast legal teams capable of delaying investigations and have the financial resources to absorb large fines without fundamentally altering their core business models. In addition, these companies wield considerable influence over standard-setting bodies and trade policy, further shaping the rules that govern their operations. Their complex global infrastructure is also difficult to fully audit or oversee, creating additional challenges for regulators seeking to ensure compliance and accountability.

Meanwhile, smaller companies and startups often bear the brunt of enforcement, either due to lower legal defenses or their inability to navigate complex compliance regimes. This creates a paradox: laws meant to curb systemic power end up being selectively enforced on the less powerful, while dominant players find ways to work around them.

Cross-Border Confusion and Jurisdictional Conflicts

The global nature of data flows creates another obstacle: who has jurisdiction over whom?

A platform based in the United States might collect data from users in the EU, store it on servers in Singapore, process it through a third-party vendor in India, and monetize it via advertising networks in Brazil.

In this scenario:

- Which regulator is responsible?
- Which country's laws apply?
- Who responds when a user files a complaint?

This jurisdictional complexity leads to delay, finger-pointing, or total inaction. Many companies exploit this ambiguity by offshoring responsibility, claiming that local rules don't apply or that they're only "data processors", not "data controllers".

Although agreements like Standard Contractual Clauses (SCCs) under GDPR, for example, aim to manage cross-border data flows, their legal durability is constantly tested.

One prominent example is Schrems II, a 2020 ruling by the Court of Justice of the EU. In this case, the EU-U.S. Privacy Shield framework was invalidated because U.S. surveillance laws were found not to provide an adequate level of protection for European personal data, highlighting the complexities and risks of transferring data across jurisdictions.

The Enforcement-Imagination Gap

Even when laws exist and regulators act, public expectations often exceed legal possibilities.

Users might assume that laws protect them from emotional manipulation, misinformation targeting, or algorithmic bias. But most privacy laws focus on data inputs and rights, not on platform design or algorithmic outcomes.

For example, GDPR doesn't ban microtargeting, it requires transparency and consent. The CCPA doesn't regulate algorithmic amplification, it allows users to request that data not be sold. The result is a persistent "imagination gap": people expect protections the laws weren't written to provide.

This gap fosters frustration and fatigue, where users feel their rights exist only in principle, not in practice.

The Quiet Failures of Redress and Accountability

Even when users are aware of their rights and attempt to exercise them, the path to redress is often slow, unclear, or ineffective.

Filing a complaint under privacy law can be a challenging and time-consuming process. Individuals often have to navigate complex regulatory websites and interpret vague or confusing privacy notices. They may also encounter nonresponsive customer support teams, and even after submitting a complaint, it can take months or even years to reach a resolution.

Meanwhile, companies often deploy delaying tactics or deflect blame to third parties. The burden of proof typically falls on the individual, who may lack legal expertise or resources. Class-action lawsuits, while increasingly common, are difficult to launch and even harder to win in regions with weak legal protections.

Hopeful Shifts: Litigation, Whistleblowers, and Civil Society Pressure

Despite the challenges of enforcing privacy rights, several actors are beginning to close the enforcement gap. Advocacy groups such as None of Your Business (NOYB) and Privacy International use strategic litigation and research to hold companies accountable for GDPR violations and other privacy breaches, often setting legal precedents that strengthen enforcement.

In 2025, NOYB filed GDPR complaints against TikTok, Grindr, and mobile analytics firm AppsFlyer, alleging that TikTok accessed sensitive user activity from other apps without consent, which users often only discovered after persistent requests. Similarly, Austria's Supreme Court ruled that Meta's personalized advertising model violated the GDPR by collecting and combining sensitive data, including political views and health information, without proper consent—a case backed by privacy advocate Max Schrems and NOYB, illustrating both the slow pace and complexity of enforcing privacy rights against major platforms.

Whistleblowers—insiders who disclose confidential information about unethical or illegal practices—have also played a crucial role in exposing violations and prompting regulatory action. Media investigations, such as the Pegasus Project, have revealed widespread abuse of spyware targeting journalists, activists, and politicians, raising public awareness and applying reputational pressure on companies and governments. Finally, civil society campaigns, such as the UK's Open Rights Group—which leads ongoing efforts against intrusive surveillance, targeted advertising, and digital ID initiatives—and Digital Rights Ireland, which pushes back against mass surveillance and unlawful data retention practices, mobilize citizens and stakeholders to demand stronger privacy protections and challenge both corporate and government abuses.

These efforts highlight the importance of bottom-up accountability, where change is driven not just by regulators, but by journalists, researchers, citizens, and ethical insiders.

Laws Are Not Enough

The enforcement and compliance landscape of global privacy regulation is a paradoxical space: ambitious in theory yet limited in practice. Laws like GDPR and PIPL contain the mechanisms to protect users, but without strong enforcement, political independence, and public support, those mechanisms remain underused.

The reality gap persists not because laws are meaningless, but because systems of accountability are incomplete, users are still expected to navigate complex terms, regulators are still playing catch-up, and corporations are still driven by profit over principle.

Bridging this enforcement gap will require more than fines and policies. Regulators must be better resourced and coordinated globally, while stronger protections for whistleblowers are essential to ensure that unethical practices are exposed. Users also need accessible, user-friendly mechanisms for redress, and companies should be subject to transparency mandates that go beyond mere compliance. Above all, closing the gap demands a cultural shift in which privacy is no longer treated as a luxury or a check-box exercise, but as a nonnegotiable feature of digital citizenship.

Digital Rights and Cultural Interpretations of Privacy

Privacy is often framed as a universal right, enshrined in global declarations and echoed in modern data protection legislation. Yet, as we explored earlier, privacy is a culturally embedded concept, shaped by history, religion, language, governance, and collective memory. What one culture considers an intolerable invasion may be seen as routine in another. These differences are not merely academic, they inform the way laws are drafted, how people use technology, and what rights they are willing to defend.

In the context of global digital governance, understanding how privacy is perceived across cultures is crucial. Laws like the EU's GDPR or the United States' patchwork of privacy protections are not just legal frameworks, they are expressions of political philosophy and cultural norms. When these laws are exported, adapted, or resisted elsewhere, it is often due to deeper value-based tensions, not just logistical challenges.

Digital rights, and especially the right to privacy, are interpreted differently around the world. It also examines the implications of these variations for policymaking, enforcement, cross-border data transfers, and platform design. Ultimately, we can argue that without cultural awareness, global privacy governance risks becoming a tool of digital colonialism rather than a protector of human dignity.

Privacy as a Cultural Construct

In Western liberal democracies, privacy is often equated with individual autonomy, freedom from surveillance, and control over personal information. It is rooted in enlightenment ideas of the self as sovereign, bounded, and distinct from the collective. This worldview underpins legal doctrines that define personal data as something owned by the individual and therefore subject to their consent.

However, in many non-Western societies, privacy is understood less as a matter of individual control and more as a question of relational boundaries. In collectivist cultures, common in Asia, Africa, and Latin America, identity is not defined solely by the self, but by one's role in a family, community, or social network. Here, privacy is often experienced as selective visibility: not secrecy from the group, but control over how one is seen within it.

For example, in rural India, the idea of a locked bedroom might be considered isolating, not protective. In Japan, personal information may be closely guarded in one context (e.g., health or finances) but openly shared in others (e.g., blood type or family role). In sub-Saharan Africa, privacy may revolve around reputation, respect, and honor, more than informational control.

These cultural orientations shape how digital rights are understood. In some contexts, people may not demand privacy in the Western sense, not because they lack awareness, but because their risk calculations and social priorities are different.

Historical and Political Legacies

In Europe, particularly in Germany and Poland, strong privacy laws are in part a response to 20th-century regimes that exploited personal data for state surveillance, repression, and control. The GDPR is not just a technical regulation, it is a historically informed safeguard rooted in a collective memory of totalitarianism.

By contrast, in the United States, privacy evolved through court rulings focused on property, consumer rights, and free speech, rather than human dignity. The Fourth Amendment to the U.S. Constitution protects citizens from unreasonable searches and seizures by the government, requiring warrants based on probable cause for most intrusions into private spaces (U.S. Const. amend. IV). However, much of U.S. privacy discourse today is driven by market norms and the logic of user choice, emphasizing consumer consent and corporate self-regulation over broader protections grounded in human rights.

In China, the state's dominant role in both public life and digital infrastructure creates a different configuration altogether. Privacy is not framed as a constraint on state power but as a protection from corporate overreach. The PIPL reflects this duality: it imposes strict rules on organizations but grants the state wide access to personal data for security and governance.

In countries with legacies of colonialism or authoritarianism, such as India and Kenya, trust in institutions can be fragile. This affects how people perceive surveillance: some may accept state monitoring as a source of protection or modernization, while others see it as an extension of historical control. Cultural variations in privacy expectations are summarized in Table 7.5.

Religion and Privacy Norms

Religious traditions also inform privacy expectations. In Islamic contexts, privacy is often linked to concepts like *awrah* (modesty) and *hurma* (sacredness). This extends beyond personal data to bodily integrity, gendered spaces, and social conduct. In such settings, privacy is both a spiritual and communal value, intertwined with morality and honor.

In contrast, Buddhist or Confucian-influenced societies may place greater emphasis on social harmony, hierarchical relationships, and situational discretion.

Table 7.5 Cultural Variations in Privacy Expectations

Region/Country	*Dominant Cultural Norm*	*Privacy Focus*	*Interpretation*	*Example*
Western Europe	Individualism	Autonomy, data control	Privacy as right	GDPR enforcement
East Asia	Confucian harmony	Social cohesion	Privacy as discretion	Real-name laws
Middle East	Islamic tradition	Modesty, honor	Privacy as spiritual and familial	Gender-based access controls
Africa	Communal values	Reputation, respect	Privacy as relational	Family-shared phones
USA	Market-driven liberalism	Consumer choice	Privacy as preference	Opt-out models

Privacy is maintained not through assertion of individual rights, but through etiquette, indirectness, and mutual understanding.

These variations influence everything from the design of digital interfaces (e.g., real-name policies vs. anonymous spaces) to what data users are willing to share and with whom. For example, an app requiring biometric authentication may feel intrusive in one culture and trustworthy in another.

Language and the Limits of Translation

The language of privacy does not translate neatly across borders. In many languages, there is no direct equivalent to the English word "privacy". Instead, multiple terms may convey different dimensions, solitude, secrecy, modesty, autonomy, or intimacy.

In Japanese, the word プライバシー (puraibashii) is a borrowed term from English and is often associated with celebrity gossip or tabloid media rather than legal rights. In Zulu, the word for privacy relates to being "hidden from view", not necessarily freedom from interference. In Hindi, privacy is often framed as *nijta* (personal space), which may apply more to physical proximity than to data.

This creates a translation gap in regulatory frameworks. When global laws are transplanted into new legal systems, their meaning can shift. Consent, for example, may carry different implications depending on cultural norms around authority, gender, and negotiation.

Platform Design and Cultural Mismatch

Global tech platforms often design for a universal user, assuming common values around transparency, consent, and personal control. But when these assumptions clash with local expectations, users may feel alienated or misunderstood.

For instance, in many parts of South Asia or Latin America, users often share devices among family members. Yet most apps assume individual use, tying access to a single fingerprint, email address, or account. Privacy settings that are granular and technical may be useless in cultures where digital literacy is low or communal usage is the norm.

Content moderation is another area of tension. What counts as hate speech, nudity, or misinformation is culturally loaded. Automated systems trained on Western datasets may mislabel or censor content inappropriately in non-Western contexts.

Moreover, platform nudges (e.g., encouraging profile completeness, birthday announcements, friend suggestions) may feel helpful to some users and invasive to others, depending on cultural norms around public visibility and self-disclosure.

Consent in Context: Real Choice or Ritual Compliance?

Consent is a cornerstone of modern privacy law, but it does not operate in a vacuum. In many cultures, especially where power distance is high, consent may be given out of respect, obligation, or fear, rather than informed choice.

This is especially true in employment or educational settings, where people can feel compelled to accept terms to avoid conflict or penalty. In low-income communities, users may trade privacy for access, seeing data collection as the cost of opportunity. Free apps, free public Wi-Fi, or access to education platforms may all come with hidden data trade-offs.

In such systems, consent is reduced to a ritualized formality rather than a genuine right, a performance of agreement in contexts where refusal is effectively impossible.

Collective vs.Individual Privacy

Another key cultural divergence is between individual privacy and collective privacy. In many indigenous and tribal communities, data is not owned by individuals, but held by the community. This is true for genetic information, traditional knowledge, or stories shared orally over generations.

Global privacy laws rarely account for collective rights. The focus on individual consent and access rights can undermine community control, allowing corporations to extract data with the permission of a single person. For example, genetic testing platforms may legally use the DNA of one tribal member without consulting the wider community.

The same issue arises in family-based cultures, where decisions about privacy are made communally, not individually. One person's choice to share data may expose others, and laws focused on individual rights may not reflect these social dynamics.

The Risk of Digital Colonialism

When dominant privacy frameworks are imposed globally, either through trade agreements, corporate policies, or regulatory harmonization, they can become a form of digital colonialism: exporting values, assumptions, and power structures without regard for local needs.

This is not to say that rights-based privacy laws are unimportant, they are essential. But uncritical standardization can erase differences and marginalize voices that don't necessarily fit the dominant paradigm. The result is often compliance without justice: laws that exist on paper but fail to resonate with the people they're meant to protect.

To avoid this, privacy governance must be culturally adaptive. It must engage with local stakeholders, listen to lived experience, and co-design protections that reflect social realities. Otherwise, global frameworks will continue to protect some users more than others, often along lines of race, class, geography, and language.

Toward a Pluralist Approach

Rather than pursuing a single universal model, privacy governance could benefit from a pluralist approach that recognizes diverse traditions, values, and needs. This involves translating legal terms into culturally relevant concepts, supporting bottom-up privacy movements that emerge from local contexts, and recognizing collective data rights alongside individual rights. It also includes designing platforms with privacy defaults tailored to different user realities and providing training for regulators and companies in cultural privacy competence. In practice, implementing such an approach is complex: it may rely in part on geolocation or other contextual signals to apply relevant defaults, but it also requires careful mapping of legal, cultural, and social norms, as well as ongoing engagement with local communities. Pluralist privacy is not a form of relativism; it continues to uphold fundamental rights while acknowledging that meaningful protection must be adaptable to the social, cultural, and political contexts in which it operates.

Many Paths to the Same Principle

Privacy is a dynamic, evolving expression of what it means to maintain personal integrity, set boundaries, and exercise agency in one's social world. While legal frameworks are essential, they must also be grounded in cultural awareness if they are to protect people effectively.

As global platforms and policies continue to shape the digital experience, we must move beyond one-size-fits-all models. We need to listen more, assume less, and design systems that recognize the plurality of human experience.

In the following section, we turn to how these cultural tensions intersect with power, exploring how the "Big Tech" companies influence not only policy but the very language and logic of privacy around the world.

The Role of Big Tech in Shaping Global Privacy Norms

Multinational technology companies, often referred to as Big Tech, have become more than service providers. They are de facto policymakers, regulators, and standard-setters. Their influence extends far beyond the platforms they operate, shaping the norms, language, and even the legal structures surrounding data privacy worldwide. Companies including Meta, Google, Apple, Amazon, Microsoft (who own LinkedIn), and TikTok wield immense power not only in markets but in regulatory environments, especially where national laws are weak, evolving, or unenforced.

Big Tech companies have taken on an outsized role in defining what privacy looks like in practice; they influence legislation, standardize compliance procedures, engage in regulatory lobbying, and export specific values, intentionally or not, through their platform architecture, APIs, user interfaces, and policy frameworks.

While they often claim to champion privacy, their impact is more complex: at times advancing protections, at other times stalling or diluting reforms. The result is a contested global landscape where privacy is increasingly shaped not by public interest, but by corporate design choices and strategic interests.

Privacy by Platform Design

At the most fundamental level, Big Tech companies shape privacy through design decisions. The structure of privacy settings, defaults, nudges, and permissions within apps has a profound impact on user behavior and understanding. As we have already shared, research consistently shows that most users do not adjust default privacy settings. This gives these companies enormous power: by setting what is visible, hidden, or opt-in by default, they can influence how much data is shared, how easily users can assert their rights, and how transparent the system appears.

Take, for example, the design of cookie banners under the GDPR. While legally required, many platforms use "dark patterns": interfaces designed to steer users toward the most data-generous option. Accepting all cookies is made quick and easy, while rejecting them requires multiple clicks, obscure menus, or confusing language. The result is technically compliant but ethically questionable.

Moreover, platforms often present privacy as a series of binary choices, public or private, on or off, ignoring the contextual complexity of real-world information sharing. This simplifies privacy to a checklist rather than a social or cultural practice, limiting how users can negotiate visibility in nuanced ways.

Lobbying and Regulatory Capture

Beyond design, Big Tech exerts influence through direct regulatory lobbying. In both the Global North and South, tech giants spend millions shaping legislation in ways that align with their business models. In the EU, lobbying around GDPR enforcement has included attempts to narrow definitions of consent or expand "legitimate interest" as a basis for data processing. In the United States, Big Tech has helped prevent the passage of comprehensive federal privacy legislation, preferring a fragmented state-by-state approach that is easier to navigate and influence.

In emerging economies, the dynamic is even more pronounced. Tech firms often enter with offers of infrastructure, free services, and economic development, all of which entrench their presence and increase leverage over regulators. Governments, eager to attract investment or accelerate digitization, may delay or water down privacy protections in response to corporate pressure.

Regulatory capture is not always visible, but it is effective. By framing themselves as allies in innovation, education, or public health, Big Tech firms often position themselves as essential infrastructure providers rather than actors subject to scrutiny. This reframing reshapes the very terms of the privacy debate.

The Export of Compliance Norms

Because Big Tech platforms operate globally, they also export their compliance models to other regions, often serving as the benchmark for what privacy looks like. Their privacy policies, transparency reports, and data subject request procedures become informal standards, especially in countries without strong regulatory frameworks.

While this can raise the baseline of user protection, it also risks universalizing a narrow model of privacy, often rooted in U.S. or European conceptions of individual rights, market logic, and technological neutrality. These models may not account for collective data ownership, low digital literacy, or shared device use, common in many parts of the Global South.

Moreover, compliance models tend to favor procedural over substantive privacy: detailed documentation, dashboards, and tick boxes rather than real limits on data extraction or use. This can result in a bureaucratization of privacy where companies are judged by their paperwork rather than their practices.

Strategic Compliance and Performative Ethics

Even when companies claim to champion privacy, such as through Apple's App Tracking Transparency initiative, these efforts are often strategic rather than purely altruistic. Privacy features can be deployed to gain a competitive edge by restricting rivals' access to valuable data, to improve brand trust especially following public scandals, or to preempt or soften regulatory pressure. Scholars refer to this phenomenon as "privacy washing", where organizations market themselves as privacy-conscious while continuing practices that undermine meaningful user control.

For example, a company might encrypt messages while still collecting metadata, or offer opt-outs that are technically available but practically difficult to use. Such strategic compliance can weaken public trust and dilute the impact of genuine regulatory efforts. As users become cynical and perceive privacy protections as largely cosmetic, the resulting disengagement reduces pressure on companies to make meaningful improvements

Intermediating Digital Rights

Big Tech also plays a significant role in shaping the accessibility and enforceability of digital rights. While laws may grant users the right to access or delete their data, in practice, platforms mediate this access. They decide how easy it is to file a request, how long it takes, what formats data is provided in, and how responses are communicated.

This gives platforms discretion over the implementation of law, particularly in regions where enforcement is weak or courts are slow. For many users, their experience of privacy rights is not with a regulator, but with a customer support form, an automated email, or a generic settings page. In this way, platforms become the gatekeepers of rights that are supposed to be universal.

Narrative Power and Public Discourse

Beyond policy and interface, Big Tech shapes privacy through narrative power. They frame the discourse: what counts as a privacy risk, what solutions are viable, and who is responsible. Their public messaging often emphasizes personal responsibility, "You control your data", "Your choices, your settings", while obscuring structural asymmetries in information, power, and consent.

This framing individualizes privacy, presenting it as a matter of consumer preference rather than a systemic issue. It downplays concerns about algorithmic opacity, predictive profiling, and the extractive architecture of data-driven advertising and analytics. Users are encouraged to "manage" their privacy without questioning the broader mechanisms through which personal data is collected, processed, and monetized.

Meta provides a clear example of this narrative strategy. In public communications, the company emphasizes the control users have over their privacy settings and the transparency of its data practices. Yet investigations and regulatory actions have revealed that Meta continues to collect and leverage extensive user data for targeted advertising, demonstrating the gap between marketed privacy and underlying data practices

Big Tech often frames privacy as compatible with surveillance-based business models. They argue that data collection can be respectful, transparent, and consensual, so long as users are informed. This reframing undermines more radical critiques that see privacy and targeted advertising as fundamentally at odds.

Global Fragmentation and Regulatory Arbitrage

Operating across borders, Big Tech companies also engage in regulatory arbitrage, adapting their privacy posture to the weakest applicable standard or exploiting jurisdictional gaps. For instance, a platform may promise GDPR-level protections in Europe while offering far less transparency or user control in other markets.

In some cases, this results in two-tier privacy: one level of protection for users in countries with strong laws and another for those in countries with weak or no regulation. This reproduces existing inequalities and creates a race to the bottom in jurisdictions hungry for investment.

At the same time, companies may lobby for global harmonization, not to strengthen protections, but to reduce compliance costs. They push for interoperable frameworks that simplify cross-border data transfer but rarely advocate for raising the global standard.

Opportunities for Reform

Despite these concerns, Big Tech's central role also presents opportunities. Because they operate at scale, small changes to platform design or policy can have massive positive ripple effects. Transparency reports, audit tools, encryption protocols, and educational campaigns, when genuine, can empower users and set new industry norms.

Moreover, public pressure, media scrutiny, and shareholder activism have begun to shift priorities. Calls for ethical AI, algorithmic accountability, and privacy by design are gaining traction, particularly in response to whistleblower disclosures and high-profile scandals.

To harness this potential, civil society, regulators, and academics must continue to challenge, monitor, and collaborate with platforms, pushing for meaningful privacy rather than procedural compliance.

Governing the Ungoverned

In today's digital ecosystem, Big Tech companies are not merely governed entities, they are governing institutions. They shape privacy norms not just by responding to law, but by writing the scripts through which privacy is imagined, enacted, and enforced. This is both a risk and a responsibility.

If privacy is to be a global right rather than a corporate courtesy, then regulation must be bold, agile, and culturally responsive. But just as importantly, platform governance must be reframed: not as self-regulation, but as public infrastructure subject to democratic oversight.

As we move toward a future of ever more integrated digital services, the question is no longer whether Big Tech shapes privacy, but whether we can shape Big Tech to protect the dignity, agency, and autonomy of all users.

Algorithmic Governance and Legal Blind Spots

As algorithms increasingly shape the flow of information, opportunities, and risk in our digital lives, questions of governance become more urgent. Who decides how algorithms work? Who is accountable when they fail? And are existing privacy laws equipped to manage the rise of predictive, opaque, and adaptive systems that operate far beyond traditional notions of user consent?

This section examines the blind spots in current data protection frameworks when it comes to algorithmic governance. While regulations such as the GDPR, CPRA, and China's PIPL acknowledge the presence of automated decision-making, their capacity to regulate it effectively remains limited. As algorithms evolve in complexity and scale, they expose fundamental gaps between what privacy law protects and how digital systems actually operate.

From Data Protection to Decision Protection

Most modern privacy regulations are built around the idea of data protection, controlling how personal information is collected, stored, and shared. But in the algorithmic age, harm is increasingly caused not just by the collection of data, but by what is done with it.

Recommendation engines, credit scoring algorithms, content moderation models, and predictive policing tools all use personal and behavioral data to make decisions or inferences that affect people's lives. These systems may not store or share the data in obvious ways, but they still process it to produce consequential outcomes, such as limiting visibility, determining eligibility, or steering user behavior.

This shift from data collection to data interpretation demands a layer of governance that addresses not only the protection of raw data, but the accountability of the systems that act upon it.

The Transparency Problem

One of the most persistent challenges in algorithmic governance is transparency. Many algorithmic systems, particularly those based on machine learning, operate as "black boxes", their inner workings are difficult to understand, even for their creators.

For users and regulators, this opacity creates a significant barrier. If you don't know how an algorithm makes decisions, you can't contest or correct its outcomes. GDPR's Article 22, for example, gives individuals the right not to be subject to decisions based solely on automated processing that significantly affects them. But in practice, platforms often obscure when and how such decisions are made, claiming proprietary secrecy or technical limitations.

Even when explanations are offered, they are typically too vague, too technical, or too generic to be useful. Telling a user they were denied a loan, for example, because they didn't meet a model's threshold does not constitute meaningful transparency, especially if the model is trained on biased data or includes variables that indirectly encode race, gender, or socioeconomic status.

Inference and Profiling: The Unregulated Core

One of the least addressed issues in data privacy law is the use of inferred data, information that is not collected directly, but predicted or deduced by algorithms.

Inferences might include:

- Likely political affiliation
- Sexual orientation
- Health status
- Emotional state
- Risk of default
- Propensity to buy

These inferences are often more sensitive and revealing than the raw data from which they are derived. Yet, most privacy laws do not explicitly regulate inferences unless they fall under narrow definitions of "sensitive personal data".

As a result, platforms and data brokers can legally trade, apply, or act on inferred data without user awareness or consent. This creates a shadow layer of profiling that is ungoverned by most existing rules, even as it becomes central to algorithmic decision-making.

Bias, Discrimination, and the Limits of Individual Rights

Another blind spot in current regulation is the issue of AI-driven algorithmic bias and structural discrimination. Algorithms often reflect and reproduce historical inequalities embedded in their training data. Whether it's facial recognition systems that misidentify darker skin tones or recruitment algorithms that seem to favor male candidates, these outcomes are rarely caused by malicious intent, they are systemic.

Yet privacy laws are often built around the individual: the individual's right to access, correct, delete, or object. While important, these rights do little to address collective harms or embedded bias. A person may not know they were excluded from a housing ad, denied a job interview, or flagged by an algorithmic risk score, because the harm is ambient, indirect, or invisible.

Effective algorithmic governance requires more than individual rights, it requires systemic oversight, auditing, and structural accountability. But few jurisdictions currently mandate such measures, and those that do often lack the enforcement capacity to follow through.

Consent as an Insufficient Safeguard

Consent is the bedrock of most privacy frameworks. Yet in the context of algorithmic governance, consent is often symbolic rather than substantive. This point bears repeating: users often accept terms of service without comprehension of how their data contributes to AI training, behavioral profiling, or algorithmically curated content.

Moreover, algorithms do not only act on your data, they act on correlated patterns, including data from people "like you". Even if you decline to participate, your profile may be inferred from others. This networked nature of prediction undermines the notion of individual control and challenges the efficacy of consent as a primary safeguard.

Platform Discretion and Self-Regulation

In the absence of robust legal requirements, many platforms have introduced their own guidelines and internal review processes for AI and automated systems. These include fairness toolkits, bias audits, and ethics boards. While welcome, such efforts often lack transparency, independence, and enforceability.

Critics argue that self-regulation amounts to corporate ethics theatre, designed to deflect criticism without challenging core business models. For example, a platform may claim to reduce algorithmic bias while continuing to monetize engagement through sensational or divisive content. The root issue is not the algorithm, it is the incentive structure behind it.

Without external scrutiny, internal governance mechanisms may not fully address user interests. This underscores the need for algorithmic governance to move beyond voluntary guidelines and goodwill, toward legally binding standards, independent audits, and transparent accountability measures.

Regulatory Efforts and Emerging Frameworks

Some regions are beginning to address these blind spots. The EU's AI Act proposes a risk-based framework that classifies AI systems according to their potential impact, with stricter obligations for high-risk applications. These obligations include requirements for transparency, human oversight, robustness, and documentation. However, critics note that the Act still relies in part on industry self-assessment and may not fully encompass consumer-facing systems such as social media recommendation algorithms or targeted advertising.

At the time of writing, the AI Act has entered into force (August 2024) and is being implemented in stages: bans on unacceptable AI practices and foundational provisions applied from February 2025, risk- and governance-related requirements for general-purpose AI began in August 2025, and most high-risk AI obligations are set to take effect through August 2026 and into 2027, meaning its full regulatory impact is still unfolding.

In the United States, several proposals for algorithmic accountability have been introduced but have yet to gain traction. Civil rights organizations have called for impact assessments, data minimization, and restrictions on algorithmic profiling, especially in housing, education, policing, and employment.

Meanwhile, countries including Canada and Brazil are exploring hybrid models that combine data protection, human rights, and AI-specific regulation. These efforts reflect a growing recognition that data protection alone is not enough, what is needed is a broader governance framework that integrates ethics, transparency, and democratic oversight.

What Algorithmic Governance Could Look Like

Filling the current regulatory gaps requires a comprehensive approach to algorithmic governance.

Platforms should be subject to transparency requirements, disclosing when algorithmic decisions are made, the data that informs them, and the outcomes users can expect. Explanations must be understandable to non-experts and directly relevant to the user's experience. High-impact algorithms, in particular, should undergo independent audits to assess fairness, bias, and compliance with legal and ethical standards. Before deployment, platforms should conduct public impact assessments of algorithmic systems, especially in sensitive sectors, to identify potential harms. Users should also have accessible redress mechanisms to challenge algorithmic decisions and hold companies accountable. Finally, limits should be placed on inferences drawn from sensitive characteristics such as race, gender, health, or political views, unless their use is explicitly justified and consented to.

In the absence of these safeguards, automated decision-making may become effectively unchallengeable, perpetuating social inequities while appearing technically neutral.

Seeing Beyond the Code

Algorithms are not neutral tools, they are products of human choices, corporate priorities, and cultural values. Yet the laws designed to protect privacy often treat them as background systems, not central actors. This legal lag allows significant power to operate without scrutiny or consequence, creating blind spots in both regulation and public understanding.

As algorithmic systems become more embedded in governance, education, healthcare, employment, and daily life, we must move beyond the limits of traditional data protection. We need frameworks that treat algorithmic harm as real, measurable, and preventable, and that recognize the structural nature of digital inequality.

The Future of Global Privacy Governance

As personal data becomes the most valuable currency of the digital economy, the challenge of governing its use has grown more complex, urgent, and contested. National laws attempt to set boundaries, but the global nature of the internet renders many of these boundaries porous. Platforms and data flows transcend borders, while enforcement remains confined within them. Meanwhile, emerging technologies—including AI, biometrics, digital identity systems, and quantum computing, which could disrupt encryption and data protection—are advancing faster than regulatory frameworks can adapt.

In this evolving landscape, the future of privacy governance depends on more than just updating existing laws. It demands a rethinking of how we conceptualize rights, responsibility, accountability, and global cooperation in the face of unprecedented technological convergence.

This final section outlines the key paths forward, risks to avoid, opportunities to embrace, and principles that might guide the global governance of privacy in the years to come.

Beyond Fragmentation: The Case for Interoperable Standards

One of the major challenges in global privacy governance today is regulatory fragmentation. Countries adopt different definitions of personal data, consent, breach notification, and user rights. While this reflects cultural and political diversity, it also creates compliance burdens, legal uncertainty, and enforcement loopholes, especially for multinational companies.

To address these gaps, a growing number of scholars, including Helen Nissenbaum and Daniel Solove, civil society organizations such as Privacy International and NOYB, and international bodies like the OECD and the UN Special Rapporteur on the Right to Privacy are advocating for interoperable privacy frameworks. Such frameworks would not require uniform laws, but would establish a set of shared baseline principles—such as data minimization, purpose limitation, transparency, and the right to redress—that can be locally adapted while remaining globally recognized.

Early efforts in this direction include the OECD Privacy Guidelines, APEC Cross-Border Privacy Rules, and UN-led digital cooperation forums. However, these initiatives currently lack the legal force, public legitimacy, and inclusive governance mechanisms necessary for meaningful global coordination. Moving forward, interoperability must be inclusive, rights-based, and democratically governed, rather than driven solely by trade facilitation or corporate convenience.

Rebalancing Power between States, Markets, and Citizens

The future of privacy cannot be secured by laws alone. It requires a deeper rebalancing of power between states, corporations, and individuals. Today, Big Tech firms often operate as quasi-sovereigns, setting de facto privacy norms through platform policies, product design, and lobbying. Governments, meanwhile, move between lax regulation and mass surveillance, often framing privacy as a threat to security or economic growth.

To counter this imbalance, stronger public institutions are needed, independent data protection authorities with cross-border mandates, adequate resources, and the ability to sanction systemic abuse. Equally important is the empowerment of civil society, activists, journalists, educators, and communities who can hold both states and corporations accountable, amplify marginalized voices, and shape the norms that law alone cannot reach.

Citizens, too, must be reimagined not just as consumers of privacy products or subjects of regulation, but as rights-bearing participants in the governance of data. This requires investment in digital literacy, public consultation, and participatory governance models where people help define what responsible data use looks like in their own context.

Embedding Ethics into Design and Infrastructure

Many current privacy challenges are not the result of broken systems, but of systems working exactly as designed. Platforms that nudge users to share more, algorithms that sort people based on predicted behavior, or data brokers that aggregate identities across platforms all emerge from design choices rooted in extractive logic.

The future of governance must extend beyond legal frameworks to address the technological architecture itself. This involves embedding ethical values across multiple layers of digital systems. Default settings should incorporate privacy by design and by default, ensuring that protective measures are built in from the outset. User interfaces must prioritize transparency and usability so that users can understand and control how their data is used. Data architecture should support decentralization, robust access controls, and strong encryption to safeguard information.

AI systems, meanwhile, require bias auditing, explainability, and fairness assessments to ensure that automated decisions align with ethical and legal standards.

This shift from reactive regulation to proactive design can create environments where doing the right thing is the easiest thing, not just the legal thing.

Anticipating Emerging Risks

As the digital landscape evolves, so too do the risks. Emerging technologies like brain-computer interfaces, emotion AI, digital twins, and biometric surveillance pose new questions that existing laws are ill-equipped to answer. The future of governance must be anticipatory, not merely reactive.

This requires regulators to develop horizon scanning and foresight capabilities, enabling them to anticipate emerging risks and technological trends. It also calls for investment in multidisciplinary research that integrates legal, technical, social, and ethical perspectives, funded through a combination of national government budgets, research councils, international organizations, and philanthropic foundations.

Regulatory sandboxes, which provide controlled and transparent environments for testing new technologies and business models under regulatory oversight, allow regulators to observe emerging systems, assess potential risks, and guide development before widespread deployment.

Embedding human rights impact assessments into the early stages of high-risk system development ensures that potential harms are addressed proactively. Such forward-looking approaches, adequately resourced, are essential not only to prevent harm but also to cultivate trustworthy innovation ecosystems, where privacy and technological progress are mutually reinforcing rather than in conflict.

Protecting Vulnerable Populations

Privacy risks are not evenly distributed. Marginalized communities—including children, people with disabilities, and those living under authoritarian regimes—face disproportionate exposure to data-based harms. These groups often lack the resources, awareness, or legal recourse to protect themselves, particularly when it comes to sensitive or protected personal characteristics.

The future of privacy governance must be explicitly equity-focused. This includes implementing stronger safeguards for sensitive and context-specific data, developing community-led oversight models, creating inclusive policies that center lived experience, and localizing rights in culturally appropriate and linguistically accessible formats.

Global governance is not just about setting universal standards; it is about ensuring that those standards are accessible, meaningful, and effective for all communities.

Co-governance and Multi-stakeholder Models

Given the cross-border and cross-sectoral nature of data ecosystems, no single entity can govern privacy effectively on its own. Multistakeholder approaches, which bring together governments, technology companies, civil society, academia, and affected communities, offer a more democratic and inclusive path forward

However, these models must go beyond consultation and tokenism. True co-governance requires shared decision-making power, transparent procedures, accountability mechanisms and safe participation for those historically excluded.

International examples such as the Internet Governance Forum (IGF) or the Global Partnership on Artificial Intelligence (GPAI) offer partial templates but often suffer from lack of enforcement or uneven representation. Future models must embed power-sharing, not just dialogue, into their structures.

Shaping a Privacy-Respecting Digital Economy

The economic logic of the digital age is built on datafication: the conversion of human experience into measurable, trackable, and monetizable units. This model has powered extraordinary innovation, but also extraordinary concentration of power, erosion of autonomy, and loss of trust.

However, these models must go beyond consultation or tokenistic participation. True co-governance requires shared decision-making power, transparent procedures, accountability mechanisms, and safe participation for groups that have historically been excluded.

Toward a Just Data Future

Privacy governance is no longer just a matter of protecting individual secrets, it is about designing fairer systems, distributing power, and preserving human dignity in a digital world. The choices we make now will shape not only how data flows, but how identity, freedom, and citizenship are defined for generations to come.

The future cannot be left to default settings. It must be built, intentionally, collaboratively, and inclusively. From the halls of regulation to the labs of innovation, from classroom curricula to community activism, privacy must be treated not as a product feature, but as a public good and a global right.

References

Ada Lovelace Institute. (2021). The data divide: Public attitudes to tackling social and health inequalities in the COVID-19 pandemic and beyond. https://www.adalovelaceinstitute.org/report/data-divide/

Asia-Pacific Economic Cooperation. (2005). APEC privacy framework (Report). APEC. https://www.apec.org/publications/2005/12/apec-privacy-framework

Brazilian Government. (2020). *Lei Geral de Proteção de Dados* (LGPD): Brazil's General Data Protection Law.

California State Legislature. (2018). California Consumer Privacy Act (CCPA) and California Privacy Rights Act (CPRA). https://oag.ca.gov/privacy/ccpa

Clegg, N. (2025). *How to save the internet: The threat to global connection in the age of AI and political conflict*. The Bodley Head.

Data & Society Research Institute. (2018). The consent paradox.

Digital Rights Ireland. (n.d.). Campaigns. https://www.digitalrights.ie/campaigns/

Eubanks, V. (2018). *Automating inequality: How high-tech tools profile, police, and punish the poor*. St. Martin's Press.

European Commission. (2024, August 1). AI Act enters into force. https://commission.europa.eu/news/ai-act-enters-force-2024-08-01_en

European Parliament. (2020). The CJEU judgment in the Schrems II case. *European Parliamentary Research Service*. https://www.europarl.europa.eu/thinktank/en/document/EPRS_ATA%282020%29652073

European Union. (2016). General Data Protection Regulation (GDPR). *Official Journal of the European Union*. https://gdpr.eu

Forbidden Stories & Amnesty International. (2021). Pegasus Project: International journalistic investigation into NSO Group spyware and global surveillance abuses. https://en.wikipedia.org/wiki/Pegasus_Project_%28investigation%29?

Global Partnership on AI. (2022). Responsible AI and governance frameworks. https://gpai.ai

Green, B., & Viljoen, S. (2020). Algorithmic realism: Expanding the boundaries of algorithmic thought. *Media, Culture & Society*, *42*(7–8), 1167–1182. https://www.researchgate.net/publication/338841806_Algorithmic_realism_expanding_the_boundaries_of_algorithmic_thought

Government of India. (2023). Digital Personal Data Protection Act, 2023 (Act No. 22 of 2023). https://www.indiacode.nic.in/bitstream/123456789/22037/1/a2023-22.pdf

Internet Governance Forum. (n.d.). Annual reports. https://www.intgovforum.org

Mozilla Foundation. (2022). Privacy not included: Big Tech's impact on children's apps and devices. https://foundation.mozilla.org

Narayanan, A., & Shmatikov, V. (2008). Robust de-anonymization of large sparse datasets. In *Proceedings of the IEEE Symposium on Security and Privacy* (pp. 111–125).

Nissenbaum, H. (2010). *Privacy in context: Technology, policy, and the integrity of social life*. Stanford University Press.

None of Your Business (NOYB). How we work. https://noyb.eu/en/how-we-work

Open Rights Group. (n.d.). What we do. https://www.openrightsgroup.org/what-we-do/

Organisation for Economic Co-operation and Development. (2013). OECD privacy guidelines (original work published 1980). https://www.oecd.org/sti/ieconomy/privacy-guidelines.htm

Pasquale, F. (2015). *The black box society: The secret algorithms that control money and information*. Harvard University Press.

Privacy International. (n.d.). – About us. https://privacyinternational.org/our-demands/data-should-be-protected

Reuters. (2025, December 17). TikTok monitored Grindr activity through third-party tracker, privacy group says. https://www.reuters.com/sustainability/boards-policy-regulation/tiktok-monitored-grindr-activity-through-third-party-tracker-privacy-group-2025-12-17/

Reuters. (2025, December 18). Austria's top court rules Meta's ad model illegal, orders overhaul of user data. https://www.reuters.com/sustainability/boards-policy-regulation/austrias-top-court-rules-metas-ad-model-illegal-orders-overhaul-user-data-2025-12-18/

Solove, D. J. (2021). *Understanding privacy*. Harvard University Press.

Standing Committee of the National People's Congress. (2021). Personal Information Protection Law of the People's Republic of China.

Tufekci, Z. (2015). Algorithmic harms beyond Facebook and Google: Emergent challenges of computational agency. *Colorado Technology Law Journal, 13*, 203–218. https://ctlj.colorado.edu/?p=1520

UK Information Commissioner's Office. (2021). Age appropriate design code (Children's Code). https://ico.org.uk

United Nations. (2021). Roadmap for digital cooperation. https://www.un.org/en/digital-cooperation

United Nations Human Rights Council. (2021). The right to privacy in the digital age: Report of the High Commissioner for Human Rights. https://undocs.org/A/HRC/48/31

United Nations. (2025, December 4). UN launches new portal for digital cooperation. https://unctad.org/news/un-launches-new-portal-digital-cooperation

United Nations. (n.d.). About the Internet Governance Forum. https://www.intgovforum.org/en/about

United States Federal Trade Commission. (1998). Children's Online Privacy Protection Act (COPPA). https://www.ftc.gov/legal-library/browse/rules/childrens-online-privacy-protection-rule-coppa

Wachter, S., Mittelstadt, B., & Floridi, L. (2017). Why a right to explanation of automated decision-making does not exist in the General Data Protection Regulation. *International Data Privacy Law, 7*(2), 76–99. https://doi.org/10.1093/idpl/ipx005

Warren, S. D., & Brandeis, L. D. (1890). The right to privacy. *Harvard Law Review, 4*(5), 193–220. https://doi.org/10.2307/1321160

Wikipedia contributors. (2023, December 17). Snowden effect. Wikipedia. https://en.wikipedia.org/wiki/Snowden_effect

8 Social Media Incidents and Privacy Breaches: Lessons Learned

For some social media users, whether it's for personal or professional purposes, the idea of using social media can provoke concern.

The media often shares stories about "things gone wrong"; sometimes these incidents start on social media, sometimes they begin elsewhere but quickly shift online.

Accounts hacked. Personal data leaked. Posts destroying careers or damaging reputations. For some, the easiest response is to stay away altogether.

But avoidance isn't easy, especially when social media is an important tool for connection, visibility, and growth in today's digital economy. Rather than shutting the door on opportunity, it's more useful to understand the risks, assess them rationally, and take informed steps to reduce exposure.

This chapter aims to unpack some of the most common fears associated with social media, particularly those linked to data privacy and security. We'll explore the different types of incidents that can occur, from high-profile data breaches to more everyday issues such as phishing attacks and reputation damage.

We'll also examine how platforms such as Facebook, Instagram, LinkedIn, TikTok, and X are responding to concerns, and what role regulation plays in shaping platform policies, protecting users, and enforcing accountability.

Understanding the Threats

It's important to recognize that not all risks are unique to social media platforms. Many of the threats that manifest on social media—such as data breaches or reputational damage—also exist in other parts of the digital world. What makes social media different is the speed at which information travels, the scale of potential exposure, and the ease with which bad actors can exploit human behavior.

One of the most commonly feared threats is the risk of a data privacy breach. This is when personal or sensitive information is accessed, shared, or leaked without permission. In the world of social media, this can happen in a variety of ways. Sometimes the platforms themselves are the problem—collecting more data than users realize, or failing to be transparent about how that data is shared with third parties. Other times, it's the result of third-party apps or tools—such as games, quizzes, or marketing integrations—that request access to your profile and quietly harvest information behind the scenes.

DOI: 10.4324/9781003654322-9

Data breaches can also occur when accounts are hacked. A weak password or a moment of inattention—clicking on a suspicious link in a direct message, for example—can result in someone taking control of your personal or business account. Malicious links can hide behind shortened URLs, leading unsuspecting users to fake login pages or downloading harmful software. This isn't just an inconvenience. In some cases, hackers use access to impersonate individuals, steal customer data, or post malicious content that damages trust and credibility. And because many people reuse passwords across platforms, even one compromised account can create a ripple effect of vulnerability.

Sometimes, the risk doesn't come from the platform or external apps at all, but from the user themselves. Oversharing can create vulnerabilities—such as posting real-time updates about a holiday, which can signal an empty house to potential burglars, or sharing work-related information that unintentionally exposes confidential company details. Even something as simple as tagging a location or revealing personal milestones can provide bad actors with enough data to build a profile for phishing attempts or identity theft.

Another type of incident that causes significant concern is reputational harm. One post, one image, one ill-judged comment—shared either by a brand or someone connected to it—can spread like wildfire. What begins as a small mistake can escalate rapidly, particularly if it touches on a sensitive issue or attracts media attention. Even when posts are deleted, screenshots survive.

But not all reputational damage comes from within. Sometimes the problem lies in how others behave toward or around your brand. An unhappy customer might post a negative review or publicly call out a poor experience. If that post gains traction, it can affect how others view your business—even if the issue was minor or already resolved.

Impersonation is another risk. Fake accounts can be set up to mimic brands or public figures, attempting to scam followers. Phishing attempts—where attackers pose as legitimate contacts or brands to trick users into handing over sensitive information—often originate through direct messages or sponsored posts.

Sometimes, the threat comes from closer to home. Employees, whether intentionally or accidentally, can cause incidents that put an organization at risk. A seemingly innocent post showing a desk setup might reveal confidential documents or customer information in the background. In more serious cases, disgruntled staff members may use their access to post offensive content or leak sensitive material. These insider risks can be difficult to anticipate, especially in smaller organizations without formal social media policies or access controls.

Despite all this, most incidents are avoidable with a combination of awareness and good practices. And even when things go wrong, there are usually steps that can be taken to repair the damage.

To move forward, we need to learn from the past. In the next section, we'll explore one of the most infamous social media privacy breaches in history: the Cambridge Analytica scandal. It's a case that highlights how data can be misused, how public trust can be eroded, and how regulation and public pressure can start to shift behavior in the tech industry.

Table 8.1 Common Cyber and Privacy Threats across Social Media Platforms

Threat	*Description*	*Case Studies*
Data protection breach	Unauthorized access, sharing, or leaking of personal or sensitive information by platforms or third parties.	Cambridge Analytica (Meta)
Insider threat	Employees or insiders intentionally or accidentally posting sensitive information, leaking data, or posting harmful content.	TikTok X (Twitter)
Data leak	Large-scale exposure of user accounts or information due to hacking, scraping, or technical vulnerabilities.	LinkedIn X (Twitter)
Zero-day/ technical vulnerability	Exploitation of previously unknown platform vulnerabilities, potentially affecting security or user data.	TikTok
Impersonation	Accounts created to mimic individuals or brands, often for scams, phishing, or social engineering.	LinkedIn Engagement bait (competitions)

Table 8.1 highlights key examples of threats across platforms, from data protection breaches to insider threats and data leaks, zero-day attacks, and fake accounts.

Cambridge Analytica: A Landmark Privacy Breach

In March 2018, the world learned how vulnerable social media data could be when news broke of one of the largest ever breaches of personal information: the Cambridge Analytica scandal. This case didn't just uncover a data misuse—it sparked a global awareness with how platforms collect, share, and protect our digital footprints.

It began with a seemingly innocuous personality quiz—the app was called "This Is Your Digital Life", developed in 2013 by Aleksandr Kogan, a data scientist at the University of Cambridge. To complete the quiz, Facebook users consented to their data being collected for academic use. However, through the use of a developer's application programming interface (API), the app also collected the personal information of test-takers' Facebook friends, collecting data on tens of millions of users. This contravened the social network's "platform policy" which banned the collection of friends' data for any reasons aside from improving user experience. Kogan's company, Global Science Research, passed the data to political consultancy, Cambridge Analytica.

The use of harvested Facebook data was first reported in 2015, sharing information that Cambridge Analytica were working for U.S. Senator Ted Cruz. Further reports from the news media followed. According to PolitiFact, in his 2016 presidential campaign, Donald Trump paid Cambridge Analytica for data on Americans and their political preferences. Cambridge Analytica also had connections to AggregateIQ, a Canadian firm that worked with different leave campaigns in the June 2016 European referendum (Brexit).

The 2018 news triggered a global backlash. The hashtag #DeleteFacebook trended on Twitter, and Facebook lost around 20% of user engagement during the following month. Its stock price plunged, wiping out over $100 billion in market value. It was later discovered that when the unauthorized data use by Cambridge Analytica was first flagged to Facebook (in 2015), they had failed to alert users and only took limited steps to recover and secure private information of millions of individuals.

The UK's Information Commissioner's Office raided Cambridge Analytica's offices and fined Facebook £500,000—the maximum under the 1998 Data Protection Act—while the U.S. Federal Trade Commission levied a $5 billion fine, then the largest ever penalty for privacy violations, and imposed a sweeping 20-year consent decree demanding structural and operational changes at Facebook.

Cambridge Analytica galvanized interest in data protection. Its fallout inspired stronger legislation like Canada's privacy reforms, the California Consumer Privacy Act, and fed into the conversation around the European Union's (EU) General Data Protection Regulation (GDPR) and the forthcoming Digital Services Act (DSA). For other platforms, the scandal triggered reforms too: Twitter (now X) banned political ads altogether, Google limited microtargeting options, and all major platforms introduced transparency tools to show users what political ads were being run on their accounts.

In the wake of the scandal, Cambridge Analytica dissolved, filed for bankruptcy, and rebranded as Emerdata before ultimately ceasing operations. The negative public response to media coverage also led to Mark Zuckerberg agreeing to testify before the United States Congress on April 10–11, 2018. Lawmakers convened the hearings to investigate how Cambridge Analytica accessed and misused the personal data of millions of Facebook users without their consent, and to examine Facebook's role in enabling such data collection through its platform. During the testimony, Zuckerberg was questioned about Facebook's data policies, oversight mechanisms, and the broader implications for user privacy and electoral integrity, underscoring the urgent need for stronger safeguards and accountability on digital platforms.

Insider Incident: Surveillance from Within

In December 2022, TikTok's parent company ByteDance admitted that some employees had improperly accessed user data to track down the source of media leaks. The incident occurred when ByteDance staff used the platform's internal systems to monitor two journalists—one from *BuzzFeed* and another from the *Financial Times*—to try and identify who had shared confidential company information. These employees dug into TikTok account details, including IP addresses and physical location data. According to Reuters, this breach resulted in the employees' dismissal—while one manager in China resigned—and sparked public concern over privacy controls at TikTok's core.

Despite TikTok's insistence that this was a limited incident tied to internal leak investigations, the episode shone a harsh light on inherent vulnerabilities. In platforms operated by global tech giants, employees often have extensive access privileges. A moment of improper or malicious intent can lead to privacy breaches affecting public figures or everyday users alike. In this case, journalists, whose independence depends on confidentiality, found themselves under digital surveillance—raising critical questions about the adequacy of oversight mechanisms, data minimization policies, and ethical training for employees.

This isn't unique to TikTok. In 2022, the U.S. Justice Department charged an ex-Twitter employee, Ahmad Abouammo, for spying on Saudi dissidents. The ex-employee misused internal access to extract personal details—email, phone number, IP address—for those posting under pseudonyms. He then passed that information to a close aide of Saudi Crown Prince Mohammed bin Salman. A jury found Abouammo guilty, after revelations that he received luxury gifts and transfers exceeding $300,000 in return for his actions.

The employees in these examples betrayed trust by exploiting their roles for surveillance. For organizations, the lesson is clear: insider threats are not just technical—they're behavioral. Access controls—such as strong role-based permissions, auditing, and ethical training—are essential. Log collection, anomaly detection, and the separation of duties are not optional; they're lifelines against internal misuse.

For users, these stories are a reminder that digital platforms are more than just code: they are human institutions with internal politics and power dynamics.

The Risks of Public Information: Scraping and Leaks

In 2021, LinkedIn faced headlines around a data leak that exposed the personal information of 500 million users. This wasn't the result of a traditional hack—no passwords or financial information were compromised. Instead, it was the consequence of large-scale scraping, where data from public LinkedIn profiles was harvested and packaged for sale on dark web forums. The leaked data included names, email addresses, phone numbers, job titles, and other details that, while technically public, became dangerous when aggregated and contextualized.

This was not an isolated incident. LinkedIn data has appeared for sale or leaked multiple times and is part of a broader trend where platforms—especially professional or business-facing ones—have become targets for industrial-scale scraping. Once scraped, these details can be used to build profiles of targets, gain trust, and infiltrate inboxes with convincing phishing emails.

Similarly, Twitter, now X, experienced data leaks in late 2022 and early 2023 that exposed over 200 million user records, including email addresses and usernames. That data was also scraped, not hacked—again blurring the lines between what counts as a breach and what doesn't.

The danger with all of these examples is that the data isn't inherently sensitive in isolation—but combined and exploited, it becomes a threat. It's easy to forget that our LinkedIn profiles are a rich source of personally identifiable information: our career timelines, education history, professional contacts, even the patterns of our engagement. Once scraped, these details can be used to build profiles of targets, gain trust, and infiltrate inboxes with convincing phishing emails.

Zero-Day Attack: Breach of High-Profile TikTok Accounts

In June 2024, TikTok confirmed a high-stakes breach when hackers exploited a yet-to-be-discovered zero-day vulnerability to compromise prominent user accounts, including those of Paris Hilton, CNN, and Sony. The attack operated through direct messages containing malicious code: a single open, with no clicks required, could grant the hackers account control.

Zero-day attacks are named for their ruthless efficiency: exploiting system flaws before developers (and defenders) are even aware of them. This breach targeted TikTok's direct messaging system—normally considered a private, secure channel. That the attackers did not need any user to click a link made the attack especially alarming: it bypassed classical forms of user responsibility (like skepticism or cautious clicking) and hit the platform's core architecture.

Upon discovery, TikTok responded swiftly—cooperating with the affected users to restore control and initiating internal investigations. The company stated that no malicious content was posted, and there was no evidence of data harvesting. But the implications were still severe. High-profile breaches convey messages of technical fragility to all users, regardless of their account size or public visibility.

The Professional Imposter: Scams, Espionage, and Fake Accounts

Fake profiles have become an increasingly widespread issue on multiple platforms, ranging from clumsy bots to state-sponsored operatives running long-term deception campaigns. While some fake profiles are designed to spam, others are part of more sophisticated scams involving job fraud, espionage, and data extraction. Much of the information used to craft these believable profiles—career history, connections, and interests—is harvested from users' own social media activity, showing how publicly shared data can be exploited.

A 2023 *Wired* investigation uncovered how advanced some of these fake profiles have become. In one example, a woman named "Camille Lons" reached out to a journalist on LinkedIn. Her profile appeared entirely legitimate: a plausible career trajectory, a well-written summary, a professional-looking photograph, and shared connections. But it was all fabricated. "Camille" was part of an Iranian-linked operation designed to extract sensitive information from academics, journalists, and government workers. The scam involved sending tailored PDF documents and arranging Zoom calls that acted as delivery mechanisms for spyware.

It's not just government-linked threats that are cause for concern. The Federal Trade Commission has warned about the rise in job scams, where users are contacted by fake recruiters offering high-paying roles. These often come with requests for personal information or fees for bogus training courses and equipment.

In the wake of mass layoffs and a volatile job market, many users are eager for new opportunities—and scammers are eager to exploit that vulnerability.

Engagement Bait and Competition Scams: When Likes Become Liabilities

A brand promises a free iPhone. All you must do is like their page, share the post, tag a few friends, and fill out a form. You've likely seen this kind of giveaway dozens of times on Facebook, Instagram, and even LinkedIn. Increasingly, these engagement-driven contests are scams designed to harvest personal data or lure users into phishing traps.

UK consumer watchdog Which? has warned about the rise of fake social media giveaways that mimic the look and feel of genuine promotions. They use slick graphics, familiar brand names, and often go viral quickly as users share them in good faith. But behind the scenes, the goal is far from generous. Once people click through, they're often taken to fake websites where they're asked to enter their personal information—names, addresses, emails, even bank details—to "claim" their prize. Some are duped into downloading apps or signing up for premium-rate SMS services. Others simply have their data sold on to third-party marketers or cybercriminals.

What makes these scams particularly effective is how closely they resemble legitimate marketing tactics. Real companies often run competitions, giveaways, and social media engagement campaigns, especially to grow followers or promote a product launch. In some cases, scammers even create lookalike pages with near-identical branding, fooling even savvy users into thinking they're interacting with the real deal.

The human psychology behind engagement bait is simple. We're drawn to the idea of a free reward—especially if it seems like all we need to do is interact with a post. Add in a deadline, a sense of urgency, and a few hundred visible likes or comments, and it starts to feel real. Scammers exploit that moment of lowered guard.

The consequences can range from mild annoyance (spammy emails) to serious damage (identity theft, malware). While social media platforms do offer guidelines as part of their community policies, and act on reports and take down scams, the sheer volume and virality make prevention difficult. Often, by the time a page is reported and removed, it has already harvested thousands of entries.

What Social Media Platforms and Regulators Are Doing to Manage Threats

The Cambridge Analytica scandal prompted platforms to reconsider not only political advertising but also the broader question of user trust. In response, social media companies introduced transparency tools, allowing users to see the ads targeted at them.

Beyond advertising controls, platforms invested in more robust privacy dashboards to help users understand what information is collected and how it is used. They opened up access to independent researchers to study platform content and algorithms, aiming to shed light on previously opaque processes. Algorithmic explainability and reporting initiatives were also introduced, offering insights into how content is recommended and prioritized.

Meanwhile, moderation systems—combining human teams with AI-assisted tools—were expanded to detect misinformation, harmful content, and coordinated inauthentic behavior.

These efforts, though uneven, signal a growing recognition that sustaining user confidence and platform legitimacy depends not just on compliance with regulation, but on proactive governance, accountability, and transparency.

We will now examine some examples of how major social media platforms—Meta, LinkedIn, TikTok, and X—are responding to these threats, the actions they are taking to comply with regulations, and the fines or enforcement measures they have faced when requirements have been breached.

> These examples represent only a portion of the total activity, as the social media landscape, platform practices and regulatory environment are constantly evolving.

Meta: Policies, Reporting, and Tech Investments

Meta underpins its approach with a structured ecosystem that includes Community Standards, regular Transparency Reports, and massive investment in trust and safety infrastructure. Its Community Standards articulate clearly what's not allowed—including violence, hate, bullying, disinformation, and more—and are applied across Facebook, Instagram, Messenger, WhatsApp, and Threads.

Every quarter, Meta publishes a Community Standards Enforcement Report alongside other transparency documents, showing not just policies but results: for example, how much harmful content is removed, how frequently government requests are complied with, and how enforcement metrics change over time. Regulators in the EU and United States continue to press for improvements in ad verification, fraud detection, and transparency.

In 2025, Meta shifted its moderation strategy by ending its longstanding third-party fact-checking program and beginning to test a Community Notes approach on Facebook, Instagram, and Threads. Community Notes is being rolled out incrementally in select regions and languages rather than globally, with Meta gathering feedback and refining the system before broader deployment. While some markets now see community-generated context on posts, the transition from fact-checkers to community moderation is ongoing and varies by region.

Over the years Meta has been subject to multiple regulatory and legal penalties across different jurisdictions, reflecting broad scrutiny of its data, competition, and privacy practices.

In Australia, Meta agreed to a significant privacy settlement to resolve allegations under the Privacy Act 1988 related to the Cambridge Analytica incident, including provision of an enforceable undertaking and compensation scheme for affected users—a regulatory action demonstrating that Australian authorities are willing to challenge international platforms over data handling practices.

In 2024, Brazil's National Data Protection Authority took action against Meta for noncompliance with the Lei Geral de Proteção de Dados, issuing provisional orders and investigations into data practices, including concerns around transparency and lawful processing of personal data for new AI features.

In April 2025, the European Commission fined Meta €200 million under the Digital Markets Act (DMA) for its "Consent or Pay" advertising model, ruling that the company's implementation did not comply with the DMA's requirements that users must have genuine choice and control over how their personal data is used for personalized ads.

In addition to DMA enforcement, Meta has faced ongoing privacy-related penalties from EU data protection authorities. In late 2024, Ireland's Data Protection Commission (DPC) imposed fines totaling €251 million for failures associated with a 2018 Facebook data breach that exposed millions of accounts, and this regulatory action continued into 2025 as Meta appealed the decisions, with courts allowing the legal process to move forward.

At the time of writing, Meta is also responding to court rulings such as a Spanish commercial court's order (November 2025) that Meta pay hundreds of millions in damages for unfair data practices that gave it an unlawful market advantage in behavioral advertising—a decision the company is planning to appeal.

These enforcement actions come amid wider regulatory pressure. For example, in October 2025, the EU preliminarily found that Meta (alongside TikTok) breached transparency obligations under the DSA by failing to provide adequate research access and properly police illegal content—requiring corrective measures to avoid further sanctions.

LinkedIn: Professionalism through Transparency

LinkedIn positions itself as the professional social network, and its Professional Community Policies prohibit fake accounts, content violations, spam, scams, and misleading job offers. Enforcement leverages a mix of automated detection, human review, and member reports via embedded tools.

The platform's Transparency Center offers semi-annual Government Requests and Community Reports, detailing content removal, account takedowns, and volumes of fake profile removals. Compliance with the EU's DSA is reflected in DSA Transparency Reports, which provide metrics by violation type.

LinkedIn has also accelerated its profile verification initiatives. Originally rolled out in 2022 to confirm workplace affiliations via company emails or government IDs, the program has expanded globally, with India emerging as the fastest-growing market in 2025. LinkedIn's verification efforts now extend beyond its platform through programs like "Verified on LinkedIn", which allows partner services such as Zoom, Adobe, and G2 to display verification badges, and a self-serve API to facilitate integration into external systems.

This layered approach—automation, human oversight, and verification—strengthens the detection of impersonation and professional misrepresentation while promoting trust and credibility across the network.

While LinkedIn has not faced major fines comparable to other platforms, regulators continue to monitor adherence to EU transparency rules and GDPR compliance, particularly around data access and advertising practices.

TikTok: Aggressive Enforcement and Regional Transparency

TikTok has scaled its trust-and-safety operations around both robust internal enforcement and external transparency, particularly in response to regulatory expectations such as the EU's DSA and long-standing transparency commitments.

In its Q2 2025 Community Guidelines Enforcement Report (covering April–June 2025), the platform reported removing 76,991,660 fake accounts, along with 25,904,708 accounts suspected to belong to users under the age of 13. The same report also noted that 45% of the removed videos were flagged as misinformation and 23.8% were flagged as edited or AI-generated content, while other content was removed for violating safety, privacy, or mature-themed policies—all underscoring TikTok's emphasis on enforcing its rules at scale.

Globally, TikTok continues to invest heavily in trust-and-safety infrastructure. Enforcement data show TikTok continues to remove vast amounts of content for guideline violations. In Q1 2025, TikTok removed approximately 211 million videos globally, with most taken down before user reports. In Q2 2025, around 189 million videos were removed worldwide, with 163.9 million taken down by automated systems within 24 hours of posting, and the platform also removed tens of millions of inauthentic and under-age accounts. These figures build on earlier platform reporting that in 2024 TikTok removed more than half a billion videos and committed roughly US $2 billion a year to trust-and-safety efforts, illustrating both the scale and persistence of proactive enforcement.

On the transparency side, TikTok regularly publishes enforcement and moderation data as part of its DSA Transparency Reports. Its fifth such report, covering the first half of 2025, provides detailed metrics on content moderation actions in the EU—including the number of pieces of content removed, the volume of illegal content reports, and improvements in response times to government orders. These reports are hosted in TikTok's Transparency Centre, which shares data with regulators, researchers, and civil society to illustrate how policies are enforced and updated under legal frameworks like the DSA.

TikTok has been fined under data protection regulations, most notably in 2025 under the EU's GDPR. In May 2025, Ireland's DPC—the lead EU privacy regulator for TikTok—fined the company €530 million for breaching GDPR by failing to sufficiently protect the personal data of European users when transferring it to China and failing to meet transparency requirements about those transfers. The decision found that TikTok could not demonstrate that European users' data, which was accessed remotely by staff in China, was afforded a level of protection equivalent to that guaranteed under EU law, and that users were not adequately informed about the data transfers. At the time of writing, TikTok plans to appeal the ruling.

This is one of the largest GDPR fines ever imposed and underscores the seriousness with which EU authorities enforce data protection law against major platforms.

Prior to the 2025 GDPR fine, TikTok was fined €345 million in 2023 by the Irish DPC for failing to protect children's privacy—another GDPR-based penalty related to default privacy settings for underage accounts.

In late 2025, privacy advocacy group None of Your Business filed new complaints against TikTok alleging GDPR violations for tracking user activity from other apps without consent, potentially exposing sensitive personal data and prompting calls for further fines.

X: Transparency and Reinvention

X has continued to evolve its approach to trust and safety under Elon Musk's ownership, balancing its stated emphasis on free speech with regulatory obligations such as those imposed under the EU's DSA.

The platform's content moderation framework is set out in its publicly accessible X Rules, which prohibit behaviors including violence, harassment, fraud, and other policy violations. Enforcement is implemented through a mix of automated detection and human review, supported by reporting and appeals mechanisms for users. X uses Community Notes—a community-based fact-checking tool—to add context to potentially misleading content.

Under the DSA, X publishes periodic Transparency Reports detailing its moderation actions. For the reporting period April–June 2025, X's DSA report describes how content moderation systems blend automation and human oversight, while also outlining investments in technology to detect and remove violent extremist and abusive content. These reports are part of compliance with obligations to disclose how policies are enforced in the EU.

Although detailed global enforcement numbers for 2025 (such as total accounts suspended or posts removed worldwide) are not centrally published, past reporting indicates substantial moderation activity—for example, during Q1 and Q2 of 2024, X suspended over 5.3 million accounts and removed or labeled approximately 10.6 million posts for rule violations.

Like other platforms, X has also faced a number of regulatory consequences. In the U.S., They agreed to pay a $150 million civil penalty and implement comprehensive new privacy and security measures under a settlement with the Federal Trade Commission and the Department of Justice, resolving allegations that it deceptively used account security data to help advertisers target users.

In December 2025, the European Commission fined X €120 million (approx. US $140 million) for violating the DSA, chiefly citing deceptive design in its blue checkmark verification system, inadequate advertising transparency, and failure to provide researchers access to public data — marking one of the first penalties under the new law.

In addition, civil society groups have filed formal complaints alleging that X's targeted advertising practices may breach GDPR and DSA requirements by using sensitive personal attributes (e.g., political opinions, sexual orientation) for ad targeting.

Overall, X's moderation and transparency approach remains under intense scrutiny from regulators, researchers, advertisers, and civil society, highlighting ongoing tensions between platform governance, user rights, and regulatory compliance.

Lessons to Learn from Social Media Incidents

Social media is a powerful tool that brings both opportunity and risk. Across the incidents explored in this chapter—from insider misconduct and fake profiles to large-scale data leaks and regulatory breaches—it is clear that misuse can occur at multiple levels: by malicious actors, through technical vulnerabilities, or due to lapses in policy or oversight. The lessons drawn from these cases help both individuals and organizations shift from fear to awareness, and from reactive responses to proactive preparation.

At the individual level, personal digital hygiene remains the first line of defense. Users must actively manage passwords, enable two-factor authentication, and limit permissions granted to third-party apps. Treating social media as a semi-public space, exercising caution over what is shared, and engaging critically with content are essential for protecting personal information and avoiding misinformation or scams.

For organizations, the stakes are higher. Breaches of trust can result in reputational damage, legal consequences, and financial penalties. Governance frameworks, access controls, and scenario-based training for employees are crucial for mitigating risk. Crisis response plans, including defined roles, escalation procedures, and transparent communication, are essential for acting swiftly when incidents occur. Fostering a culture that embeds digital safety into daily behavior ensures that responsibility is shared across teams rather than concentrated in IT departments alone.

Platforms themselves have invested heavily in systems designed to keep users and communities safe. Automated detection, human review, and transparency reporting create guardrails that enable informed engagement. While these systems may be imperfect—mislabeling content, exhibiting bias, or lagging behind emerging threats—they do provide mechanisms for reporting, resolving, and learning from incidents.

Regulatory enforcement, including fines by authorities across jurisdictions, demonstrates that platform accountability is not optional. It is important to note the fines highlighted are examples—it's not an exhaustive list—but they highlight the seriousness with which regulators treat breaches, privacy failures, and transparency shortcomings.

Ultimately, navigating social media safely requires a combination of awareness, due diligence, and engagement with the tools and protections available. Individuals and organizations that understand the rules, leverage platform safeguards, and model responsible online behaviour by reporting harmful content, promoting respectful engagement, and supporting accurate information can harness the benefits of social media while minimizing exposure to risk.

The goal is not to avoid social media, but to use it confidently, responsibly, and strategically.

References

Bangkok Post. (2024, October 24). *TikTok touts $2 billion of online safety and trust measures*. https://www.bangkokpost.com/business/general/3078565/tiktok-touts-2bn-of-online-safety-and-trust-measures

Borger, J. (2018, May 3). *Cambridge Analytica: What happened and what comes next?* The Guardian. https://www.theguardian.com/uk-news/2018/may/03/cambridge-analytica-closing-what-happened-trump-brexit

Borger, J. (2022, August 9). *Ex-Twitter employee found guilty of spying on Saudi dissidents. The Guardian*. https://www.theguardian.com/us-news/2022/aug/09/twitter-saudi-arabia-dissident-spying

Cecchinato, F. (2022, December 22). *ByteDance finds employees obtained TikTok user data of two journalists. Reuters*. https://www.reuters.com/technology/bytedance-finds-employees-obtained-tiktok-user-data-two-us-journalists-2022-12-22/

European Commission. (2025, December 5). *European Commission fines X €120 million for transparency violations under Digital Services Act. Le Monde*. https://www.lemonde.fr/en/economy/article/2025/12/05/european-commission-fines-x-120-million-for-transparency-violations_6748186_19.html

Federal Trade Commission. (2022, May 25). *FTC charges Twitter with deceptively using account security data to sell targeted ads*. https://www.ftc.gov/news-events/news/press-releases/2022/05/ftc-charges-twitter-deceptively-using-account-security-data-sell-targeted-ads

Hern, A. (2024, June 5). *TikTok hackers target Paris Hilton, CNN and other high-profile users. The Guardian*. https://www.theguardian.com/technology/article/2024/jun/05/tiktok-hackers-target-cnn-paris-hilton-cyber-attack

Hern, A. (2025, May 2). *TikTok fined €530m for failing to protect user data from Chinese state. The Guardian*. https://www.theguardian.com/technology/2025/may/02/tiktok-fined-530m-for-failing-to-protect-user-data-from-chinese-state

Hutchinson, A. (2025, March 5). *X shares latest info on content removals and government requests. Social Media Today*. https://www.socialmediatoday.com/news/x-formerly-twitter-account-removals-government-requests-data/741721/

Irish Data Protection Commission. (2025, May 2). *TikTok fined €530 million and ordered to bring data processing into compliance following GDPR inquiry* [Press release]. https://www.dataprotection.ie/en/news-media/latest-news/irish-data-protection-commission-fines-tiktok-eu530-million-and-orders-corrective-measures-following

Kakadia, K. (2025, August 18). *TikTok privacy concerns exposed: What users need to know*. Sociallyin. https://sociallyin.com/resources/tiktok-privacy-concerns/

LinkedIn Ireland Unlimited Company. (2025, February). *Digital Services Act transparency report* [PDF]. LinkedIn. https://content.linkedin.com/content/dam/help/tns/en/February-2025-DSA-Transparency-Report.pdf

LinkedIn Corporation. (2025). *Community report*. LinkedIn. https://about.linkedin.com/transparency/community-report

LinkedIn Corporation. (2025). *Government requests report*. LinkedIn. https://about.linkedin.com/transparency/government-requests-report

LinkedIn Corporation. (n.d.). *Our transparency center*. LinkedIn. https://about.linkedin.com/transparency

Meta Platforms, Inc. (2025, March 13). *Testing begins for Community Notes on Facebook, Instagram and Threads* [Blog post]. Meta Newsroom. https://about.fb.com/news/2025/03/testing-begins-community-notes-facebook-instagram-threads/

Meta Platforms, Inc. (n.d.). *Community standards*. Meta Transparency Center. https://transparency.meta.com/policies/community-standards

Meta Platforms, Inc. (n.d.). *Policies*. Meta Transparency Center. https://transparency.meta.com/policies

OAIC. (2024). *Meta and the Australian privacy settlement under the Privacy Act 1988*. MinterEllison. https://www.minterellison.com/articles/metas-50m-reckoning-the-oaic-gets-tough-on-privacy

Reuters. (2025, July 15). *X hit by complaints to EU over user data and targeted advertising*. https://www.reuters.com/sustainability/boards-policy-regulation/x-hit-by-complaints-eu-over-user-data-targeted-advertising-2025-07-15/

Singh, J. (2025, December 18). *LinkedIn's profile verification push is accelerating — and India is leading the charge in 2025*. TechCrunch. https://techcrunch.com/2025/12/18/linkedins-profile-verification-push-is-accelerating-and-india-is-leading-the-charge-in-2025/

Solon, O., & Graham-Harrison, E. (2018, May 3). *The six weeks that brought Cambridge Analytica down. The Guardian.*https://www.theguardian.com/uk-news/2018/may/03/cambridge-analytica-closing-what-happened-trump-brexit

TBS News. (2025, April 10). *TikTok releases Q1 2025 Community Guidelines Enforcement Report*. https://www.tbsnews.net/economy/corporates/tiktok-releases-q1-2025-community-guidelines-1196201

TikTok touts $2 billion of online safety and trust measures. (2025, March). *Bangkok Post*. https://www.bangkokpost.com/business/general/3078565/tiktok-touts-2bn-of-online-safety-and-trust-measures

TikTok. (2025). *TikTok Q2 2025 Community Guidelines Enforcement Report. The News Digital. (2025, October 21). Tik Tok released its latest Q2 2025 report amid global crackdown. The News International*. https://www.thenews.com.pk/latest/1352601-tik-tok-released-its-latest-q2-2025-report-amid-global-crackdown

TikTok. (2025, August 29). *Digital Services Act: Our fifth transparency report on content moderation in Europe. TikTok Newsroom*. https://newsroom.tiktok.com/digital-services-act-our-fifth-transparency-report-on-content-moderation-in-europe

TikTok. (n.d.). *TikTok Transparency Centre*. https://www.tiktok.com/safety/en/transparency

TIME (2018, March 22). *Mark Zuckerberg just revealed 3 steps Facebook is taking to address the Cambridge Analytica crisis*. https://time.com/5209729/mark-zuckerberg-facebook-cambridge-analytica/

Trade Chronicle. (2025, July 15). *TikTok releases Q2 2025 Community Guidelines Enforcement Report*. https://tradechronicle.com/tiktok-releases-q2-2025-community-guidelines-enforcement-report/

Wikipedia contributors. (n.d.). *Facebook–Cambridge Analytica data scandal*. In *Wikipedia*. https://en.wikipedia.org/wiki/Facebook%E2%80%93Cambridge_Analytica_data_scandal

Wikipedia contributors. (n.d.). *PolitiFact*. In *Wikipedia, The Free Encyclopedia*. https://en.wikipedia.org/wiki/PolitiFact

X. (n.d.). *X rules*. X Help Center. https://help.x.com/en/rules-and-policies/x-rules

X Internet Unlimited Company. (2025). *DSA Transparency Report: Content moderation and enforcement (April–June 2025)* [Report]. https://transparency.x.com/dsa-transparency-report-2025-october.html

9 Tools for Protecting Privacy: Empowering the User

This chapter shifts the lens to the practical side of privacy, offering individuals and organizations tangible tools to reclaim control over their data.

As we have explored throughout this book, in the age of algorithmic profiling, behavioral tracking, and mass data collection, the erosion of personal privacy can feel inevitable. For many users, especially those active on social media, privacy seems like a fading ideal, an abstract principle overwhelmed by convenience, connectivity, and digital dependence.

Corporations engineer platforms for maximum engagement and data extraction; governments surveil in the name of security or efficiency. Meanwhile, users are often left with a sense of powerlessness, believing that privacy is something they lost long ago, or that reclaiming it requires technical expertise beyond their reach. But this narrative is somewhat misleading and, perhaps, one of the greatest enablers of surveillance culture. The truth is, privacy is not dead. It is under pressure, yes, but it is also evolving. And like all rights, privacy must be exercised to be protected.

That's where this chapter begins not with fear, but with agency. The tools exist. The strategies are within reach. The question is not whether we can protect our privacy, but whether we are equipped to do so.

This chapter is about taking back control not by retreating from the digital world, but by engaging with it more consciously. It offers readers a practical toolkit for understanding and adjusting privacy settings, using protective technologies, and building everyday habits that reduce data vulnerability. Whether you're a casual social media user, a content creator, a parent, a student, or a business professional, the tools and tactics in this chapter are designed to be accessible, applicable, and adaptable.

Importantly, this chapter also challenges the myth that privacy is only for the paranoid or the guilty. Too often, we hear the refrain: "I have nothing to hide". But privacy isn't about hiding, it's about boundaries, dignity, and choice. Just as we close the door to our homes, choose what to share with friends, or keep certain thoughts private, we deserve the same control in digital spaces. A social media profile should not be an open book for advertisers, data brokers, or even future employers. Nor should digital life mean surrendering our autonomy to algorithms we can't see and didn't consent to.

DOI: 10.4324/9781003654322-10

Of course, tools alone cannot solve systemic issues. Privacy settings won't dismantle surveillance capitalism, and a virtual private network (VPN) won't stop every form of tracking. But small, informed actions can significantly reduce exposure and restore a sense of control. Moreover, they send a signal to platforms, policymakers, and peers that privacy matters. And as more people demand better tools and stronger protections, individual actions can drive collective change.

We will explore the range of technical tools available, demystify the privacy options embedded in everyday apps, and examine behavioral patterns that shape our digital footprint. We will also reflect on the limitations of these tools, the risks of over-reliance, and the broader cultural shifts needed to reclaim privacy as a social norm, not just a setting buried in a menu.

Privacy begins with awareness. It grows with action. And it thrives when we stop accepting lack of control over our personal data as the cost of participation.

Understanding Platform Privacy Settings

For many of us, the phrase "privacy settings" conjures up an image of obscure menus, toggle switches we don't fully understand, and long-forgotten boxes we ticked years ago just to get past a prompt. The reality is that most users interact with social media through the surface-level experience posting, scrolling, liking, sharing without ever venturing deep into the architecture that quietly governs what is seen, by whom, and how often. But buried behind those interfaces are the real levers of control that shape not only our visibility, but also our vulnerability.

We tend to think of these settings as optional tweaks, something to adjust only if we're feeling particularly cautious. Yet, in truth, they serve as our first and most immediate form of defense: our digital lock on the front door, our curtain drawn over the window. The paradox is that while these settings are designed *for* us, they are rarely designed *with* us in mind. They are complex by design, ambiguous by intention, and often obscured under layers of cheerful user interface design. The average user often never even realizes the full extent of their exposure.

Let's take Facebook as a starting point, the world's most active social media platform. Facebook provides a suite of tools with names like "Privacy Checkup" and "Profile Visibility", inviting users to manage who sees what. At a glance, it feels empowering. But open the settings, and you'll quickly find yourself scrolling through an ocean of options: who can see your posts, who can find your profile, who can tag you, how your face is recognized in others' photos, whether advertisers can target you based on your web activity, and so on. These controls exist, yes but they're often set to share more than we might realize, hidden under optimistic assumptions of default openness. Even something as seemingly harmless as letting others tag you in photos can lead to a cascade of unintended visibility, especially when posts are cross-shared or accessed by third-party apps.

On Instagram, part of Meta's family of apps, the aesthetic minimalism of the app hides a similar complexity. It feels intuitive, clean feeds, simple icons, easy interactions. But its privacy assumptions are just as porous. For many, their

Instagram profile begins as public by default. This means that unless you actively restrict visibility, your photos, stories, likes, and comments are accessible to strangers and automated scrapers alike. The platform allows you to make your account private, hide stories from specific followers, and disable read receipts, but only if you know where to look. And herein lies the problem: the responsibility to protect ourselves is placed entirely on us, while the platforms can benefit from our default exposure.

TikTok introduces another layer. Known for its addictively tailored "For You" feed and its influence over younger audiences, it builds user profiles rapidly sometimes after just a handful of videos are watched or liked. The app's data collection practices are the subject of ongoing scrutiny, yet millions continue to use it without adjusting even the most basic privacy settings. Many are unaware that the app tracks off-platform behavior, records how long you linger on a post, and even analyses your facial expressions. The interface may allow you to limit who can comment or "duet" your videos, but few users consider what happens to their biometric data in the background.

Then there's LinkedIn, often seen as the "safe" network for business professionals. But it, too, makes assumptions about your willingness to be seen. Every time you view someone's profile, your name is logged, unless you change your settings. When you update your title or job, it's broadcast to your entire network. Unless you actively disable it, your connections list is visible to others, providing insight into your social graph. For those working in sensitive roles or undergoing career transitions, this visibility can be more than inconvenient; it can be compromising.

X, which offers a more transparent range of controls, defaults to openness. Posts are public unless protected. Likes are visible. Lists can be followed. And, unless you dig into the settings, your location might be embedded in posts. The platform allows users to exercise restraint but again, only if they know they should, and where to do so.

What's striking across all these platforms is a shared pattern: the illusion of choice. Yes, the tools exist. But they are rarely presented at the right time, with the right explanation, or in the right context. Privacy settings are often introduced reactively after a scandal, a breach, or a regulatory requirement rather than integrated into the natural rhythm of user interaction. They are framed as options rather than safeguards, as something extra rather than something essential.

This isn't simply a design flaw. It's a business model. Platforms thrive on data. The more public your activity, the more that can be tracked, analyzed, and monetized. Openness is the default because it's profitable.

So What Can We Do?

We can begin by refusing to accept these defaults as inevitable. We can treat every platform not as a neutral playground, but as a space where boundaries must be deliberately drawn. Privacy isn't a one-time decision, it's a practice. It requires regular review, especially after updates, re-brands, or acquisitions. It means checking who can tag you, who can message you, what permissions your apps have—as shown in Table 9.1—and what you've shared publicly without perhaps realizing it.

Table 9.1 Key Privacy Controls across Social Media Platforms

Platform	*Default Visibility*	*Sensitive Controls You MUST Change*	*Risk Level (Low/Medium/High)*
Facebook	Friends/Public	Face recognition, tag review, ad preferences	High
Instagram	Public	Account privacy, story visibility	Medium
TikTok	Public	Personalized ads, data sharing	High
LinkedIn	Public	Profile viewing options, network visibility	Medium
X/Twitter	Public	Location tagging	Medium

The risk level assigned to each platform reflects the likelihood and potential impact of unintended data exposure if default settings remain unchanged. Platforms categorized as high risk, such as Facebook and TikTok, combine extensive data collection with features like facial recognition, behavioral profiling, and personalized advertising, increasing the chances of surveillance, misuse, or secondary data sharing. These platforms also tend to encourage public visibility and continuous engagement, amplifying exposure over time.

Platforms assessed as medium risk, including Instagram, LinkedIn, and X, still default to public visibility but offer more granular user controls that can meaningfully reduce exposure when actively configured. While the risks here are less severe than in high-risk environments, they remain significant, particularly for professional profiling, location inference, and social engineering.

No platform is categorized as low risk by default, underscoring the broader argument that privacy protection requires deliberate user intervention. The risk levels therefore serve as a practical guide, signaling where immediate action is most critical and reinforcing the need for regular review of platform settings as part of ongoing digital hygiene.

It also means recognizing that the most powerful setting isn't hidden in a menu—it's the decision about what to share in the first place. Protecting privacy isn't only about turning off features or limiting access; it's also about being intentional with your digital presence. For organizations, this means preparing clear social media policies that define what can and cannot be posted, how employees engage with platforms, and how sensitive data is handled. For individuals, it means considering what you will and won't share, what you choose to engage with, and how to maintain a footprint that reflects your priorities.

Sometimes, protecting your privacy means choosing silence, choosing absence, or keeping a smaller digital footprint—not to hide, but to preserve what is valuable: your identity, your independence, and your space outside the constant tracking of metrics and algorithms.

In the next section, we'll go beyond what platforms offer and look at external tools and technologies that add an extra layer of protection, built not by corporations, but often by open-source communities, privacy advocates, and ethical technologists who believe we all deserve more than a false sense of control.

The Quiet Revolution of the Private Browser

Most of us use the browser our device came with: Chrome, Safari, maybe Edge. These browsers are functional and familiar, but they are also deeply entwined with surveillance ecosystems. Chrome, for instance, is made by Google, a company whose business model relies on collecting user behavior for targeted advertising. Every click, search, and login feeds the profile.

Enter the privacy-first browsers. Tools like Brave, Firefox, and Tor offer alternatives that don't track your activity or monetize your movement. Brave blocks trackers and ads by default, making browsing faster and less cluttered. Firefox offers a suite of privacy controls, including anti-fingerprinting technology and enhanced cookie protection. Tor, the most radical of them all, routes your traffic through multiple encrypted layers, masking your location and identity. It's slower, but more secure, often used by journalists, researchers, and anyone seeking digital invisibility.

Switching browsers is one of the simplest but most powerful things you can do. It doesn't change your daily habits, it just means those habits aren't being watched quite so closely.

VPNs: The Illusion of Being Somewhere Else

If browsers are your windows to the internet, a VPN is your curtain. It doesn't stop you from being online, it just obscures where you're coming from. A VPN encrypts your internet traffic and routes it through a remote server, masking your IP address and location. This means websites can't easily trace your activity back to your device. It also helps you access content restricted by geography like news sites blocked in authoritarian countries or video services that vary by region. But not all VPNs are created equal. Free ones often log your data and sell it on. Reputable paid services like ProtonVPN, Mullvad, or IVPN are more transparent, often refusing to collect logs at all.

The key is to choose a service that puts privacy before profit. Using a VPN isn't about hiding criminal behavior. It's about reclaiming the right to explore, read, and communicate without being constantly geo-tagged and profiled.

> In some countries, the use of VPNs is restricted or even banned outright, particularly where governments seek to control information flows and limit access to independent news. Nations such as China, Russia, Iran, and the United Arab Emirates have implemented legal or technical measures to block or regulate VPN use, requiring providers to register with authorities or restricting unapproved services. These restrictions illustrate that digital privacy tools are not universally protected, and that using a VPN may carry legal or technical risks depending on where you are.

VPNs are also becoming part of debates about online safety. As governments introduce age-based restrictions on access to social media and other online services, concerns have emerged that young people can use VPNs to bypass these measures by masking their location or identity. This has prompted policymakers and regulators to consider how VPN use can be addressed within broader approaches to digital governance, while raising ongoing questions about privacy, security, individual freedoms, and the practical limits of regulating online behaviour.

Password Managers: The Locks That Matter Most

We live in a world where our digital lives are held together by a handful of characters: passwords we reuse, simplify, and forget. Many people still rely on the same password for multiple accounts, or use predictable combinations like names, birthdays, or "123456", In doing so, they leave their doors wide open.

A password manager is a vault; a secure app that stores, encrypts, and generates strong passwords for you. Tools like Bitwarden, 1Password, and Proton Pass allow you to create unique passwords for every service you use, without needing to memorize them all.

When combined with two-factor authentication (2FA) where a code is sent to your phone or generated by an app like Authy or Google Authenticator, your digital identity becomes significantly harder to compromise.

We have summarized some example privacy tools in Table 9.2.

However, no tool is infallible. Even password managers, designed to secure your credentials, can be compromised. In December 2025, the UK's Information Commissioner's Office fined LastPass £1.2 million following a data breach dating back to 2022, which exposed personal information for approximately 1.6 million users. While encrypted passwords themselves were not reportedly decrypted, the incident highlights that personal data linked to accounts can still be at risk when a provider's security is breached.

A password manager is still a critical tool: it stores, encrypts, and generates strong, unique passwords for every service, making it far harder for attackers to compromise multiple accounts. Combined with 2FA, your digital identity becomes significantly more secure. Yet users should remain vigilant, update their software, and recognize that security is never absolute.

Encrypted Communication: Privacy in Conversation

Not all messages are created equal. When you send a text, post a photo, or make a call, the content often passes through multiple servers, sometimes unencrypted, sometimes stored indefinitely. Popular messaging apps such as WhatsApp, iMessage, and Telegram all vary in how much privacy they provide.

Table 9.2 Example Privacy Tools (Browsers, VPNs, Password Managers)

Category	*Example Tools*	*Strength*	*Limitation*
Browsers	Brave, Firefox, Tor	Anti-tracking, open source	Tor slower
VPNs	ProtonVPN, Mullvad	No logs, encrypted tunnels	Can reduce speed
Password managers	Bitwarden, 1Password	Strong passwords, 2FA integration	Requires trust

WhatsApp uses end-to-end encryption by default for messages and calls, meaning that only the sender and recipient can read them, though metadata (who you contact and when) is still visible to the platform. iMessage also provides end-to-end encryption for messages between Apple devices, but like WhatsApp, it collects certain metadata and is limited to the Apple ecosystem. Telegram offers optional end-to-end "secret chats" but stores standard messages on its servers, which could potentially be accessed.

Apps like Signal offer true end-to-end encryption, meaning only you and your recipient can read the message. Not even Signal knows what you're saying; it collects virtually no metadata; it doesn't store who you talk to, when, or for how long. It's open-source, donation-funded, and designed with surveillance resistance in mind.

Knowing these distinctions allows you to make more informed choices about which platform best fits your privacy needs.

For email, services like ProtonMail and Tutanota offer encrypted messaging and privacy-conscious policies. Unlike mainstream providers, they don't scan your inbox to serve targeted ads, reducing the risk that your personal communications are used to build marketing profiles. For social media users, this is particularly relevant: the more platforms you link to your email—whether for login, password recovery, or notifications—the greater the risk that data from those platforms could be aggregated or exploited.

Tracker Blockers: Decluttering the Web

Ever searched for a new pair of shoes and then seen ads for similar shoes follow you across websites and social media feeds for weeks? That's not coincidence—it's tracking, often powered by a technique called retargeting, where advertisers use cookies and other trackers to show you ads based on your previous online activity.

Websites embed trackers from advertising networks, data brokers, and analytics services. These tiny scripts watch what you click, how long you stay, and where you go next. Over time, they create a behavioral fingerprint.

Tracker blockers like uBlock Origin, Privacy Badger, and Ghostery disrupt this. They block known trackers, prevent invisible scripts from running, and reduce the amount of data leaking from your browsing session. These extensions are free, easy to install, and often customizable.

They won't make you invisible but they'll make you harder to follow. And they'll make your internet cleaner, faster, and less targeted.

Mobile Privacy: The Device You Never Leave Behind

Smartphones are intimate. They're with us in the bathroom, the bedroom, and the boardroom. They know where we are, who we talk to, what we search, and when we sleep. And yet, most users never question the permissions granted to their apps.

Both iOS and Android allow you to review and restrict app access to your location, camera, microphone, and more. It's worth taking the time to audit this.

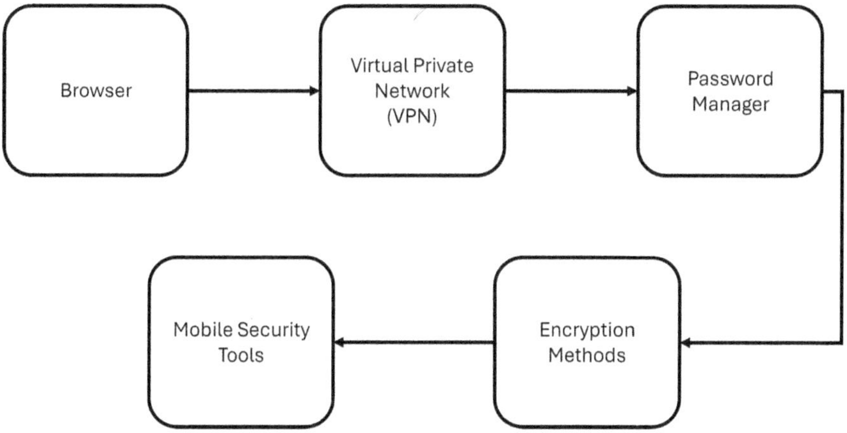

Figure 9.1 Privacy Tech Stack.

Why does a flashlight app need to know your location? Why is your weather app accessing your contacts?

Apps like Jumbo Privacy and DuckDuckGo App Tracking Protection act as mobile guardians. They scan your device, flag risky behaviors, and help you adjust settings for better control, as shown in Figure 9.1.

Putting It All Together: A Holistic Approach

Unfortunately, no single tool offers total protection. A VPN doesn't help if your passwords are weak. Encrypted messaging is moot if your phone is compromised. Privacy isn't a product, it's a practice, a mindset that combines tools with habits.

The goal is not to disappear. It's to create friction in systems that assume passive compliance. It's to make surveillance more expensive, less rewarding, less inevitable. Each tool you adopt chips away at the data industrial complex.

Learning and Adapting

Tools evolve, and so should we. The digital privacy landscape is always shifting: apps get acquired, settings change, new vulnerabilities emerge. Staying protected means staying curious.

Follow independent tech journalists, privacy blogs—such as the Cyber Management Alliance cybersecurity blog—and advocacy organizations like Electronic Frontier Foundation or Access Now. They publish regular updates, reviews, and guides. Join online communities such as r/privacy on Reddit or explore resources like PrivacyGuides.org, a volunteer–run, nonprofit project offering independent news, reviews, and discussions about privacy tools and practices. These sources can help you stay informed about developments, assess tools critically, and learn from others' experiences.

There is no endpoint, only progress. And progress begins with user awareness.

Social Engineering and Behavioral Awareness

Despite the sophistication of encryption tools and the complexity of digital safeguards, one of the most common points of failure in privacy isn't technological, it's human. No firewall is impenetrable when someone opens the door from the inside. No system is secure when its weakest link is compromised. And that is exactly what social engineering exploits: the soft, emotional, trusting, distracted, and deeply human parts of us. It's not about code; it's about behavior.

In everyday terms, social engineering refers to the manipulation of people into revealing confidential information or performing actions that compromise security. It's phishing emails designed to look like legitimate login prompts. It's messages from 'support teams' asking you to verify your account. It's someone posing as a friend or colleague, or even as yourself, in order to trigger trust. And the scariest part? It often doesn't look or feel like an attack. It feels like routine. It feels like helping.

Many of us imagine that we'd never fall for common social engineering tactics as shown in Table 9.3. We believe we're too careful, too smart, too skeptical. But attackers don't target gullibility, they target routine. They exploit the very habits we build to survive online: speed, convenience, multitasking, and emotional response. You're tired, trying to clear your inbox, and you get a notification that your account has been locked. Without thinking, you click the link. You're sent to a login page that looks identical to your bank's website. The URL is slightly off, or uses unusual characters—subtle cues you might not notice in the moment, but it's a classic phishing attack… You enter your credentials. Just like that, someone else has access. It wasn't your fault. It wasn't even your lack of knowledge. It was timing, emotion, and the invisible architecture of urgency that modern digital life embeds into our nervous systems.

On social media, the manipulations are subtler but no less effective. Consider what we choose to share without hesitation: birthdays, vacation plans, new purchases, pet names, childhood schools. To us, these are just reflections of our lives. To attackers, they are answers to security questions, patterns in passwords, or breadcrumbs that lead to deeper impersonation. A simple "Which Harry Potter house are you?" quiz can be a front for data mining. That feel-good "Comment your first car" thread is a harvest of personal history. Harmless fun on the surface, dangerous if misused.

Table 9.3 Common Social Engineering Tactics and How to Respond

Attack Type	*How It Works*	*Red Flags*	*User Response*
Phishing	Fake login pages	Urgency, unknown links	Verify URL
Impersonation	Fake friend/colleague message	New number, unusual request	Confirm via call
Baiting	"Free gift" or quiz	Requests personal info	Ignore/delete
Pretexting	Pretending to be authority	Threats, demands	Ask for verification

But, social engineering isn't always adversarial. Sometimes, the manipulation is built into the platform itself, as we learned in Chapter 5. This is where behavioral awareness becomes even more critical. Dark patterns are design choices that subtly steer users toward less private, more profitable outcomes. You might find it incredibly easy to accept all cookies, but laborious to reject them. You might be guided toward sharing your contacts, granting location access, or allowing microphone use through cheerful pop-ups, default settings, or time-limited incentives. None of it is technically forced. But much of it is engineered to be the path of least resistance.

Understanding these tactics means becoming digitally literate. It means pausing before clicking. It means reading URLs, hovering over links, and asking whether the request in front of you makes sense. It means verifying before trusting, especially when the message stokes fear or urgency. It means asking why a service needs what it's asking for and whether you can say no.

Behavioral awareness also involves managing our own impulses. Social media platforms thrive on attention, outrage, and rapid reaction. Every time we post in anger, share without checking, or forward something that confirms our biases, we become part of the machine. And when we overshare—whether it's a new job, a child's school, or a health scare—we build a narrative of ourselves that others, including advertisers or online predators, can discern, repurpose, or exploit. Privacy isn't just about data it's about discernment.

This doesn't mean we stop posting. It means we shift from unconscious sharing to intentional communication. We ask: What am I revealing? To whom? For how long? What is the emotional state I'm in while posting? Sometimes, it means sharing the same photo but cropping the background. Sometimes, it means delaying a post until you've left a location. Sometimes, it means withholding altogether not out of fear, but out of a healthy sense of boundaries.

One of the most powerful ways to build behavioral awareness is to trace your digital trail backwards. Go through your social media accounts and see what's visible publicly. Search your name and see what surfaces. Check what apps have access to your profile. Ask yourself whether a stranger could guess your hometown, your best friend, or your employer based on what you've shared. Privacy leaks rarely happen in one big spill. They happen in drips: cumulative, overlooked, and quietly extractive.

The encouraging truth is that awareness scales. The more you see, the more you start to notice. You begin to catch the manipulative language in email subject lines. You start to question why a gaming app needs access to your microphone. You recognize that a post asking for your "superhero name" based on your pet and street name might be scraping data. You stop handing out information simply because the interface smiles at you.

Building behavioral awareness also means sharing what you learn with others. Talk to your colleagues, friends, and your family. Most people don't fall for scams because they're foolish, they fall because they're unaware that they're being targeted. The more we normalize conversations about privacy risks, the stronger our collective resilience becomes. It's not just about protecting yourself. It's about improving online safety for everyone.

Workplace Guidance

For many, privacy is imagined as something personal—a matter of what we choose to share on social media or how we protect our own devices. But privacy is also a professional concern. The boundaries between personal and work-related digital spaces are increasingly blurred, particularly in the age of hybrid work and social media as a professional branding tool. Phones, laptops, and social accounts follow us across meetings, video calls, and client interactions. Privacy in this context is not just a preference; it's a professional imperative.

Employees should receive clear guidance on social media use, both in relation to their job roles and personal accounts. This includes understanding what can be linked to the company—corporate devices, emails, cloud storage—and how posts, messages, or activity might reflect on their employer. Even seemingly innocuous interactions, like responding to DMs or posting about work-related events, can create a digital footprint that is traceable and potentially monitored. Clear policies help employees navigate these risks while maintaining professionalism and protecting both personal and organizational privacy.

All employees, regardless of role, have a part to play in understanding the regulations that govern privacy (see Chapter 7). Awareness of laws, internal policies, and industry best practices helps ensure that social media activity is responsible, ethical, and aligned with both personal and organizational privacy expectations.

For roles such as marketing, HR, communications, or leadership, the stakes are often higher. Professionals managing public-facing accounts, interacting with stakeholders online, or using advertising platforms like Meta Business Suite, or LinkedIn Campaign Manager must handle large volumes of personal data responsibly.

Using these tools ethically and transparently is not just good practice—it safeguards brand reputation and trust.

So How Can We Navigate this Space Responsibly?

First, it begins with clarity and boundaries. If you're using a company-issued device, assume that activity can be monitored. If you're using a personal device for work (as in Bring Your Own Device policies), understand what data the company has access to and what you're agreeing to by installing corporate apps. Ask questions. Read policies.

Second, practice separation of spaces. Use dedicated accounts for professional communication. Avoid mixing personal and work profiles on platforms like Instagram or X unless explicitly required. Where platforms allow it, use built-in separation tools—such as Facebook's multiple profile option—to distinguish professional activity from personal expression and reduce unintended overlap between audiences. Store work-related files in approved cloud services rather than personal drives. This not only protects the organization but also protects your own privacy should an audit, legal request, or security breach occur.

Third, if you're responsible for managing digital platforms within or on behalf of an organization, make ethical choices by default. Don't collect more data than necessary. Avoid harvesting or purchasing audience data through scraped social media profiles, third-party lists, or unofficial tools. Be transparent about how cookies, pixels, lead forms, and social media tracking features are used, and ensure data is handled only in approved systems

Finally, create or support internal cultures that care about privacy. Advocate for digital hygiene sessions during onboarding. Choose collaboration platforms that offer privacy-respecting features. Encourage use of a password manager tool and 2FA.

Best Practices for Workplace Social Media Privacy

- Know the policy: Familiarize yourself with your organization's social media guidelines and any legal or regulatory obligations.
- Separate accounts when possible: Use dedicated professional accounts for work-related social media activity; keep personal accounts private.
- Think before posting: Consider whether posts, comments, or shares could be linked to your employer or affect your professional reputation.
- Manage digital footprints: Be aware that messages, photos, and interactions—even on personal accounts or messaging apps—can be traceable or archived.
- Use secure credentials: Avoid logging in to work systems with personal social media accounts unless explicitly allowed; enable strong passwords and 2FA.
- Report incidents promptly: If you notice suspicious activity, data breaches, or unintended sharing of company information, notify IT or compliance teams immediately.
- Stay informed: Regularly update yourself on privacy regulations, platform changes, and emerging risks.

Digital Hygiene Checklists

Much like physical health, digital well-being depends not on grand gestures but on consistent, everyday maintenance. We brush our teeth, wash our clothes, and sort our mail not because we expect disaster, but because upkeep is part of everyday life. The same is true of our digital lives. Over time, accounts accumulate, permissions linger, devices slow, and data spills quietly into places we've forgotten. What begins as convenience can end in clutter, and, if left unchecked, in compromise.

Digital hygiene is the practice of periodic digital housekeeping. It's a blend of routine and reflection: auditing your online presence, cleaning up your data trails, and reevaluating how your information is shared, stored, and secured. It's not about achieving perfection or disappearing from the grid, it's about ensuring that the systems you rely on aren't silently working against your privacy.

The good news? You don't need to be technical to begin. You just need to start small, and make it a regular habit. This section offers a practical checklist to build your own rituals of digital care—both at work, and at home.

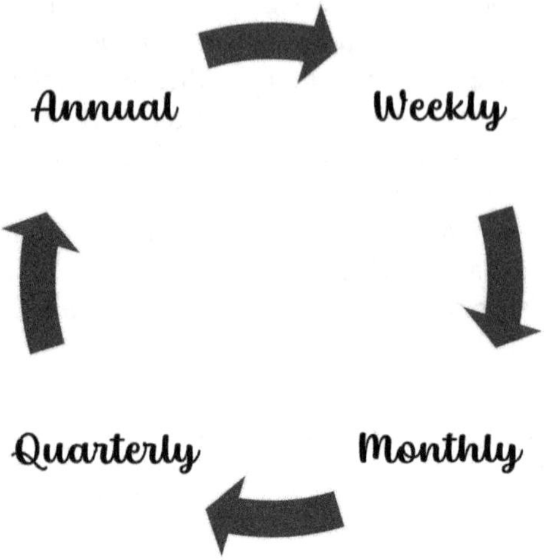

Figure 9.2 Digital Hygiene Lifecycle.

Start with Your Devices

Your phone and computer are like your digital homes. If they're compromised, everything else is too. Begin by reviewing the basics regularly as shown in Figure 9.2.

- Update regularly. Outdated software is a primary entry point for hackers. Enable automatic updates for your OS, apps, and antivirus tools.
- Remove what you don't use. Uninstall apps that you no longer need, especially those with access to your camera, microphone, or location.
- Review permissions. On both Android and iOS, check which apps are allowed to track your location, access your contacts, or use sensors.
- Clear your cache and history. These build up over time and can reveal more about you than you realize.
- Restart occasionally. It seems trivial, but rebooting devices can refresh system processes and apply necessary patches.

Clean up Your Online Accounts

Most of us have far more online accounts than we remember. Each one is a potential weak link into your devices.

- List your accounts. Think of every service you've signed up for: email, shopping, subscriptions, forums. Use a password manager to help surface forgotten logins.
- Delete what's obsolete. Close accounts you no longer use. Many platforms have a "Delete My Account" option buried in settings.
- Use unique passwords. If you're reusing the same password across multiple sites, change that. A password manager can help automate this.

- Enable 2FA. 2FA adds a critical layer of protection by requiring a second form of verification in addition to your password.

Review Your Social Media Footprint

Social platforms are some of the most visible aspects of your digital identity, where exposure can have the greatest impact.

- Check your visibility. Who can see your posts? Your friends list? Your profile photo? Adjust these privacy settings based on your comfort level.
- Delete old content. That political rant from 2016? The party photos from university? If it no longer represents you, consider removing it.
- Revoke app access. Over time, third-party apps and games gain access to your account data. Remove anything you don't use.
- Audit tagged content. Remove yourself from photos or posts that are public by default or no longer relevant.
- Review account type and subscription features. Consider whether premium features, linked services, or automatic renewals still meet your needs and privacy preferences.

Tidy Up Your Email Inbox

Email remains a central hub of personal and professional life, but it's also a magnet for spam, scams, and surveillance.

- Unsubscribe ruthlessly. If you're not reading it, stop receiving it.
- Organize folders. Don't let your inbox become a bottomless pit. Sort by topic or urgency to keep important emails from getting lost.
- Watch for phishing. Check sender addresses, hover over links, and never download attachments from unexpected messages.
- Use alias addresses. For newsletters, trials, or one-time purchases, consider using disposable or secondary emails.

Check for Breaches

Even the most careful user can be affected by leaks from companies or services they once used.

- Search your email on "Have I Been Pwned." This tool reveals whether your credentials have been part of a known data breach.
- Change compromised passwords. If your email or password shows up in a leak, update it immediately, especially if reused elsewhere.
- Monitor account activity. Many platforms (like Google, Facebook, and Microsoft) offer security dashboards showing where and when you've logged in. Spot anything suspicious? Revoke access and change your password.

Reset Your Sharing Habits

Perhaps the most powerful act of digital hygiene is not deletion, but intention.

- Pause before posting. Ask yourself: is this something I'm comfortable with a stranger seeing ten years from now?
- Turn off auto-sync. Do you need every photo backed up to the cloud? Are your voice recordings being stored? Decide what deserves a digital trail.
- Delay location tagging. If you want to share travel or event posts, consider doing it after you've left, not in real time.
- Avoid public Wi-Fi without protection. If you must use it, pair it with a trusted VPN to keep your connection secure.
- Review your algorithmic and default settings. Adjust your feed preferences, notification settings, and content order (e.g., chronological vs. algorithmic) to take back control over what you see and share.

Create a Schedule

Digital hygiene isn't a one-time detox. Like any kind of care, it benefits from rhythm.

- Weekly: Clear your browser cache, update apps, review social media tags, delete old screenshots or downloads, and report any content you find inappropriate or harmful.
- Monthly: Check your permissions, change key passwords, run a security scan, review connected devices.
- Quarterly: Audit your accounts, clean your inbox, delete unused apps, reset ad preferences.
- Yearly: Close old accounts, review your digital legacy settings (e.g., what happens to your account if something happens to you), and evaluate whether your privacy tools still meet your needs.

Put a reminder on your calendar. Make it part of your seasonal reset. You don't need to do it all at once, just do it regularly.

Limitations of Tools—No Magic Bullet

One of the first limitations of privacy tools lies in their very architecture: most are reactive, not proactive. They attempt to patch vulnerabilities that already exist, rather than prevent them from emerging in the first place. A VPN won't make you invisible, it will simply obfuscate your location. A password manager won't stop a phishing attack, it will only reduce the damage if one occurs. Tools rarely address the underlying issue: that our digital world is built around extractive design, behavioral prediction, and data maximization. They operate within that system, not outside it. They are, to some extent, playing by the rules of a game that was never designed with user privacy in mind.

And then there's usability. Many privacy tools, especially the most secure ones, come with a learning curve. They require configuration, habit changes, sometimes even discomfort. Tor, for instance, offers near-anonymous browsing, but it's slow and incompatible with many sites. Encrypted email like ProtonMail is safer than Gmail, but limited in cross-platform compatibility. Signal is secure, but only if your contacts also use it. VPNs add latency. Tracker blockers can break websites. Stronger passwords are harder to remember. In short, privacy comes with friction, and that friction often turns people away.

This isn't just an issue of design; it's an issue of trust. Tools that claim to protect you must also be trusted not to betray you. But how many of us know who maintains the code? Who funds the service? Has the software been independently audited? Trust becomes a paradox: we install privacy tools because we don't trust Big Tech, but we must then place our trust in smaller players, often with fewer resources, less transparency, and no brand recognition. In some cases, tools marketed as privacy-preserving are anything but. They promise anonymity while quietly collecting telemetry. They claim to block ads but inject their own. They boast encryption but lack proper implementation. Navigating this minefield requires not only digital literacy, but also a kind of ethical intuition: the ability to ask, What's their incentive? What's their business model? Who benefits if this tool grows?

The second layer of limitation lies in context. Privacy tools work differently depending on where, how, and by whom they are used. A VPN that protects a student in the UK might raise suspicion in a country with strict internet controls. A secure messaging app might be legal in one country and banned in another. Even simple practices, like using a pseudonym or hiding your status, can be interpreted as evasive, suspicious, or even criminal depending on the context. There is no one-size-fits-all solution. Cultural, legal, infrastructural, and political differences shape the effectiveness and safety of privacy behaviors.

Tools also fail to address the networked nature of exposure. You might lock down your own profile, but what about your friends? Your family? Your co-workers? Social media, by design, encourages information about you to be shared by others. You can restrict tags, but not prevent someone from posting your image. You can delete a post, but not the screenshots taken before. You can leave a platform, but not the data trails that linger in group chats, mentions, or search histories. Tools give the illusion of individual control in a space that is fundamentally collective. Privacy, in this sense, is only as strong as the least careful person in your circle.

Moreover, privacy tools don't address the emotional and psychological side of surveillance. They cannot prevent the anxiety that can come with always being visible, nor the exhaustion of managing dozens of settings, permissions, and notifications. They cannot stop you from comparing yourself to algorithmically curated feeds or feeling exposed after a vulnerable post. They do not replace the need for boundaries, support, and community norms that value discretion. In short, tools cannot care for you. Only people can.

Then there's the issue of accessibility. Many of the most recommended tools are not available in all regions, languages, or platforms. They may require paid subscriptions, high-speed internet, or advanced devices. They assume a baseline of digital fluency that not everyone possesses. For people with disabilities, older users, or those in low-connectivity areas, the very tools meant to empower may become a barrier. When privacy becomes a luxury product, available only to those with time, money, or technical expertise, it deepens digital inequality.

This is not to say tools are useless. Far from it. They are powerful, necessary, and in many cases lifesaving. But placing all responsibility on tools, and by extension, on users, risks reinforcing a dangerous narrative: that privacy is a personal failure, not a structural issue. It lets platforms off the hook. It shifts the burden to individuals. And it hides the fact that no matter how vigilant we are, our data is still being collected, sold, and analyzed in ways we can neither see nor stop.

That's why privacy needs to be reframed not as a product you download, but as a politic you live. It's about the questions you ask, the defaults you challenge, the platforms you pressure, the norms you model. Tools help you resist, but resistance is bigger than software. It includes the parent who refuses to post photos of their child without consent. The employee who enforces strong, secure password practices in the workplace. The teacher who explains to students how TikTok's algorithm works. The developer who chooses not to collect analytics. The policymaker who drafts legislation that mandates true user control. The activist who demands ethical design. The friend who shares a privacy guide, not because they expect perfection, but because they care.

So Where Does This Leave Us?

It leaves us in a place of sober clarity. The tools are important, but partial. They are a response, not a revolution. They are the armor, not the battlefield. Rely on them, but don't romanticize them. Use them, but don't stop there.

Advocate. Educate. Organize. Reflect.

And perhaps most of all, be kind, to yourself, and to others. Because digital life is complicated, messy, and evolving. You will make mistakes. You will overshare. You will click the wrong link. You will forget a setting. That's okay. Privacy, like any form of care, is not about perfection. It's about intention, practice, and resilience.

There is no magic bullet. But there is something better: the slow, steady work of reclaiming your digital self, tool by tool, post by post, decision by decision.

From Protection to Presence: Reclaiming the Digital Self

We began this chapter with a simple proposition: that privacy is not dead, merely under pressure. That it can still be reclaimed, not only through laws and platforms, but through personal agency, intentional action, and digital rituals.

And throughout these pages, we have explored the many ways individuals can protect themselves: from understanding the logic behind privacy settings, to deploying tools that guard our communications, conceal our footprints, and resist manipulation. We've traced the practices that shape digital hygiene, considered how these apply both at home and in the workplace, questioned the limitations of tools, and acknowledged the emotional labor involved in navigating the surveillance-saturated terrain of everyday life.

And yet, as we come to the end of this exploration, it becomes clear that privacy, real privacy, is not just a matter of defense. It is also a matter of presence. Of how we exist online, not only how we avoid being exploited. Of who we choose to be when the metrics are invisible, when the likes are absent, when the profile becomes more than just a curated façade. It is about the quality of our digital lives, not just their security.

This is a critical shift. Because when privacy is framed solely as protection—protection from surveillance, from corporations, from governments—it begins to feel like retreat. As if to be private is to withdraw, to shrink, to opt out. But privacy is not the opposite of participation. In its most generative form, privacy is what makes participation meaningful. It is the space from which expression can emerge without coercion. It is what allows us to speak without pandering, to share without performance, to experiment without the algorithmic gaze dictating outcome.

When we feel safe, we are more ourselves, not less. When we are not watched, we are not invisible, we are free.

This reframing also demands that we rethink our relationship with digital platforms. We must stop imagining them as public squares, where speech flows democratically, and instead recognize them as corporate theatres, where engagement is choreographed, where identity is performed, where visibility is monetized. In such spaces, privacy is not merely about hiding, it is about negotiating performance. Who am I in this space? Who do I become when I know I am being watched? What do I withhold, not because it is shameful, but because it is sacred?

These are not hypothetical questions. They are the invisible code behind every post, every story, every shared location, every bio update. And increasingly, they are the questions that define the mental and emotional texture of digital life. For younger generations especially, social media is not a tool they log into, it is the interface of the self. And within that interface, privacy becomes both harder and more necessary.

The tools we have explored in this chapter are vital. But they are not the destination. They are the foundation upon which we build a healthier relationship with technology and, by extension, with ourselves. They allow us to create space, space to feel, to think, to breathe, to choose. They return to us a sense of rhythm in a digital world that moves too fast to notice. They give us back our attention, piece by piece. And with that attention, we can begin to ask deeper questions.

What does it mean to be a person in a quantified world? What happens to identity when it is always exposed to interpretation, ranking, or rejection? How do we craft our digital presence in ways that honor who we are, not just who we are expected to be?

These are the questions we take with us into our final chapter. Because privacy is not simply the backdrop to digital identity, it is its precondition. Without privacy, self-expression becomes performance. Without privacy, experimentation becomes a risk. Without privacy, community becomes a spectacle. To reclaim privacy is not just to secure our data, it is to reclaim our narrative.

We will explore how identity is shaped, fractured, and reassembled across platforms. How the architecture of social media demands particular kinds of selves, marketable, legible, strategic. How race, gender, sexuality, and class are made hypervisible or rendered invisible by the logic of algorithms. And how the promise of self-expression can sometimes turn into a burden of self-optimization.

We will also ask: what does it mean to be *seen* online? Is visibility always empowerment? Is anonymity always protection? Can we be authentic in systems that reward consistency over complexity?

Once we understand how to protect our digital space, the next question is what we *do* with that space. What does it mean to show up online, not just safely, but truthfully? Can we imagine identities that are not just reactions to surveillance, but affirmations of autonomy, creativity, and care?

These questions are not easy. But they are necessary. For if we are to live meaningful digital lives, not just efficient or optimized ones, we must be allowed to be messy, evolving, unfinished. We must be allowed to step away from the performance. We must be allowed to choose when, how, and whether to be seen.

And we must recognize that privacy is not about erasure, it is about agency. It is not a wall; it is a door. And what we do once we open that door is what truly defines us.

Now, we turn the page, not to exit the conversation on privacy, but to deepen it. Because the question is no longer just *How do I protect my data?* but *Who am I when I do?*

References

Access Now. (n.d.). *Digital security & privacy resources*. https://www.accessnow.org/digital-security/

Apple. (2024). *Apple platform security*. https://support.apple.com/guide/security/welcome/web

CISA. (2023–2025). *Social engineering & phishing guidance*. U.S. Cybersecurity & Infrastructure Security Agency. https://www.cisa.gov/topics/cyber-threats-and-adversarial-behavior/social-engineering

Cloudflare. (2023–2025). *Zero trust & personal security guides*. https://www.cloudflare.com/learning/

Cyber Management Alliance. (n.d.). *Cyber security blog*. https://www.cm-alliance.com/cybersecurity-blog

Electronic Frontier Foundation. (n.d.). *EFF: Defending digital privacy and free speech*. https://www.eff.org/

FTC. (2023–2025). *Online scams & social engineering reports*. Federal Trade Commission. https://www.ftc.gov/news-events/topics/scams-fraud

Gen Digital. (2023–2024). *Password security & digital hygiene reports*. NortonLifeLock/Avast. https://www.gendigital.com/research

Google. (2023–2025). *Safety center – Security, privacy & account protection*. https://safety.google/

Information Commissioner's Office. (2025, December). *Password manager provider fined following data breach*. ICO. https://cy.ico.org.uk/about-the-ico/media-centre/news-and-blogs/2025/12/password-manager-provider-fined/

Kaspersky Security. (2023–2024). *Social media threat reports*. https://www.kaspersky.com/resource-center

LinkedIn. (2024). *Data privacy & security practices*. https://www.linkedin.com/help/linkedin/answer/66

Meta Platforms. (2023–2025). *Privacy, security, and account settings*. https://transparency.meta.com/policies/

Microsoft. (2023–2025). *Identity protection & account hardening*. Microsoft Security Blog. https://www.microsoft.com/en-us/security/blog/

Mozilla Foundation. (2023–2025). *Privacy not included (privacy ratings for tools)*. https://foundation.mozilla.org/en/privacynotincluded/

NCSC. (2023–2024). *Social media security guidance*. National Cyber Security Centre. https://www.ncsc.gov.uk/collection/top-tips-for-staying-secure-online/social-media

Norton Labs. (2023–2024). *Social engineering trends & online safety reports*. https://us.norton.com/blog

Ofcom. (2026, May 21). Experiences of age assurance, use of VPNs, and attitudes to the Protection of Children Measures. https://www.ofcom.org.uk/online-safety/protecting-children/experiences-of-age-assurance-use-of-vpns-and-attitudes-to-the-protection-of-children-measures

Privacy Guides. (n.d.). *Privacy Guides: Independent privacy & security resources*. https://www.privacyguides.org/

Reddit. (n.d.). *r/privacy* community. https://www.reddit.com/r/privacy/

TikTok. (2024). *Safety center*. https://www.tiktok.com/safety/

X Corp. (2023–2025). *Safety and cybersecurity policies*. Twitter/X. https://help.twitter.com/en/safety-and-security

10 The Future of Privacy in Social Media

Social media is entering its most transformative era yet. Privacy is evolving with every technological leap, every design change, every global event, and every new form of digital expression. As platforms reshape themselves in real time, so too must our understanding of surveillance, autonomy, and digital identity.

This chapter explores the breakthroughs, tensions, and cultural shifts that will define the next decade of privacy in social media, and what they mean for the future of our digital selves.

The Rapidly Evolving Landscape of Social Media Privacy

The future of privacy in social media is unfolding faster than anyone might have anticipated. Only a few years ago, conversations about digital privacy were centered on familiar concerns: targeted advertising, third-party cookies, or the data breach that briefly dominated headlines. But between 2023 and 2025, the landscape has shifted dramatically. Social media is no longer just a space of connection or self-expression, it has become an ecosystem intertwined with artificial intelligence (AI), geopolitical tension, algorithmic governance, deepfakes, immersive technologies, and biometric surveillance.

The result is a rapidly evolving terrain where privacy is no longer a passive background issue, but a defining feature of the digital world's next chapter.

And perhaps the most striking change is this: privacy is no longer simply about what we choose to share, it is about what platforms can infer, predict, and generate about us without ever needing our explicit input.

The introduction of sophisticated AI models across all major platforms has transformed social media into a predictive environment. Platforms can infer emotional states from facial expressions on video, assess personality traits from interaction patterns, and even attempt to anticipate real-world behaviors such as political leanings, purchase decisions, or relationship intentions.

As generative AI tools have become embedded within apps, users' creative outputs, photos, voices, writing styles, and even movements, have become new sources of behavioral data. In other words, the future of privacy is not primarily about *posts*, it is about the invisible metadata shaping who we become online.

At the same time, platforms themselves are undergoing upheaval.

DOI: 10.4324/9781003654322-11

TikTok's evolving position in the United States, the European Union's (EU) regulatory crackdown on behavioral advertising practices, and the rise of decentralized networks like Bluesky and Mastodon show that social media is no longer a stable industry dominated by a few tech giants.

Regulatory bodies in Europe, India, Australia, Canada, Brazil, and California have all expanded their definitions of personal data to include inferred data, biometric identifiers, and sensitive behavioral signals.

The EU's Digital Services Act (DSA) and Digital Markets Act (DMA) now require unprecedented transparency from platforms regarding algorithmic systems. Meanwhile, the EU AI Act, the world's first comprehensive regulation on AI, directly impacts how social platforms deploy content moderation AI, facial recognition tools, and recommendation engines. These shifts make it clear that privacy futures are now inseparable from AI governance.

At the same time, digital identity is entering a new phase. Deepfake technology, once niche and experimental, has become mainstream. In 2024 alone, major platforms reported exponential increases in AI-generated identity abuse, from impersonation scams to fabricated political content. Governments have begun crafting synthetic media policies, requiring watermarking, labeling, and provenance tracking for AI-generated content. Yet even with these measures, the lines between authentic and artificial identities are increasingly blurred.

Simultaneously, immersive technologies from augmented reality (AR) headsets to next-generation wearables are expanding the boundaries of what social media and connected devices can detect. Beyond traditional clicks and likes, these systems capture subtle behavioral signals—eye movements, hand gestures, facial expressions, and spatial patterns—that reveal more about users than ever before. These signals, while essential for device functionality, are uniquely intimate forms of behavioral data. Again, regulators have struggled to keep pace, and platform policies remain inconsistent. This signals a profound shift: the future of privacy will not only concern what platforms *take* from us, but what they *sense* about us.

Technological innovation has also opened the door for alternative social media models. As users grow frustrated with centralized platforms such as Facebook, Instagram, and X, where control over data and algorithms is concentrated, alternative models that prioritize user autonomy and privacy are gaining traction. Decentralized networks, including Mastodon, Bluesky, and the Fediverse more broadly, offer a glimpse of what a privacy-respecting future could look like, where individuals have greater control over their identities, data, and online interactions, even as challenges around moderation, usability, and regulatory compliance remain.

Companies are increasingly treating privacy-enhancing technologies (PETs) as a strategic advantage: platforms that can protect user data while still delivering personalized experiences are better positioned to maintain trust, engagement, and regulatory compliance.

Amid these shifts, a new idea is emerging: privacy as a cultural value rather than a personal task. Over the past decade, individuals have carried the burden of managing privacy, adjusting settings, learning tools, navigating consent banners. But the future demands a collective reframing. Privacy is relational. The photos we share reveal others. The contacts we upload expose entire networks. The facial recognition tools we use can identify bystanders who never opted in.

Protecting privacy going forward will require shared norms, shared expectations, and shared rights, not just individual choices.

And, as we step into this future, this chapter asks a guiding question: *What will privacy mean in a decade where artificial intelligence, decentralization, immersive technology, global regulations, and cultural shifts converge?*

The future of privacy will not be defined by a single innovation or law, but by the interplay between technology, policy, industry, psychology, and user behavior. It is a future still in the making.

In the final pages ahead, we will explore the key trends and innovations shaping the next era of privacy in the age of social media. We will examine how AI transforms both protection and surveillance; how emerging laws redefine platform responsibilities; how decentralized networks challenge corporate power; how deepfakes, biometrics, and immersive data reshape identity; and how cultural movements toward conscious sharing may shift the psychological foundations of online life.

To understand the future of privacy, we must first understand the technologies rewriting its foundations. What follows are the major developments reshaping how data is collected, processed, inferred, and utilized across modern social spaces.

AI-Driven Privacy

AI is transforming social media—not just as a tool for content filtering or recommendations, but as a system capable of generating insights about users that they never explicitly provide. AI can detect patterns in engagement, predict behaviors, and even anticipate life events, from career changes to mental health signals.

For social media users, this means that the data they consciously share is only part of what platforms know; AI creates a shadow profile of inferences drawn from activity, interactions, and engagement patterns.

Platforms are also experimenting with AI-driven privacy assistants, designed to help users navigate complex privacy settings. These systems can recommend safer configurations, alert users when app permissions change after updates, and flag interactions that may expose personal information. Instagram's Safety Check, introduced in 2024, illustrates how AI can proactively guide users toward safer digital behavior.

Yet for every protective application, there is a risk. Generative AI can now create highly realistic synthetic content: voices can be recreated from seconds of audio, images generated from minimal prompts, and user writing styles predicted from a handful of posts. Combined with AI-driven emotional profiling, these capabilities allow platforms to subtly shape what users see, hear, and feel. The challenge for privacy is therefore twofold: managing both the data users deliberately provide and the invisible inferences AI derives from it.

Regulation, such as the EU AI Act—which limits emotion recognition in workplaces, schools, and public settings—offers some safeguards, but social media largely remains a gray area, leaving users exposed to sophisticated profiling and manipulation.

The Rise of Decentralized Social Platforms

Disillusionment with social media—driven by political controversies, opaque algorithms, and the monetization of personal data—has spurred interest in decentralized networks. These platforms aim to give users more control over their identities, data, and social environments.

A key example is the Fediverse, a network of interconnected platforms such as Mastodon, Pixelfed, PeerTube, and Lemmy that communicate using the ActivityPub protocol, a standard that enables different servers to share content and interact seamlessly while each maintains its own rules. Between 2023 and 2025, the Fediverse experienced notable growth. Mastodon's user base surged after instability on Twitter/X, Meta's Threads platform integrated with the Fediverse in 2024, signaling growing mainstream recognition of decentralization, and Bluesky launched its AT Protocol, allowing portable identities across servers.

Decentralization offers clear privacy benefits. Users who control their hosting reduce reliance on ad-driven business models, and smaller networks mean less risk of large-scale breaches. Data portability also allows users to migrate between platforms without losing their social identity. Yet decentralization is not a panacea: local server administrators can still access data, moderation practices vary widely, and compliance with global privacy rules is complex. Autonomy comes with trade-offs, including potential gaps in content moderation and uneven protections against harassment.

Ownership of Digital Identities

Building on the principle of user control, emerging technologies such as blockchain and self-sovereign identity (SSI) are beginning to offer ways for social media users to own their digital identities and manage their data more directly. Blockchain is a technology that provides a tamper-resistant framework for secure and transparent data exchanges, while SSI process will allow individuals to hold and share credentials on their own terms (e.g., proving age or membership without revealing unrelated personal data). Together, these approaches reinforce the decentralization ethos, giving users more autonomy, privacy, and flexibility in online social networks.

Privacy-Enhancing Technologies

Social media platforms are increasingly exploring ways to protect user data while still enabling analytics. PETs offer approaches that reduce exposure without sacrificing functionality.

Differential privacy is already in use by major tech companies. Apple applies it to iOS usage statistics, Google uses it in Chrome and for mobility reports, and the U.S. Census Bureau uses it to protect individual identities in population data. By adding a small amount of "noise" to datasets—essentially tiny, random modifications—platforms can analyze overall trends without revealing personal details. On social media, this could allow platforms to study engagement patterns or detect harmful trends without tracking specific users.

Federated learning is also partially implemented today. Google uses it for predictive text on Android keyboards, and social media platforms are experimenting with it for personalization algorithms. Instead of sending raw data to central servers, the learning happens locally on users' devices, and only aggregated updates are shared. This enables services like predictive text or safety monitoring without exposing individual data.

Zero-knowledge proofs (ZKPs) are emerging, primarily in blockchain and cryptographic applications, but they hold promise for social media. ZKPs let a platform verify a fact—like a user being over 18—without ever seeing the underlying information, preserving privacy while confirming eligibility.

Homomorphic encryption is still largely experimental. It allows calculations on encrypted data, meaning platforms could analyze user activity or train recommendation models without ever decrypting personal information. While resource-intensive, it represents a potential future step toward truly privacy-conscious analytics.

Together, these technologies signal a shift from indiscriminate data harvesting to privacy-aware computation. Some, like differential privacy and federated learning, are already shaping practices today, while others, like ZKPs and homomorphic encryption, represent the frontier of what might soon be possible.

Biometrics, Wearables, and Emotional Data

Perhaps the most contentious frontier of digital privacy involves behavioral and biometric data generated by next-generation devices. From Apple's Vision Pro to Meta Quest 3 and SamsungXR, these technologies capture unprecedented signals: eye movements, facial expressions, spatial mapping, body motion, and even micro-saccades—tiny, involuntary eye movements that reveal attention and subtle emotional reactions.

When this data intersects with social media ecosystems, platforms gain unprecedented insight into user attention and emotion. Companies can track what captures a user's gaze, how long attention is sustained, and how facial or bodily responses indicate emotional states. In practice, this means platforms could infer which content provokes anxiety, which influencers inspire trust, or when a user's physiological response signals excitement or stress. It is attention-economy optimization taken to its extreme.

Internal research at Meta, revealed through leaked documents and whistleblower testimony, demonstrates that AI systems are capable of interpreting emotional and behavioral cues to guide engagement strategies—even in sensitive contexts such as interactions with minors. While platforms may publicly deny using emotion recognition for advertising, these examples illustrate the underlying capability and potential for misuse.

Privacy experts warn that emotional data may become the most exploited category of personal information in the coming decade. Unlike demographic or behavioral data, it reveals how users feel, not just what they do. Advertisers could target sadness, loneliness, or insecurity; political campaigns could identify emotional vulnerability; algorithms could subtly shape content to maintain particular engagement states. Although the EU AI Act restricts emotion recognition in workplaces, schools, and public spaces, social media remains largely unregulated.

The stakes are profound: biometric and emotional data blur the line between outward expression and internal states. When platforms understand users' emotions as well—or better—than the users themselves, manipulation becomes easier, subtler, and far harder to detect. The ethical challenge is clear: the more precise the measurement of our emotional lives, the greater the responsibility to protect them.

The rapid expansion of AR and virtual reality devices, wearables, and emotion-recognition technologies has brought biometric privacy into sharp focus. These systems extract deeply personal signals—ranging from gaze tracking and facial micro-expressions to voice patterns and inferred emotional states—often without users' explicit awareness of the extent or sensitivity of the data involved.

Regulators are responding with a mix of prohibitions and heightened safeguards. These include bans on real-time biometric monitoring in public spaces under the EU AI Act, stricter consent requirements for facial and voice recognition, formal investigations into the use of emotion recognition in education, retail, and workplace contexts, and ongoing debates about whether emotional data should be recognized as a distinct legal category. Underpinning these responses is a growing understanding that biometric and emotional data are psychologically intimate and uniquely vulnerable to exploitation.

A Privacy Landscape in Motion

The technological shifts shaping the future of social media-from AI to decentralized networks, PETs, blockchain identity, emotional data, wearables, and synthetic media-reveal a world where privacy is simultaneously at risk and undergoing reinvention.

Each advancement opens powerful opportunities for empowerment, autonomy, and personalization. Yet each also introduces new vulnerabilities, inequities, and forms of control.

The future of privacy will depend on how society negotiates these tensions: how regulators constrain exploitation, how platforms adopt ethical design, how businesses prioritize trust, and how users redefine their boundaries in an increasingly immersive digital world.

The Future Regulatory Landscape

The regulatory environment surrounding social media privacy is transforming rapidly. Between 2023 and 2025, governments around the world have moved from treating social media as a communication tool to recognizing it as a powerful, AI-driven infrastructure with profound implications for public health, democracy, and personal autonomy.

The laws emerging today reflect a growing awareness that privacy cannot be protected solely by limiting data collection; it must now address data inference, algorithmic influence, biometric surveillance, synthetic media, and cross-border digital power.

The future of privacy will be shaped by policymakers who understand that social platforms are no longer passive intermediaries—they are active systems that shape behavior, emotion, and identity.

The Global Shift toward Comprehensive, AI-Aware Privacy Frameworks

A new generation of privacy regulation is taking shape, one that is explicitly designed for platforms powered by AI. Rather than focusing solely on how data is collected and stored, these frameworks increasingly address how personal information is created, inferred, and operationalized by algorithmic systems.

The EU has been at the forefront of this shift. Together, the DSA, the DMA, and the AI Act mark a significant redefinition of platform accountability, extending regulatory oversight beyond traditional data protection into the logic and consequences of automated decision-making.

And, at the heart of this regulatory evolution is a move from data protection toward inference protection. Lawmakers are beginning to acknowledge that AI-driven platforms do not merely process existing personal data; they generate new forms of personal information through prediction, profiling, and behavioral inference. As a result, newer rules introduce explicit restrictions on practices such as biometric categorization, emotion recognition, and sensitive behavioral profiling, particularly where these techniques risk discrimination, manipulation, or loss of autonomy.

This AI-aware approach is no longer confined to Europe. Comparable reforms are emerging globally, including the United Kingdom's proposed Data Protection and Digital Information Bill, Canada's Bill C-27, India's Digital Personal Data Protection Act, and strengthened enforcement of Brazil's Lei Geral de Proteção de Dados (LGPD).

Across Southeast Asia, regulators are also beginning to update privacy frameworks with AI-specific provisions. Collectively, these developments signal a regulatory turn that targets not just how platforms *collect* data, but how they conceptualize, infer, and monetize personal information at scale.

Algorithmic Transparency and Independent Oversight

Alongside these substantive shifts, transparency has become a central regulatory demand. One of the most consequential developments is the requirement for visibility into how social media algorithms shape information flows, attention, and behavior. Under the DSA—fully enforceable since 2024—the largest platforms must now explain how their recommendation systems and content moderation models function, particularly where they pose systemic risks.

Regulators are increasingly insisting on independent algorithmic audits, formal risk assessments covering areas such as misinformation, mental health impacts, and democratic integrity, and structured access for approved researchers to platform data. Transparency obligations now extend to the logic behind content ranking and demotion, advertising delivery, and the models used to assess and manage systemic risk.

Similar expectations are emerging beyond Europe, with countries including Australia, Singapore, and South Korea moving toward stronger algorithmic accountability regimes. What was once treated as proprietary opacity is becoming legally and politically untenable.

The Era of Dynamic, Real-Time Consent

The idea that privacy consent can be meaningfully captured through a single checkbox at sign-up is increasingly seen as outdated. Regulators now recognize that data practices on social media are continuous, adaptive, and often opaque, and that consent mechanisms must reflect this reality. As a result, there is growing pressure on platforms to design systems that allow users to understand, approve, or refuse data use at the moment it occurs, rather than retrospectively or abstractly.

This shift is visible in emerging regulatory expectations around contextual prompts when data is accessed, layered consent interfaces for high-risk processing, and the use of simplified, accessible language tailored to different user groups. Clearer opt-out mechanisms and more visible explanations of how data is processed are also becoming standard requirements rather than optional best practice.

Countries including Japan, Australia, and members of the EU are exploring structured consent models in which particularly sensitive data—such as biometric information, behavioral inference, or location data—requires recurring approval. Consent, in this framing, is no longer a one-off transaction but an ongoing relationship between users and platforms.

Cross-Border Data Governance and Digital Sovereignty

At the same time, data has become a strategic and geopolitical resource. Governments are increasingly asserting sovereignty over how data generated within their borders is stored, transferred, and analyzed, reshaping the global architecture of social media platforms.

This trend is evident in India's selective data localization requirements, China's tightened controls on data exports, Brazil's evolving cross-border transfer rules under the LGPD, and ongoing efforts such as the EU–U.S. Data Privacy Framework to stabilize transatlantic data flows.

These developments have practical consequences for platform design and operation. Social media infrastructures may fragment along regional lines, cloud storage and AI training pipelines may face jurisdictional constraints, and companies must navigate an increasingly complex patchwork of national and regional compliance obligations. The future of social media governance will therefore unfold in a world where data flows are not merely technical challenges, but deeply political ones.

Artificial Intelligence Regulation as the New Frontier

Between 2023 and 2025, social media platforms underwent one of the fastest technology migrations in history: nearly all major platforms integrated generative

AI into their core products. The transformation continues; AI now shapes content, interactions, trends, moderation, and even user identity.

AI's sweeping influence includes:

- Personalization algorithms becoming predictive rather than reactive
- Generative engines assisting users in creating visuals, videos, and messages
- Synthetic influencers competing with human creators
- Automated content polishing, translation, and caption generation
- Voice-cloning features emerging in TikTok, Snapchat, and Meta tools.

AI is not just a feature-it has become the operating system of social media.

The integration of AI into social media platforms introduces complex privacy implications. Platforms can now access behavioral cues such as tone, cadence, and writing style, enabling more nuanced profiling of individual users. Generative tools collect stylistic data that may be used to infer personality traits, often without users' explicit consent. AI assistants are increasingly capable of analyzing emotional states to "improve" content, raising questions about the boundary between personalization and surveillance.

Meanwhile, advancements in voice and image modeling expand the categories of biometric data being captured, adding another layer of sensitivity to the information platforms hold.

The challenge for users is that AI blurs the boundaries between what is explicitly shared and what is inferred, often without their awareness. The challenge for platforms is that AI integration demands new safeguards, greater transparency, and alignment with emerging global regulatory frameworks. These developments underscore the growing need for clear data practices and robust protections in an era of AI-driven digital interaction.

AI has also become central to privacy governance debates. The regulatory concern is no longer limited to what data platforms collect, but extends to how AI systems use that data to generate insights, predictions, and synthetic outputs that can shape users' experiences and opportunities. This has prompted fundamental questions: whether AI-generated predictions should be treated as personal data; whether individuals should have rights to correct or delete algorithmic inferences; whether platforms must disclose when content is curated or prioritized by AI; and whether synthetic media, such as deepfakes or AI-generated avatars, should be legally labeled.

Regulatory responses are beginning to emerge. The EU AI Act mandates transparency measures such as watermarking for certain forms of AI-generated content and places strict limits on emotion-recognition systems. In the United States, federal standards for AI transparency and accountability are under active development, while countries such as Japan, Singapore, and Canada have introduced frameworks intended to balance innovation with safety. Taken together, these efforts reflect a growing recognition that AI governance and privacy regulation are now inseparable.

From Compliance to Stewardship: Evolving Corporate Responsibility

Finally, regulators are beginning to treat large social media platforms as systemically important infrastructures rather than ordinary private actors. This shift carries new expectations. Companies are increasingly required not only to comply with specific rules, but to demonstrate ongoing responsibility for the broader privacy impacts of their technologies.

In practice, this means conducting continuous algorithmic impact assessments, publishing detailed risk and transparency reports, eliminating harmful design patterns, submitting to independent third-party audits, and embedding privacy-by-design principles into products and features from the outset.

Enforcement is intensifying, with significant fines and investigations already underway across jurisdictions including the EU, India, and Brazil.

As a result, corporate privacy governance is moving away from being treated as a peripheral compliance cost and toward becoming a core function of organizational stewardship and accountability.

Protecting Young Users of Social Media

Regulators and platforms alike are responding to the distinctive needs of younger social media users, recognizing that their digital experiences are qualitatively different from those of adults. In the UK, the Online Safety Act has introduced legally binding duties for platforms to protect children from harmful content, requiring proactive risk assessments, moderation, and safety-by-design features. Platforms are increasingly creating age-specific spaces or features, such as restricted content feeds, default private profiles, and parental oversight tools, reflecting a broader recognition that one-size-fits-all approaches are insufficient for younger audiences.

Internationally, protections around digital privacy and safety are evolving rapidly—and one of the most high-profile examples comes from Australia. In December 2025, the Australian Parliament enacted what is widely described as a world-first social media age-restriction law, to introduce a "social media minimum age" that effectively prevents children under 16 from holding social media accounts on major platforms. Under this new framework, platforms such as Facebook, Instagram, TikTok, Snapchat, YouTube, X (formerly Twitter), Reddit, Twitch, Threads, and others are legally required to take "reasonable steps" to ensure that Australians under the age of 16 cannot create or maintain accounts. If they fail to comply, companies face stiff civil penalties—up to tens of millions of Australian dollars—placing the responsibility squarely on platforms rather than families or young people themselves.

While many parents and child safety advocates have welcomed the move as a decisive step to safeguard young people, it has also sparked debate and criticism. Some tech companies and civil liberties organizations question the feasibility of reliable age verification and argue that children may simply migrate to unregulated corners of the internet or use workarounds such as virtual private networks

(VPNs). In some cases legal challenges are already underway, and observers from other democracies are watching closely as they consider whether to adopt similar policies.

As we prepare the final edits for this book, the UK has announced a ban on social media access for under-16s, expected to come into force in Spring 2027.

Regulatory developments also mirror broader cultural shifts among younger generations, who are increasingly rejecting the "share everything" ethos that dominated the early 2010s. Gen Z, in particular, prefers closed communities, ephemeral content, pseudonymous profiles, and platforms with tighter boundaries. On TikTok, trends such as photo dumps, anonymous confessions, and private accounts reflect a desire for authenticity without exposure.

The rise of digital minimalism—a deliberate approach to reducing online clutter, limiting social media use, and engaging only in meaningful digital interactions—signals growing fatigue with algorithmic performance metrics and perpetual visibility. This shift is sparking new conversations not only about digital privacy but also about emotional privacy and cognitive privacy—concepts that were barely discussed a decade ago.

The Emerging Hybrid Ecosystem: Centralized + Decentralized + AI-Native

The future of social media will not follow a single model. Instead, it is likely to evolve into a hybrid ecosystem that blends centralized giants, decentralized networks, AI-native environments, and immersive AR/VR spaces. In this future, users will move fluidly between platforms depending on purpose, while portable identities allow participation across multiple ecosystems. Privacy protections will be embedded at a system level through PETs, and AI agents will help manage user preferences, privacy settings, and content filters. This multi-layered environment will challenge existing norms around content moderation, identity, and advertising, while simultaneously expanding user choice and autonomy.

The Corporate Pivot toward a Privacy-Conscious Future

Social media platforms stand at a turning point. Under pressure from regulators, users, and market forces, they are redefining not only how they operate but what values they prioritize. Privacy is no longer viewed as a barrier to innovation; it is increasingly seen as a foundation for sustainable growth, user trust, and long-term competitiveness.

This vision reveals a future where business models diversify, AI becomes foundational yet regulated, moderation grows more intelligent and accountable, identity shifts to being user-owned rather than platform-owned, and privacy emerges as a shared responsibility across the digital ecosystem.

The next decade of social media will be defined by platforms that lead this transformation-not those that resist it.

Privacy as a Social Signal: Boundaries as Identity

Privacy practices themselves have evolved into a form of identity expression, signaling maturity, self-awareness, digital literacy, and personal autonomy. Users engage in "privacy signaling" by keeping relationship updates offline, choosing not to post images of their children, avoiding luxury or travel posts to reduce envy or risk, turning off read receipts and online activity indicators, or maintaining a minimalist public profile.

These behaviors communicate emotional intelligence, self-respect, respect for others, digital hygiene literacy, and a rejection of performative engagement. They also reflect a conscious choice to resist the attention economy. In this way, privacy is becoming a status symbol—a marker of someone who knows how to navigate the complexities of the digital world with discernment and wisdom.

Relational Privacy: The Shift from Individual to Shared Responsibility

Privacy is no longer solely an individual concern; it has become a collective negotiation. When someone posts a photo of a group, they are shaping not just their own digital footprint but everyone else's as well. This awareness is reshaping user behavior. Relational privacy concerns include tagging friends without consent, posting images of children before they can understand digital life, sharing private events publicly, circulating screenshots without permission, and automatically uploading contacts to social platforms. In response, new cultural behaviors are emerging: asking permission before sharing content, blurring the faces of bystanders, avoiding location tags that reveal habits, seeking group consensus before posting group photos, and establishing "don't post me" preferences within friend circles. Relational privacy shifts the conversation from individual rights to shared boundaries, emphasizing collective responsibility in online spaces.

Backlash Against Surveillance Capitalism: Users Push Back

People are increasingly uneasy with the idea that their attention, behavior, and emotions are being monetized by corporations. In response, users are taking concrete steps to reclaim agency over their digital lives: installing tracker and ad blockers, rejecting cookies and opting out of personalized ads, choosing subscription-based models that prioritize privacy, reducing cross-platform sharing, and avoiding platforms known for aggressive tracking. This backlash is fueled by a growing understanding of how data is monetized, widespread media coverage of platform scandals, concerns amplified by AI-driven manipulation, and rising expectations for ethical design. Collectively, this cultural critique is nudging platforms and advertisers toward contextual advertising, subscription models, and ethical personalization.

Context Collapse Fatigue and Identity Fragmentation

At the same time, users are grappling with the psychological strain of performing for multiple audiences simultaneously—the phenomenon known as context collapse. People feel pressure to maintain a polished identity for coworkers, friends, and family all at once, and the fear of misinterpretation often leads to silence rather than openness. Conflicts between professional and personal identities have prompted new behavioral adaptations. Many now practice "digital fragmentation", maintaining separate accounts for family, friends, and hobbies, using pseudonyms for sensitive content, avoiding posts visible to mixed audiences, and relying more on private channels to uphold boundaries. Users are increasingly seeking digital spaces where identity boundaries are respected rather than collapsed.

Ephemerality and the Demand for Impermanent Digital Life

Ephemeral content has emerged as another response to digital pressures, reflecting a cultural desire for moments that do not last forever—mirroring the impermanence of real-life conversations. Users increasingly engage with stories, fleeting messages, temporary content, chats that disappear by default, auto-delete options in apps like WhatsApp, Signal, and Telegram, and even temporary personas or "digital moods" that expire. Ephemerality matters because it reduces long-term digital reputation risks, encourages candid expression, provides a psychologically safer space than permanent posts, and mitigates the fear of content resurfacing years later. In effect, impermanence gives users control over time, not just visibility, and represents a significant shift in how people experience and curate their digital lives.

Culture, Not Technology, Determines the Future of Privacy

The cultural and behavioral shifts outlined in this section show that privacy is no longer a fringe concern—it is a mass movement driven by psychological needs, aesthetic trends, safety concerns, and social norms.

People want more control over their visibility, autonomy over digital identity, and freedom from algorithmic judgment. They want intimacy without surveillance and authenticity without exposure.

The future of privacy will be shaped far more by how people behave than by what platforms build. Culture is moving decisively toward intentionality, boundaries, and nuance-and platforms must follow.

Predictions: What Social Media Privacy Will Look Like in 2030 and Beyond

Predicting the future of social media privacy requires understanding more than technology—it demands an appreciation of culture, regulation, geopolitics, psychology, and economics. The years between 2023 and 2025 have already shown that privacy is moving from a technical concern to a defining lens through which people interpret digital life. By 2030, the convergence of AI, decentralization, global regulation, and emotional well-being will reshape social media in ways that feel both revolutionary and inevitable. This section looks ahead to a future where privacy becomes intertwined with identity, agency, and the fundamental structures of digital experience.

The Era of Inference Privacy

The most radical privacy challenge of the next decade will not be about the data people *give* platforms, but the data platforms *extract* and *predict*. Today's AI systems already infer emotional states, personality traits, political leanings, sexual orientation, and mental health signals from speech patterns, eye movements, typing rhythms, and micro-behaviors. By 2030, inference models will be exponentially stronger—and far more ubiquitous.

Inference privacy will therefore become the main battleground. Instead of worrying about profile information or uploaded content, users will increasingly worry about what AI *believes* about them. This shift will push regulators to define boundaries around what types of inference are permissible, what must be disclosed, and what should be prohibited entirely.

We are likely to see a world in which political inference, sexuality inference, mental health inference, and emotion-targeted advertising become heavily restricted categories, similar to how biometric data is seen today. Users may also gain the right to request a "transparency snapshot" of what platforms have inferred about them, forcing companies to reveal psychological categories, behavioral clusters, and risk scores they assign to each account. By 2030, the question "What does the platform know about me?" may become as common—and as important—as questions about credit scores or medical records.

Emotional and Cognitive Privacy as Emerging Rights

If the 2010s were about data privacy and the 2020s about algorithmic transparency, the 2030s will center on emotional and cognitive privacy. As AR/VR headsets, wearable biosensors, sentiment analysis systems, and emotion-recognition algorithms become integrated into social platforms, the line between physiological data and psychological state will blur.

Emotional privacy will likely be formally recognized as a sensitive category of personal data by many jurisdictions. This means platforms may be barred from analyzing facial micro-expressions, vocal stress markers, or behavioral cues without explicit permission. The growing field of "cognitive liberty"—originally associated with neurotechnology—will begin influencing social platform governance as well. Users will demand safeguards against systems that attempt to detect mood, predict intentions, or influence decision-making based on inferred emotional vulnerabilities.

Emotion-agnostic modes, where platforms deliberately avoid analyzing behavioral signals, may become common. Users may toggle such settings to prevent mood-based content targeting during vulnerable moments like late-night browsing or post-breakup posting. Emotional privacy will evolve from a technical issue to a deeply personal right tied to dignity and autonomy.

A Deepfake-Saturated World Forces Identity Reinvention

By 2030, deepfake and synthetic media technology will be indistinguishable from real footage in most everyday contexts. Social media platforms will likely host enormous volumes of AI-generated personas, voices, and narratives. Identity verification tools—currently optional or limited to creators—may become a default feature for anyone who wants to build trust online.

Provenance tracking will be embedded into digital infrastructure, not just platforms. Browsers, messaging apps, and AR devices will automatically verify the authenticity of visual and audio content. Users will be able to hover over a video to reveal its origin, edits, and generative history. Yet, even these authenticity protocols will face challenges; malicious actors will always seek ways around them.

This future environment will create pressure on individuals to protect their likeness, voice, and narrative identity. People may watermark their own videos to prevent misuse, rely on digital signatures to verify posts, and store "authenticity keys" in their identity wallets to prove they are the human behind the account. Trust will become both scarce and valuable, pushing authenticity verification into the same category as cybersecurity or digital hygiene.

Decentralized Social Identity Goes Mainstream

Decentralized identity systems—supported by distributed ledgers, verifiable credentials, and user-held cryptographic keys—will move from emerging trend to mainstream infrastructure by 2030. Instead of logging into dozens of platforms separately, users will maintain a single, portable identity that they can move across apps like a digital passport.

This shift will be driven by regulatory pressure for data portability, cultural resistance to platform lock-in, and practical frustrations with traditional account systems. Decentralized identity will also solve a fundamental privacy problem: today, platforms own user identity; by 2030, users will hopefully own their identity independent of platforms.

This independence will reshape user expectations. Losing access to an account will no longer erase a creator's career. Moving to a new platform will not require rebuilding social graphs. Personal identity will feel more stable, consistent, and self-sovereign across the digital ecosystem. It may also make social media more competitive, as switching costs dissolve and users feel freer to move.

A Fragmented Social Ecosystem: Centralized, Decentralized, and AI-Native Worlds

Social media in the 2030s will not be one ecosystem. Instead, it will diverge into three parallel but interlinked worlds.

Centralized giants including Meta, TikTok, and X will continue to operate but under much stricter privacy and transparency rules. They will resemble regulated digital utilities, offering subscription options, contextual advertising, AI-driven content creation, and stricter child-safety environments. These platforms will still dominate global culture but with more oversight and less autonomy than before.

Decentralized networks will thrive among users who value autonomy, niche communities, and customizable social experiences. These networks will appeal to activists, privacy enthusiasts, and people seeking refuge from algorithmic amplification. They will also host a large portion of professional and academic communities who want control over moderation, data retention, and identity.

A third ecosystem will emerge: AI-native social spaces populated by synthetic personalities, personalized AI agents, emotionally intelligent companions, and generative communities. These spaces may blur the line between gaming, socializing, and self-exploration. Privacy norms in this world will look entirely different, because conversations, relationships, and social dynamics will involve AI agents capable of infinite memory, prediction, and emotional modeling.

People will maintain different identities in these three ecosystems, each with its own privacy expectations and boundaries.

Transparency Becomes a Consumer Expectation

By the end of the decade, algorithmic transparency will shift from regulatory obligation to consumer expectation. People will demand clarity about why they see certain posts, how content is ranked, and how their behavior influences feed dynamics.

Platforms may offer interactive transparency dashboards where users can adjust factors such as political sensitivity, emotional tone, or topic diversity. Recommendation engines may become configurable, allowing users to apply different "feed presets": chronological, interest-based, creator-focused, wellness-oriented, or anonymity-enhanced.

Transparency will influence cultural trust. Platforms that explain themselves will earn loyalty; those that hide their logic will lose credibility. People will treat algorithms not as invisible gods controlling their experiences, but as tools they can interrogate, reshape, and override.

Synthetic Relationships Reshape Identity and Privacy Norms

By 2030, many people will maintain ongoing relationships with AI entities—companion bots, AI influencers, learning mentors, creative assistants, and emotional support agents. These relationships will produce new privacy challenges because AI companions are—by design—always attentive, always listening, always learning.

The psychological intimacy of these interactions will create new questions: What data should an AI companion be allowed to remember? Should AI agents have the right to predict user emotions? How do you "break up" with a synthetic entity? And how should governments regulate emotional attachment data?

Users may demand the ability to edit, clear, or reset AI relational memory. Synthetic relationships will not replace human ones, but they will coexist with them, influencing how people conceptualize intimacy, vulnerability, and trust.

Portability and Interoperability Become Fundamental Rights

By 2030, users will expect seamless movement across digital spaces. Exporting one's digital identity, friendships, preferences, and content will become as normal as switching mobile carriers.

This will shift power dramatically away from platforms. No longer able to trap users through network effects, platforms will compete more aggressively on quality, privacy, safety, and user experience. People may maintain stable digital identities across dozens of spaces, reducing the emotional burden of platform migration and minimizing the risk of catastrophic account loss.

Portability will also reduce the psychological pressure to stay on platforms "because everyone is there". Instead, users will assemble personalized social ecosystems across interoperable networks.

Automated Privacy Agents Manage Complex Ecosystems

By 2030, privacy will have become too complex for individuals to manage manually. Automated privacy agents—AI systems acting on behalf of users—will take on this responsibility, managing settings, negotiating consent, filtering for emotional safety, and monitoring digital footprints. These agents will serve as personal privacy auditors, digital bodyguards, emotional safety monitors, identity verifiers, and inference blockers, providing a proactive layer of protection in an increasingly intricate digital landscape.

Users will simply describe their preferences ("Don't let apps track my emotional data", "Delete posts older than two years", "Alert me if someone tries to impersonate me"), and AI agents will implement them across platforms.

This will democratize privacy by reducing reliance on user expertise or manual vigilance.

Privacy Becomes a Form of Digital Selfhood

By 2030, privacy will no longer be defined as secrecy, anonymity, or restriction. Instead, it will become a form of digital selfhood—a holistic expression of control, autonomy, and identity across dynamic digital ecosystems.

Future privacy will be:

- emotional
- cognitive
- relational
- portable
- self-sovereign
- AI-assisted
- regulated
- culturally embedded

In this world, social media does not disappear. It becomes more human, more contextual, more controlled by individuals, and more aligned with human dignity.

Pathways Toward a Privacy-Conscious Digital Future

The future of privacy will not emerge automatically from technological evolution or regulatory intervention; it must be *built*, consciously and collaboratively, through the decisions of individuals, platforms, institutions, and societies. This section outlines the concrete pathways that can lead to a more privacy-conscious digital world—one that prioritizes human dignity, autonomy, agency, and psychological safety over unchecked data extraction and algorithmic control.

These pathways are not isolated strategies; they collectively form the architecture of a new social contract—one where individuals reclaim control over their digital selves, platforms redesign systems to respect that control, and policymakers create frameworks that recognize privacy as a fundamental human right in the digital age.

Empowering Individuals Through Agency, Digital Literacy, and Practical Tools

The first pathway toward a privacy-conscious digital future begins with individuals, because user behavior and expectations ultimately shape the incentives for platforms and policymakers. Achieving privacy does not rely on fear-based avoidance; instead, it requires embedding privacy into daily digital habits as part of intentional, empowered digital living.

Reclaiming control over one's digital identity is central to this effort. Individuals can benefit from practices that limit unnecessary exposure, such as using pseudonyms or multi-layered identities across different platforms, practicing digital minimalism by reducing over-sharing, and separating personal, professional, and creative identities. Being mindful about the permanency of posts, stories, and comments ensures that presence online is curated intentionally, rather than avoided entirely. This approach is not about hiding from the digital world but about tailoring one's digital footprint according to context.

Equally important is understanding how algorithms perceive us. As people learn that algorithms can infer personality traits, emotional states, and even mental health markers, they will begin to question why certain content appears, understand the emotional impact of recommendation systems, and interpret feed patterns as reflections of algorithmic behavior rather than personal failings. Digital literacy in the 2030s will therefore expand from simple "protect your password" strategies to understanding one's algorithmic persona and how it shapes online experiences.

Adopting privacy-enhancing tools further empowers individuals to manage their exposure. Tracker blockers, VPNs, privacy-first browsers, password managers, encrypted messaging apps, and consent managers all create micro-resistance against pervasive surveillance systems, allowing users to proactively protect their data. Alongside these technical measures, emotional privacy must be normalized. Developing habits such as thinking before posting emotionally vulnerable content, avoiding over-sharing during times of distress, setting boundaries with AI companions, and recognizing when platforms may be reading emotional cues reframes privacy not just as a data issue, but as one tied to mental and emotional well-being.

Redesigning Platforms through Privacy-by-Design Principles

The second pathway focuses on platforms themselves. Future social ecosystems must be built on the principle that privacy is foundational, not optional. Platforms should make privacy the default rather than an optional extra, minimizing data collection, limiting storage duration, removing unnecessary tracking layers, requesting permissions only when necessary, and offering default private modes for sensitive interactions. Privacy should not be the responsibility of individuals navigating complex settings; it should be embedded into the design of the systems themselves.

Rethinking feed architecture is also crucial. The way social feeds are structured profoundly shapes user psychology. Platforms can reduce behavioral amplification loops, allow chronological or hybrid views as default, provide algorithmic tuning for transparency and control, and introduce emotional-health pacing mechanisms to prevent addictive patterns. This represents a shift from engagement-maximizing design toward well-being-oriented design.

Integrating PETs into core systems further strengthens user autonomy. Federated learning, differential privacy for analytics, encrypted computation for content moderation, and on-device processing for voice and biometric data allow platforms to extract value from data without fully accessing it. Meanwhile, transparent data practices—clearly disclosing what data is collected, what inferences are generated, how long data is retained, and how algorithms classify and rank content—become trust-building mechanisms rather than mere compliance exercises.

Steering Industry Transitions toward Ethical Innovation

Industry stakeholders—including developers, advertisers, hardware manufacturers, and AI companies—must reshape business models around ethical innovation. Redefining success metrics is a first step: moving away from retention, engagement time, and click-throughs, toward measuring meaningful interactions, user satisfaction, well-being outcomes, trust, reputation, and long-term loyalty. This realigns economic incentives with human values.

Building consumer trust through honesty will increasingly differentiate companies. Transparent interfaces, clear language, and predictable behavior will outperform organizations that rely on dark patterns or hidden data flows. Ethical AI deployment is equally vital. Safeguards should prohibit emotion-based targeting, manipulation of vulnerable groups, opaque algorithmic profiling, and require clear rules for synthetic content, supported by authenticated media pipelines to reduce the harm caused by deepfakes. Brands that adopt privacy as a core part of their identity—through encrypted devices, AI agents that protect users, or minimal-data products—will set market standards and influence user expectations.

Strengthening Regulatory Frameworks for a Data-Complex Future

Regulation forms the fourth pathway. Laws must evolve to reflect technological realities, addressing not just data privacy but inference privacy, emotional privacy, biometric risk, and cross-border data flows. Emotional and cognitive data inferred by AI should be recognized as sensitive, with restrictions on emotion-recognition systems, behavioral predictions that infringe autonomy, and protections for vulnerable populations including children and minorities. Governments will also need to regulate synthetic media and deepfakes, enforcing provenance standards, authentication requirements, punishments for malicious fabrication, and global watermarking frameworks to combat identity fraud and misinformation.

Regulatory frameworks may also require interoperability and portability, enabling users to export their identity, migrate contacts, transfer messages, and move social histories, thereby shifting power from corporations to individuals. Algorithmic transparency will become mandatory, including risk assessments, fairness audits, explanations for content amplification, and the right to challenge algorithmic decisions. Child-focused rules will include age-appropriate design mandates, limits on algorithmic exposure, bans on personalized advertising, strict consent rules for biometric data, and protections against addictive design—ensuring that children are safeguarded not just from data misuse, but from psychological harm.

Building a Culture of Shared Responsibility and Collective Ethics

The final pathway is cultural. Laws and platform design alone cannot guarantee privacy; it must be reinforced through shared norms and collective behaviors. Consent in social interactions will become routine, with individuals asking permission before posting photos of others, respecting "do not post me" boundaries, avoiding tagging sensitive locations, and considering relational privacy alongside personal privacy. Authenticity will evolve in tandem, allowing people to express real experiences without overexposure, share selectively in safe spaces, show personality without compromising security, and maintain boundaries without appearing secretive.

Digital self-care will be normalized within communities, including social media breaks, detox periods, turning off notifications, and limiting emotional labor online. Community-led moderation will shift responsibility from platforms to users, who will participate in shaping guidelines, supporting respectful spaces, challenging harassment, reporting impersonation, and creating norms around AI use. Finally, as the internet becomes increasingly fragmented, multi-layered identities will flourish: public-facing profiles, private circles, pseudonymous creative spaces, professional profiles, and AI-personalized digital selves. This ecosystem of layered identities encourages nuanced privacy behaviors and reflects a mature, privacy-conscious digital culture.

A Multi-Stakeholder Approach to a Human-Centered Digital Future

The pathways outlined in this section show that building a privacy-conscious digital future requires participation from everyone—individuals who adopt intentional behaviors, platforms that redesign systems, industries that shift business incentives, regulators who anticipate the risks of inference and AI, and communities that uphold norms of mutual respect.

In the world of 2030 and beyond, privacy will not simply be a right—it will be a social value, a cultural practice, and a daily behavior. It will be as essential to digital well-being as physical safety is to everyday life. The task ahead is not only to guard against harms but to *reimagine* how digital spaces can support human flourishing.

A New Vision for Digital Privacy

For more than a decade, popular narratives framed privacy loss as a series of unfortunate accidents—an inevitable by-product of progress, an unintended side effect of convenience, or the regrettable cost of living in a connected world. But as we have shown, the truth is far more deliberate: privacy is not lost accidentally; it is engineered away through design choices, business incentives, and cultural norms that reward visibility over restraint, and extraction over autonomy.

The evolution of social media reveals a system where data collection is neither incidental nor peripheral—it is foundational. Every interface, nudge, default setting, interaction pattern, and algorithmic choice shapes how users behave and what platforms learn about them. If we are to reimagine digital privacy for the world ahead, we must recognize this fundamental reality: the architecture of social platforms determines the architecture of privacy.

Over the course of this chapter, we have traced privacy's transformation across seven major dimensions: technological shifts, regulatory evolution, platform redesign, cultural change, decentralization, emotional well-being, and predictive AI.

Together, these threads form a new tapestry—one that requires rethinking privacy as a *living ecosystem* rather than a static right.

Privacy Is No Longer Only about Data—It Is about Identity, Emotion, and Agency

Earlier models of privacy assumed that what mattered was the protection of personal information: names, locations, photos, browsing habits. But the rise of AI has expanded the scope of what is considered private.

Platforms now go beyond simply collecting data—they actively infer insights about users, including personality traits, attention patterns, emotional states, predicted behaviors, and even vulnerabilities or insecurities. These inferences shape the content users see and the experiences they have online, often without their explicit awareness.

These inferences also shape everything from content recommendations to advertising, moderation, and even interpersonal experiences online. Privacy is now intimately tied to who we are, not merely what we share.

The future demands protections for emotional and cognitive autonomy, not just informational secrecy. As AI grows more capable of interpreting micro-behaviors, privacy becomes a battle to defend inner life.

Privacy Has Become Relational, Not Individual

The shift toward relational privacy—introduced earlier in this chapter—has profound implications. One person's decisions increasingly affect the data exposure of entire groups. A photo tags not just a face but a network; a contact upload exposes the social graph of nonusers; a group chat screenshot captures private conversation dynamics.

This means privacy is no longer solely a personal preference. It requires a collective ethic, similar to public health or environmental care. Just as second-hand smoke affects bystanders, second-hand data practices can impact those who never opted in.

For privacy to thrive in 2030 and beyond, communities must cultivate norms of shared consent, mutual respect, and thoughtful boundaries.

Platforms Are Shifting from Extractive Design to Protective Design

A seismic change is underway in design philosophy. Platforms that once maximized engagement at all costs are recognizing that such strategies lead to user burnout, mistrust, political scrutiny, and mental health crises. The emerging design language—slower feeds, contextual advertising, transparency dashboards, "digital rest" modes, and minimal data interactions—signals a transition from extraction to stewardship.

Protective design redefines success:

- not minutes spent
- but well-being preserved
- not clicks generated
- but trust maintained
- not emotional manipulation
- but emotional safety

The platforms that thrive in the next decade will be those that treat privacy as a feature, not friction.

Regulatory Pressure Is Reshaping the Digital Landscape

The regulatory momentum of the 2020s—especially in the EU, the UK, Canada, India, Brazil, and parts of Asia—marks the beginning of a global shift. Regulations have evolved beyond focusing solely on data collection. Today, they also address AI inference, biometric scanning, algorithmic opacity, emotional targeting, real-time surveillance, and manipulative design patterns, reflecting the broader and more complex ways technology can impact privacy and user autonomy.

The emergence of the EU AI Act, the DSA, India's DPDP Act, and global child-safety legislation signals a world where privacy is not a vague guideline but a legal infrastructure. By 2030, platforms will be required not just to comply with rules, but to prove they act in the public interest.

Regulation is evolving from punishment to partnership, from reactive to anticipatory. It aims not to restrict technology but to shape it toward human-centered values.

Decentralization Is No Longer Fringe—It Is the Counterbalance to Platform Power

Decentralized platforms, once seen as overly technical, have grown into legitimate alternatives because they offer what mainstream platforms cannot: ownership, autonomy, and community-driven governance. These ecosystems challenge the economic and architectural assumptions underlying social media.

The future likely includes a hybrid model:

- centralized platforms for scale
- decentralized networks for autonomy
- AI-native environments for exploration

This diversity gives users unprecedented freedom to choose how visible they want to be, who controls their data, and how their identities are managed.

Culture Is the Real Engine of Privacy Transformation

Perhaps the most significant shift is cultural. Privacy is no longer just a personal choice or technical practice; it has become a marker of digital maturity, a form of social signaling, a strategy for supporting mental health, an expression of individual values, and a way to reclaim personal boundaries in an increasingly connected world.

People are moving away from performative oversharing and toward intentional presence. They are choosing micro-communities over mass audiences, pseudonymity over polished identity, ephemerality over permanence, authenticity over performance. These choices are not nostalgic—they are adaptive, reflecting an evolving understanding of what it means to be human in a computational world.

Ultimately, cultural shifts dictate platform design, regulatory priorities, and market expectations. Privacy becomes sustainable only when it aligns with how people want to live.

Reflection

Social media began as a way to connect people, but over time it grew into a web of surveillance, inference, pressure, and algorithmic influence. Yet it does not have to stay that way. As technology becomes more powerful, so too must the values that guide its use.

This chapter ends with a simple recognition:

- Privacy is not a nostalgic longing for a less connected past.
- It is the blueprint for a more humane future.

- It is the framework through which individuals reclaim agency, families protect their relationships, communities maintain trust, and societies preserve democratic integrity.

Privacy is the quiet infrastructure that allows people to be fully human—even in digital spaces where everything can be watched, measured, predicted, and monetized.

The future of privacy is not about withdrawal; it is about intentionality. It is about building a world where technology amplifies human flourishing rather than eroding it. It is about reclaiming control over the narratives and identities that define us.

As social media continues to evolve, privacy will become the compass guiding us toward a digital world that is not merely efficient or entertaining, but profoundly respectful of our complexity, vulnerability, and autonomy.

Privacy, in other words, becomes the architecture of a better internet—one that aligns with the open, user-centric vision Tim Berners-Lee imagined when he created the World Wide Web: a space designed to empower individuals rather than exploit them, where human agency is built into the very structure of the system.

Final Words—A Human Ending in a Digital World

As this book comes to a close, we arrive at a truth that has echoed throughout every chapter: privacy is not about withdrawing from the world—it is about participating in it with intention, dignity, and agency. The journey has taken us through the opaque architectures of data-driven platforms, the psychology of visibility, the politics of control, the economics of surveillance, and the spaces where identity, emotion, and technology meet.

And yet, after exploring the complexity and scale of the digital world, what remains isn't fear—it is clarity.

Privacy is not an act of hiding.

It is an act of choosing.

It is the moment we pause before posting, the instinct to protect a loved one's image, the whisper of discomfort when an app asks for too much access, the shift in behavior when we realize algorithms see us in ways we do not see ourselves. Privacy is not the end of connection; it is the beginning of authentic connection, built on boundaries that protect our humanity.

In a world where social media strives to capture every gesture, track every emotion, and anticipate every desire, privacy becomes a form of resistance—not loud, angry resistance, but quiet, consistent, grounded resistance. A resistance rooted in values rather than fear. A resistance that says: *I choose what is mine to share. I choose who sees me. I choose how I exist in this space.*

We often imagine the digital world as something overwhelming and external-an unstoppable force shaping our behavior. But the truth is more balanced: technology shapes us, yes, but we shape it in return. Every platform, every feature, every algorithmic shift is ultimately influenced by human expectation, social norms, and cultural behavior. We have always been part of the design loop, even when we didn't realize it.

As people rethink how they show up online, social platforms are evolving in turn. Companies are being forced—by users, by regulators, by their own reputational fragility—to recognize that attention without trust is worthless. They are beginning to adopt safer defaults, transparent architectures, interoperable identities, and emotional well-being features not because they want to, but because the cultural and political environment leaves them no choice. That is the power of collective behavior.

It turns out that privacy is not only a legal right or a technical configuration—it is a cultural act. A shared language. A set of expectations we build together. And perhaps most positively: it is becoming a social norm.

We are entering an era where asking "Can I post this?" is seen as respect, not awkwardness. Where children grow up with parents who understand digital boundaries. Where friendships and partnerships are anchored in mutual consent for online visibility. Where the decision not to share is not secrecy—it is self-care. And where choosing privacy is a sign of confidence, not hesitation.

There is, however, another layer to this story: privacy is deeply intertwined with well-being. Burnout, comparison fatigue, identity fragmentation, context collapse—these psychological struggles are signs that systems have not been designed with human nervous systems in mind.

When individuals set digital boundaries, when platforms redesign for emotional safety, when regulators enforce limits on surveillance, they are all participating in the same essential project: making the digital world livable.

That is the real heart of privacy.

- Privacy is not a barrier to connection; it is the condition that makes connection meaningful
- Privacy is not a barrier to creativity; it gives creators the safety to take risks without fear of misinterpretation
- Privacy is not a barrier to innovation; it forces innovators to build responsibly, sustainably, ethically
- Privacy is not a barrier to community; it builds trust, safety, and belonging within communities.

This book has shown that privacy is not a single skill but a constellation of practices—some personal, some communal, some technological, some cultural, some emotional. It is also the thread that binds our digital identities with our offline ones. The more digitally entwined our lives become, the more essential privacy will be as a stabilizing force.

And this is not a pessimistic future—it is a hopeful one.

We are seeing the rise of thoughtful design, honest interfaces, privacy-first tools, user-controlled identities, and communities built on trust rather than reach. We are seeing users reclaiming their digital agency, choosing closed groups over broadcast feeds, choosing slower social spaces over constant performance, choosing presence over visibility. In these subtle, daily actions, millions of people are rewriting the cultural script of digital life.

- *If there is one thing to carry forward from this book, let it be this: privacy is a joyful act*
- *It is joyful to choose what we share, rather than to be pushed toward constant revelation*
- *It is joyful to protect the people we love from unnecessary exposure*
- *It is joyful to know that our identity belongs to us, not to algorithms*
- *It is joyful to express ourselves in spaces that feel aligned with our values, not extracted from our vulnerabilities.*

Privacy is not something we lose to platforms; it is something we reclaim together—through laws, through design, through culture, and through everyday habits that recenter our humanity.

As this journey ends, consider that privacy is not a destination—it is a practice. A way of approaching technology with awareness instead of fear, with intention instead of impulse, with dignity instead of resignation.

We will continue to live in a world shaped by algorithms, data, AI, and digital identities. But we will also continue to shape that world in return—through our expectations, our behaviors, our boundaries, and our insistence that technology does not define us, but *serves* us.

The future of privacy is not about turning away from connection.
It is about walking toward a more mindful, balanced, humane digital life.
And in that future, we do not lose ourselves—we finally find space to be whole.

References

Malik, A. (2026, June 15). These are the countries moving to ban social media for children. TechCrunch. https://techcrunch.com/2026/06/15/social-media-ban-children-countries-list/

Berners-Lee, T. (2025). *This is for everyone*. Macmillan.

California Attorney General. (2022–2024). *Age-appropriate design code act (AADC)*. https://oag.ca.gov/privacy/children/aadc

EFF. (2023–2025). *AI and surveillance research*. Electronic Frontier Foundation. https://www.eff.org/issues/ai

European Commission. (2023). *Digital markets act*. https://digital-strategy.ec.europa.eu/en/policies/digital-markets-act

European Commission. (2023). *Digital services act: Regulation (EU) 2022/2065*. https://digital-strategy.ec.europa.eu/en/policies/digital-services-act-package

European Parliament & Council. (2024). *EU artificial intelligence act*. https://artificialintelligenceact.eu/

FPF. (n.d.). *AI & privacy research*. Future of Privacy Forum. https://fpf.org/

Government of India. (2023). *Digital personal data protection act*. https://www.meity.gov.in/data-protection-framework

Harvard Berkman Klein Center. (n.d.). *Digital governance*. https://cyber.harvard.edu/

Horwitz, J. (2025, August 14). *Meta's AI rules have let bots hold 'sensual' chats with kids, offer false medical info* [News report]. Reuters. https://www.reuters.com/investigates/special-report/meta-ai-chatbot-guidelines/

MIT Technology Review. (2023–2025). *The future of deepfakes & synthetic media*. https://www.technologyreview.com/topic/artificial-intelligence/

Meta Oversight Board. (n.d.). *Transparency reports*. https://www.oversightboard.com/reports/

Mozilla. (2023–2025). *Privacy not included reports: Detailed analysis of privacy risks in consumer tech*. https://foundation.mozilla.org/en/privacynotincluded/

OECD. (2023). *OECD principles on artificial intelligence*. https://oecd.ai/en/ai-principles

Pew Research Center. (2023, 2024). *Teens, social media, and technology*. https://www.pewresearch.org/internet/

Stanford Institute for Human-Centered AI. (2024). *Artificial intelligence index report*. https://aiindex.stanford.edu/

The White House. (2023). *Executive order on safe, secure, and trustworthy artificial intelligence*. https://www.whitehouse.gov/briefing-room/presidential-actions/2023/10/30/executive-order-safe-secure-and-trustworthy-artificial-intelligence/

UNESCO. (2023). *Guidelines for regulating digital platforms*. https://unesdoc.unesco.org/ark:/48223/pf0000383890

UNICEF. (2023). *Child online safety and privacy framework*. https://www.unicef.org/globalinsight/online-safety

WEF. (2024). *Global risks report*. World Economic Forum. https://www.weforum.org/reports/global-risks-report-2024/

Wynn-Williams, S. (2025, April 9). *Meta whistleblower says company targeted ads at teens based on their emotional state*. TechCrunch. https://techcrunch.com/2025/04/09/meta-whistleblower-sarah-wynn-williams-says-company-targeted-ads-at-teens-based-on-their-emotional-state/

Index

Note: **Bold** page numbers refer to tables and *italic* page numbers refer to figures.

For Product Safety Concerns and Information please contact our EU representative GPSR@taylorandfrancis.com
Taylor & Francis Verlag GmbH, Kaufingerstraße 24, 80331 München, Germany

www.ingramcontent.com/pod-product-compliance
Lightning Source LLC
LaVergne TN
LVHW021427121026
849957LV00028B/375
* 9 7 8 1 0 4 1 1 0 2 8 1 6 *